SHOOTING THE SUN

Smithsonian Series in Ethnographic Inquiry

William L. Merrill and Ivan Karp, series editors

Ethnography as fieldwork, analysis, and literary form is the distinguishing feature of modern anthropology. Guided by the assumption that anthropological theory and ethnography are inextricably linked, this series is devoted to exploring the ethnographic enterprise.

EDITED BY
BERNARD JUILLERAT

SHOOTING THE SUN

RITUAL AND MEANING IN WEST SEPIK

Smithsonian Institution Press
Washington and London

Published in cooperation with
the Ministère des Affaires Etrangères, Paris.

Designed by Kathleen Sims
Edited by Vicky Macintyre.
Production editing by Rebecca Browning.

Library of Congress Cataloging-in-Publication Data
Shooting the sun : ritual and meaning in West Sepik / edited by
  Bernard Juillerat.
      p. cm.—(Smithsonian series in ethnographic inquiry)
   "Published in cooperation with the Ministère des affaires
étrangères, Paris."
   Includes bibliographical references and index.
   ISBN 1-56098-168-7
   1. Yafar (Papua New Guinea people)—Rites and ceremonies.
   2. Umeda (Papua New Guinea people)—Rites and ceremonies.
   3. Symbolism. I. Juillerat, Bernard. II. Series.
DU740.42.S5   1992
299'.92—dc20   92-4511

British Library Cataloguing-in-Publication Data is available.

Manufactured in the United States of America.
96 95 94 93 92
5 4 3 2 1

∞The paper used in this publication meets the minimum requirements of
the American National Standard for Permanence of Paper for Printed Library
Materials Z39.48-1984.

Contents

Acknowledgments

Since the fundamental text (chapter 1) submitted here for discussion is based principally on fieldwork, my thanks go, first, to the Yafar, especially to those who were willing to let me attend the nonpublic parts of the Yangis festival in 1976, and who subsequently, bit by bit, unlocked the secret by providing me with the exegetical elements that made it possible to arrive at a global interpretation of the ritual. While expressing my warmest gratitude to them, I shall respect their wish to remain anonymous.

This book would never have been more than a long article, however, had my colleagues and coauthors not been kind enough to read through all the details of the ethnographic documentation and to assimilate it; and, above all, had they not taken the pains they did—in comparing the present work with Alfred Gell's parallel study of the Umeda—to add their critical comments to the interpretation I had brought to the Yafar Yangis cult. I would like to thank them sincerely for their indispensable and generous contribution. Although the text of chapter 1 has been modified very little since I first submitted it to my colleagues in 1985, I would like to say how much I owe, in particular, to André Green (who devoted several of his 1988–89 seminars in psychoanalysis at the Université de Paris VII to the Yangis ceremony) for our many discussions on the symbolic system of Yangis and how it relates to psychoanalytic concepts; his enthusiasm was a constant encouragement in my search for meaning in Yafar rituals and mythology.

I would also like to thank Richard Werbner, who introduced me to Smithsonian Institution Press and its editorial director, Daniel Goodwin, and who stoutly defended the publication of the present work. I am honored that it will be appearing under the imprint of this prestigious institution.

My thanks also go to those who helped prepare the English version of the texts by French speakers: to Alan Sheridan for translating the introduction and Green's and Manenti's contributions—and also to Kenneth Hoyle for revising the latter; and to Daniel Doyle and Nora Scott for their suggestions for improving chapter 1 and the epilogue, which I wrote in English.

I conducted my research among the Yafar as a member of the research groups R.C.P. 259 and R.C.P. 587 (now G.D.R. 116) of the Centre National de la Recherche Scientifique, to which, along with the Ministère des Affaires Etrangères (D.G.R.C.S.T.), I am grateful for the funding of my fieldwork in New Guinea. I should also like to thank the D.G.R.C.S.T. (Subdepartment of Human Sciences) for its effort in seeing this work published.

But my debts would not be fully acknowledged if I did not mention Alfred Gell, who, as he was finishing his own work among the Umeda in 1970, generously suggested the Yafar as a local society deserving separate study. Like an archaeologist unearthing a temple intact that is covered with paintings and inscriptions, he had just "discovered"—alive and well—the Ida cult of the Waina communities.

Bernard Juillerat

Introduction

Of all the cultural productions that human genius and the unconscious have been pleased to present to the observer, often in figurative language, ritual and myth have perhaps proved to be the most resistant to interpretation. Just as an understanding of mythology in general presupposes a recognition of the different kinds of mythology, each requiring a somewhat different analytical approach, so ritual in general cannot be reduced to a single type of behavior: between a simple propitiatory gesture carried out individually and a complex, public ceremony there is more or less the same distance as between the name of a god briefly invoked and the detailed account of Creation solemnly offered to a gathering of believers. But we are only too well aware of the failure of the various attempts at classification in both spheres of symbolic expression; and the fact that myth is exclusively based on language, whereas ritual is expressed by a whole range of signs—nonverbal (plants, objects, colors, gestures) and verbal—has not made the work of the mythologists any easier. The mere choice of term (myth, tale, story, fable, legend) under which a text deriving from oral tradition may be classified poses the same kind of difficulty as that of the epithet attached to the designation of a particular ritual (magical, initiatory, funerary, ancestor, cosmogonical, fertility, totemic). The linguistic forms as well as the social functions that seem to govern the enactment of ritual or myth can so seldom be isolated and so often occur simultaneously that any typological undertaking seems doomed to failure from the outset, especially because the concepts to which we refer are all of Western origin. The parallels that the communities being studied often draw between their rituals and their myths have led anthropologists to pose the wrong question, now abandoned, of the anteriority of one over the other. Although a ritual is seldom in its entirety the literal transcription of a spoken mythical account, narrative or cosmogonic elements (what Lévi-Strauss has called "implicit myth") are often indicated by informants as being capable of explaining certain ritual aspects. We shall find some striking examples of this in the case of the ceremony analyzed in this book. On the other hand, for our best Yafar informant ritual acts were a way to remember myths.

The following chapters have as their subject a single ritual from New Guinea, approached through the understanding achieved of it by two anthropologists, Alfred Gell and myself, working in two neighboring communities. This ritual has neither a therapeutic character nor an initiatory function (at least in the traditional meaning of the term). Gell sees it as an annual fertility festival possessing great sociological importance, whereas I identify it as a dualistic totemic ritual ensuring the symbolic reproduction of the society through the metaphorical expression of the ontogenetical stages. However, we both agreed that the ritual was intended to regenerate not only the sago palms (as the participants state), but the whole of society. Quite obviously, the ceremony represents what has come to be called in Melanesia a "male cult," a system of practices and representations shrouded in secrecy intended to perpetuate the dominance of men over women in the relationship that society maintains with nature through the mediation of the spirit world. Although very different both from the great initiation cyles of the Sepik River, the Gulf of Papua, or of the Highlands, and from such original rituals as the Naven of the Iatmul studied by Bateson (1936) or the emotional Gisaro of the Kaluli (Schieffelin 1976), this ritual fascinates at once by its formal, quasi-theatrical aspect and by the diversity of the masked characters and sacred gestures that are staged in a perfectly rigorous order. Does this syntagmatic structure conceal a coded message, a story, a cosmogony? Do the characters represent divinities of the local pantheon? Does the dance performed throughout a whole night, until exhaustion puts an end to it, by a pair of male dancers painted in black or the final release of arrows toward the sun by two protagonists covered entirely in red ochre possess a secret meaning for the participants, or are they both the manifestation of a tradition perpetuated without exegesis? Behind these essentially ethnographical questions stands a methodological problematic concerning the interpretation of this particular ritual and its comparison with other Melanesian cults, but also in relation to ritual in general, considered from such varied points of view as the relation between structure and meaning, social function and integration, semiotic syntax, and the relationships with other aspects of local culture. Is the ritual to be taken as the reflection, whether faithful or inverted, of the social structure, or as the cultural manifestation of individual, unconscious representations? Should the analytical approach first be sociological or psychoanalytical, give preference to Durkheim or to Freud? What place should be given to lexical similarities, binary oppositions, or Freudian interpretation in the analysis of ritual metaphors? Do the exegetical commentaries of informants have a heuristic value, or must they be excluded from the scientific model that the anthropologist is trying to construct? To what extent do regional variants constitute a signifying system? These are some of the questions that will be discussed in this book.

THE GEOGRAPHICAL AND CULTURAL CONTEXT

Before presenting Gell's methods and results and my own, it might be useful to provide the reader with a sketch of the societies concerned and of the regional context of which they form a part. West Sepik is both an administrative province (distinct from that of East Sepik since 1966) of Papua New Guinea and a geographical region corresponding to the upper course of the Sepik River, including the neighboring mountainous zones and the alluvial plain of the tributaries of the left bank of the river; to this should be added the chain of the Bewani and the western part of the Torricelli situated between the Sepik and the coast, as well as the coastal region itself, which stretches from the Indonesian frontier to the west and Aitape to the east. Despite its highly diverse terrain, the region is marked by ecological homogeneity, as characterized by the omnipresent rain forest. Geographical contrasts combined with the fortuitous events of human settlement (of which we know almost nothing) seem to have contributed to the formation of an ethnic and cultural diversity that may be divided into five areas: the coastal region and hinterland as far as the Bewani-Torricelli mountain chain (Swadling 1979; Thomas 1941);

the Torricelli Mountains (Lewis 1980; Mitchell 1978; and others); the Border Mountains, which are the habitat of the societies discusssed in this book; the strictly river zone, including the surrounding plain (Kelm 1975, 1980; and others), to which may be added the Fas communities of the eastern Bewani, which have not been studied; and the northern side of the area known as Mountain Ok, which includes the northeastern part of the Star Mountains, mainly around the sources of the Sepik (Barth 1975, 1987; Craig 1969, 1990; Gardner 1981, 1984; Jorgensen 1981a; Poole 1976, 1982; and others). However, these roughly defined areas do not coincide with the linguistic geography of the province, which is a much more complex matter (Laycock 1975).

Consider the Yafar and the Umeda. Between the great loop of the Upper Sepik and the Bewani "coastal" range (which is, in fact, quite a distance from the coastline), a hill region stretches on either side of the frontier with Western New Guinea (Indonesian Irian Jaya), culminating at an altitude of about 1,000 meters, called the Border Mountains. For geopolitical reasons, the northern part of this massif was not regularly administered by the Australians until 1962 (at which date Western New Guinea was transferred to Indonesia), having previously had only sporadic contact with the Dutch administration, which could more easily reach the region from the west (see Juillerat 1986). The various non-Austronesian languages of the Border Mountains may be divided into different stocks, the Waris family consisting in part of the languages of the northern half of the massif (including Amanab, spoken by the Yafar, and Waina, spoken by the Umeda) on either side of the international demarcation (Laycock 1975); as elsewhere in Papua New Guinea, pidgin (*tokpisin*) now serves as the language of communication. Internal cultural variations are certainly well marked.[1] Nevertheless the whole of the Border Mountains area contrasts with the societies of the Upper Sepik plain nearby (the Baibai, Kwomtari, Nagatman, Abau languages, for which we have no adequate ethnographical account), and even more with the Mountain Ok groups, which are now fairly well known (see above). Some of the dominant sociocultural features of the Border Mountains are the juxtaposition of small tribes made up of 100–300 individuals, each confined to a well-defined territory bordering on neighboring ones, the mobility of local groups and their clanic heterogeneity (except for the Waina speakers), patrifiliation, great matrimonial stability and a domestic organization based on the nuclear family, a mixed economy dominated by itinerant horticulture-arboriculture on patches of burnt land (the sago palm providing the basic food), and hunting (involving limited semirearing of pigs). There is no evidence of any institutional form of leadership, but one notes the presence of certain men possessing ritual responsibilities and secret functions. The absence of men's houses and of initiation rituals is compensated by a great diversity in therapeutic rituals and by ceremonial cycles devoted to the forest spirits and the spirits of the dead with whom men negotiate their cynegetic successes (south and center of the massif as far as the north of the Amanab area: Huber 1975, 1980; Juillerat 1986). Like the societies situated outside the Border Mountains to the northeast, the northern Amanab groups and all the Waina possess a dual organization made up of totemic moieties, which, as we shall see, are an integral part of the Ida-Yangis male cult.

UMEDA AND YAFAR

Figure 1 shows the position of the two societies that concern us here: the Umeda and the Yafar. Umeda is the main village of the Waina linguistic area; it is made up of six fixed, exogamous hamlets, each bearing the name of the clan that occupies it. Three of them belong to the male moiety (*edtodna*) and the other three to the female moiety (*angwatodna*). Each hamlet is in turn subdivided into two "hamlet moieties" linked by certain minor forms of exchange (Gell 1975). Except for a few differences, the same type of structure prevails among the other groups of the Waina language. The Yafar (approximately the same size as the Umeda, that is, 200 inhabitants) form one of the most northern Amanab-speaking societies; it is territorially bordered by the Punda, themselves intermediaries between the Umeda and the Yafar. The Umeda and Yafar do not intermarry, but the Punda intermarry with both of them. The residential instability of the Amanab local groups is, in contrast to the Waina, marked; the pluriclanic hamlets split, break apart, and are grouped together again according to the accidents of the social relations (internal conflicts, accusations of sorcery, sudden variations in the mortality rate); the subdivision into moieties ("male" *Araneri* and "female" *Angwaneri*), noted among all the central and northern Amanab groups, is in principle reproduced in each hamlet. It is understandable, then, that although the Waina hamlets are coherent with the dual and clan structure, the Yafar local groups are merely the

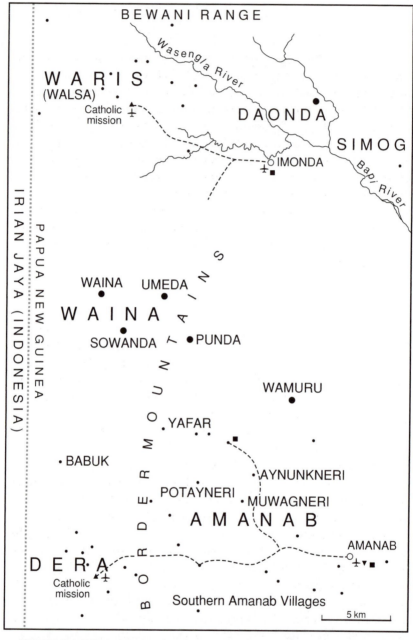

WARIS, DAONDA, SIMOG, WAINA, AMANAB, DERA: linguistic areas

- • Village
- ▼ Protestant Mission
- ✛ Airstrip
- ● Group of hamlets
- ■ Primary School
- --- Semi-passable road
- ○ Amanab: District Headquarters; Imonda: Patrol post
- ▲ Catholic Mission: Mindepoke in the Waris area; Kamberatoro in the Dera area

Figure 1. Map of the northern part of the Border Mountains and the Wasengla Valley.

product of a contingent historical process. The two communities are also distinguished by their kinship terminology (Omaha for the Umeda, Dakota-Iroquois for the Yafar)—although their system of alliance of a semicomplex (Omaha) type is similar—and by certain forms of cultural behavior relating to sexuality or to illness (open and more socialized among the Umeda, repressed and desocializing among the Yafar). On the other hand, village life is more developed in Yafar than in Umeda and in the other Waina communities that live almost the whole year in the forest in isolated families and that meet only on ritual occasions, the most important being Ida, which brings together the entire population. The Yafar celebrate this ritual, which they call Yangis, only episodically; it is not, therefore, part of the annual cycle. We shall return to the moiety totemism of the Yafar in chapter 1.

Since the 1960s, both groups have integrated the transformations that colonization and a moderate missionary influence imposed on them—Protestant (almost nonexistent until recent years) among the Yafar, and Catholic and older (though now interrupted) among the Umeda. Young men, although not many among the Umeda, went to work under contract in the plantations of the Bismarck archipelago. Such prospects of work away from home ended for the entire region in the early 1970s, but the planned construction of a road linking the Sepik region to the northern coast holds out some promise of development in the future.

THE IDA RITUAL OF THE UMEDA

Turning now to the ritual that is the subject of this book, let us begin by summarizing the description of it given by Gell in chapter 4 of *Metamorphosis of the Cassowaries*. In principle, it takes place each year during the dry season (July–August) but is announced between 8 and 10 months earlier, at the beginning of the rainy reason, with a day and a night of wooden trumpet music; the intermediary period, which is regarded as a preparatory phase, is marked by a number of taboos, especially concerning the coconut palms that surround each hamlet and the making of noise. The prospective performers in the ritual also observe eating and sexual prohibitions.

During the days preceding the beginning of the public ritual, a secret clearing (*prob,* literally "source") is made near the hamlet where the ritual will take place, with the intention of hiding from the women the making of masks and the preparation of the dancers (body paint). The materials that will be used for the masks are collected in the forests by the men and brought to the *prob*. Two days before the ritual begins, the men send the women out into the forest and then begin secretly to cut the infrapetiolar tissues of the coconut palms (*wata*), vegetal cloth that is then decorated with clan motifs and sewn together in pairs back to back to form the central part of the *tamwa* (fish) masks.

The preparation of the masks may also be the occasion for a ritual gift of the first phallocrypt (ovoid penis gourd) to a youth, a gesture performed by a "maternal uncle" and accompanied by a symbolic rebirth of the novice crawling out from between his uncle's legs.

The public ritual begins one evening with the entry (a screen of leaves hides the wings of the sacred enclosure from the spectators' view) of two pairs of characters:

First Night

1. The *eli sabbra,* "the two men," their bodies entirely blackened, wear an *ageli* mask surmounted by sago palms and dance with the black ritual phallocrypt, *pedasuh,* which is made to swing vertically so that it strikes a bone belt (*oktek*) and produces a characteristic clicking sound; the dance movement that this triggers suggests the sexual act. These two figures are defined as representing two cassowaries and dance alone in the center of the hamlet area. They are played by mature men from each moiety of the society.

2. The *molna tamwa,* "fish of the daughters," their bodies painted all over with red ochre, wear only an ordinary penis gourd (of the yellow ovoid kind) and move slowly backward and forward, keeping to the edge of the dancing ground. Their heads are covered with fish masks. Unlike the *eli,* they are followed by a retinue of young boys. These roles are played by two unmarried youths, belonging to each moiety.

Eli and *molna tamwa* dance uninterruptedly until dawn. Simultaneously, five trumpet players (undecorated men or boys, who may be replaced at any time) walk around the area breathing into their instruments, while the population as a whole sings a wordless melody. The women dance only on the periphery, in a style that consists of making their string skirts stick out horizontally. Like those men who are merely spectators, they wear only personal decorations consisting of feathers, decorative foliage, and sweet-smelling plants and are allowed to paint their faces only in a discreet way (Gell 1975: 183).

First Day

At the first light of dawn, *eli* and *molna tamwa* are dismissed from the scene and the exhausted dancers are replaced by two characters known as *aba* (sago). They wear the masks of the *eli,* but their body paint, contrasting with that of the *eli,* consists of wide, horizontal, multicolored stripes; they also dance wearing the black phallocrypt. At the same time, mature men ritually prepare a full container of sago jelly (*yis*) according to the usual method. A limbum (a receptacle made of areca palm sheath) of water is boiled by placing hot stones in it; the water is then poured into another limbum containing sago until the jelly congeals of its own accord. While the stones are being heated, the two dancers jump from time to time over the fire. According to Gell, all the men have brought some sago with them. The women disappear from view because they must not witness the making of this ceremonial *yis.* When the jelly is ready, the men and the two male dancers gather around the receptacle and the hands of the two *aba* are plunged into the hot jelly; the dancers then fling a handful of the jelly into the air. The other men responsible for this operation shout out spells invoking the growth of the sago palms and throw bits of the jelly over themselves. When this ritual is over, the *aba* dancers withdraw "off-stage" and are replaced by the two performers (each of whom always belongs to one of the moieties) called *ulateh.*

These two characters, whose name denotes firewood (*teh*), wear the same kind of masks as those of the *eli* and *aba,* except these have a long central mast surmounted by a bunch of croton and cordyline. The performers' bodies are covered with horizontal or diagonal, multicolored stripes, and they dance wearing the *pedasuh* phallocrypt for about an hour; no particular event accompanies their dance, which simply ends with the *yis* ceremony.

When the performers withdraw, it is about nine in the morning, and the rest of the day will be taken up with dancing by a number of participants wearing fish masks. They dance in a line round the arena, swinging their *pedasuh* and holding a bow and arrow. A distinction must be drawn between two kinds of Fish: (a) the *ahoragwana tamwa,* "the Fish of Ahoragwa," a mythical "bad woman" identified with the *ahora* toad, and (b) the *tetagwana tamwa,* "the Fish of Tetagwa," the beautiful cult heroine, the "melon (*tet*) woman." These two mythical female figures are associated with the culture heroes *Toag-tod* (negative) and *Pul-tod* (positive), respectively.

The *ahoragwana tamwa* first dance alone, their bodies completely painted with charcoal, dotted with white spots made with kaolin. They are gradually replaced by the *tetagwana tamwa,* whose bodies, in contrast, are marked by remarkable varied polychromatic motifs (stripes, horizontal lines, and lozenges). For both kinds of Fish role, the dancers wear a fish mask, the central part of which consists of the double fibrous tissue of the coconut tree mentioned above, decorated with the performer's clan emblem. The dancers are replaced continually, and the men, in the ritual enclosure forbidden to women, constantly decorate the bodies of the new participants, while the masks pass from one dancer to another. Meanwhile, the trumpet players are replaced from time to time on the public stage, thus ensuring the musical continuity of the ritual.

During the Fish dance, secondary characters (of which Gell describes five types) appear for a few moments, sometimes representing woodland devils for the Umeda or, according to the author, ogres and ogresses: the bodies of the performers are often covered in mud, their heads encased in vegetal materials and their choreographic style grotesque or violent. They enter the public arena directly from the forest and go back to it, often chased off by the spectators, who respond to their appearance with fear, consternation, or laughter.

The first day ends with a brief appearance of the "Termite" (*amov*) characters and of the *ipele* described below.

Second Night

The second night is taken up with the sacred *awsego* chants, whose words, Gell tells us, are difficult to make out; seven or eight senior men walk up and down emitting a series of chants until dawn. The singers wear no decoration, and no masked figure appears, except a pair of *ab* (wildfowl), which, around midnight, appear for a short time, while the chants are temporarily interrupted to make way for the trumpets.

Second Day

At daybreak, the two *eli* of the first night reappear briefly. They are immediately replaced by the *ahoragwana tamwa,* then by the *tetagwana tamwa,* as on the previous day. The *yis* ceremony and the dance of the *aba* and *ulateh* are not repeated. As on the first day, the polychrome Fish are renewed uninterruptedly throughout the day, the women dancing on the periphery.

Toward the end of the afternoon the *amov* (Termites) appear: their body paint is similar to that of the *tetagwana tamwa,* their heads hidden in material made from the underbark of *Gnetum gnemon* yellowed in the *Curcuma* and suggesting a termite's head, their headdress resembling the nonritual headdress worn by the spectators, and they wear a necklace of colored croton and cordyline leaves and the orange *subove* fruit (*Rejoua aurantiaca*). Each dancer wears an ordinary phallocrypt and holds a bow and arrow. The style of the dance, which is freer and joyful, has lost the phallic character of the Cassowaries (*eli*) or Fish, and the performers (often more than two) urge all the young boys to follow them, singing in the same way as when they accompanied the *molna tamwa* on the first night.

It is at this point in the ritual that one of the youths having received, a few days before, his first phallocrypt (see above), is allowed to walk around the dancing ground accompanied by a "maternal uncle" without decorations; the neophyte, called *nemetod* (new man), wears a *pedasuh* phallocrypt and *oktek* belt, as well as a *tamwa* mask; his body is entirely painted with red ochre, with no motif added. The *nemetod* may also be designated by the term *ipele,* just as the true *ipele,* which I am about to describe and whose appearance ends the Ida ceremony, may be called *nemetod.*

The *ipele* occupy the second level in the hierarchy of prestige or of the sacredness of the Ida ritual roles. There are two of them—a representative from each moiety—and the actors assuming this role cannot represent any other ritual character in the same ceremony. Their masks are a "miniaturized" version of the *tamwa* masks. Their bodies are entirely painted with red ochre, but with black motifs specific to each moiety: a motif known as *kwituda* (young cassowary) consisting of two vertical lines on the chest and back for the representative of the male moiety (*edtodna*), two circles painted on the abdomen and on the small of the back of the dancer for the *ipele* of the female moiety (*agwatodna*). The performers wear no penile cover, but their sex is decorated by a vegetal tie (*subnab*) drawn from the heart of the wild areca tree (*sub*). The arrow that the *ipele* hold in shooting position on their bows is of the three-pronged type, also designated by the term *ipele,* reserved for the hunting of birds and very small game. In the Ida context, the prongs of these arrows are painted red and, like the penes of the participants (Gell notes) carry a *subnab* tie.

The *ipele* performers must remain secluded under the shelter of the *prob* from the beginning of the ritual to the point at which they leave. They then walk several turns around the dancing arena, preceded by two men wearing neither mask, painting, nor ritual penile decoration, but carrying a bow and a tipless arrow whose end is smeared with mud: these are the *kwanugwi* (old men, whom Gell also calls preceptors). This role is played by two older men, who must also belong to a generation older than that of the *ipele*. Gell notes the similarity in function of the two *ipele*'s guides and of the *nemetod*'s "mother's brothers" described above. "Their function is to instruct the *ipele* in their role as bowmen, for the latter, being 'new men' must be treated as if they had not yet acquired the art" (Gell 1975:205). The *ipele* and their tutors appear on the public square on three occasions: briefly in the late afternoon on the first and on the second day, then for a longer time at sunset on the second day at the end of the ritual. These four characters do not dance but walk with a slow, measured step, arrows pointing down to the ground, alternately stretching and relaxing their bows. Meanwhile, the trumpets play an accelerated rhythm; the women must not witness the appearance of the *ipele* and disappear during their presence in the hamlet. The general atmosphere is solemn, contrasting with the joyful atmosphere that characterized the dance of the Termites.

Finally, at the end of their last appearance, the two *kwanugwi* stop and, facing the setting sun, shoot their arrows over the coconut palms toward the bush; after each of them, the *ipele* of the corresponding moiety does the same. Having released their arrows, the two bowmen drop their bows and flee to the ritual enclosure beyond the public's view. The other dancers still present (Fish, Termites) leave the public arena in turn, while the trumpets emit long, harmonious notes.

That is the end of the Ida ritual as such, as described by Alfred Gell for Umeda society. The author adds that the men set off hunting, an activity that has been suspended for several weeks, after washing in a stream, they smear themselves with the blood of small fowl, in order—they say—to cleanse themselves of the "dirt" that the ritual has left on them. This having been done, a whole day devoted to trumpet music—and corresponding to the similar opening ritual almost a year before—brings the ceremonial period to an official end.

GELL'S INTERPRETATION

When Alfred Gell began his 17-month stay among the Umeda in February 1969, no study had yet been undertaken on any of the Border Mountains societies (with the exception of Galis's investigations on the Dutch side); but during this period Hanns Peter settled among the Gargar in the extreme southwest of the massif, Peter Huber began his study of the village of Wamu among the Anggor, and I myself made my first sojourn with the Yafar (May 1970). When he arrived, Gell had no knowledge of the existence of the Ida ritual, but he soon had occasion to observe it at Umeda and in other Waina groups (Punda and Sowanda). As a result, he devoted his investigations not only to Umeda social structure and economic life, but more specifically to deciphering the symbolic system of that ritual. The main result of that research was his book *Metamorphosis of the Cassowaries: Umeda Society, Language and Ritual,* to which one should add a number of articles (see the references at the end of this volume). The book was well received by the international anthropological community and is often proposed as a methodological model for the interpretation of ritual; some authors offered commentaries on Ida and on Gell's approach in later articles (by Brunton 1980a and b; Huyghe 1982; Johnson 1981; Jorgensen 1981b; Wagner 1984; Werbner 1984, 1989, n.d.; and others). The main title of the work suggests the ultimate interpretation that Gell gave to Ida, namely, the regeneration of the Cassowary as representation of Man. The association of the terms "language" and "ritual" suggests one of the aspects of the method of analysis used by the author. By language he means the language of nonverbal signs (forms, materials, colors, gestures), as well as the lexical productions whose agglutinative character makes possible a comparison of words through the identification of recurrent segments bearing the same meaning. Following in the steps of S. Ullman, the author demonstrates this approach to the meaning of words in a chapter entitled "Language and Symbolism"; this enables him to bring out a few key notions of the Umeda symbolic system, which forms, for example, in an organic structure, the triple analogy between (a) a centrality-masculinity-vertical axis-trunk-agnatic continuity group, (b) an opposed marginality-femininity-branches of tree-lateral parts of the body group, and (c) a daughter-fruit or son-young shoot group.

Outside the semantic analysis of the terms designating objects, colors, ritual behavior, or natural species to which Ida refers, Gell tries to reconstitute the nonverbal discourse of the ritual in its paradigmatic as well as syntagmatic dimension on the basis of these last items regarded in terms of their nonlinguistic characteristics: the recapitulative table that served as his basic model is reproduced in table 1. At this level, he admits to having been inspired both by Roland Barthes's *Elements of Semiology* and by Claude Lévi-Strauss's analysis of myths. His approach is therefore clearly structuralist, although he does recognize a debt to V. Turner, who, he says, alerted him to the notion of ritual symbolism and provided him with the principle of a transformation of the ritual's "sensory meaning" into an "ideological meaning" (Gell 1975:chap. 5). However, Gell moves away from Turner—it is well known how much stress Turner puts on local exegesis—when he notes "the virtual absence of 'native exegesis' " in his approach to Ida. The esoteric knowledge secretly kept by old Umeda men (most of which seems to concern magical practice) does not seem, in Gell's eyes, to be capable of assisting the analysis, which can culminate in an interpretation only by developing an "observer's construct." But beyond the decoding of symbols and the construction of a "model system within which symbols . . . are made relative to explanatory concepts" (Gell 1975:214), Gell aspires to a sociological interpretation of Ida that, while praising G. Bateson's analysis of the *Naven* ceremony (1936), does not hesitate to follow Durkheim's approach (*The Elementary Forms of Religious Life*), but with, as he says, a "less schematic view of ritual" and with a more Malinowskian conception, seeing in society a "structure of interlocking, balanced, role-complementarities" (Gell 1975:210).

As far as the interpretation of the ritual itself is concerned (Gell 1975:chap. 5), Gell sees in Ida a fertility ritual that goes well beyond the aim given by the Umeda to encourage the growth of sago palms. It is society as a whole that is symbolically regenerated by the performance; indeed, the ritual evolves between the nocturnal dance of the Cassowaries, who represent, according to the author, male autonomy and the final appearance of the *ipele,* who represent the same pair of the regenerated birds. The roles are spread over three generations, namely, the guide, or mother's brother of the *ipele* (G + 1); the Cassowaries (*eli*) and the *ipele* in an elder-younger relationship of the same generation (G = 0); and the *molna tamwa* or "daughters" (G − 1). Elsewhere,

Table 1.
Ida Ritual of the Umeda

Name of role	Body paint style	Mask type	Mask fringe	Feathers, leaves	Treatment of dancer's penis	Bow and arrow	Dance style	Social status of actor
Night →								
Eli (cassowary)	All black	Ageli	Hubnab (pandanus)	Naveli (sago fronds)	Pedasuh and oktek	None	Energetic, unstructured, (occasionally holding hands)	Senior man
Molna tamwa (fish)	All red	Tamwa	Subnab (limbum)	Gouria hornbill, parrot, etc.	Peda	Present	Restrained, single-file followed by children	Neophyte
Dawn →								
Aba (sago)	Polychrome horizontal bands	Ageli	Hubnab	Naveli	Pedasuh and oktek	None	Energetic, leaping over the fire	Senior man
Early Morning →								
Teh (firewood)	Polychrome decorative patterns	Teh	Hubnab	Naveli and cassowary plumes	Pedasuh and oktek	None	Energetic	Intermediate
Ahoragwana tamwa (fish)	Black with random markings	Tamwa	Subnab	Gouria, hornbill, etc.	Pedasuh and oktek	Present	Energetic, single-file (aggressive)	Senior (old men)
Midday and Afternoon →								
Tetagwana tamwa (fish)	Polychrome decorative patterns	Tamwa	Subnab	Gouria, hornbill, etc.	Pedasuh and oktek	Present	Energetic, single file (aggressive)	Intermediate (young men)
Amov (termite)	Polychrome decorative patterns	Amov	Hubnab (small)	Nu-leaves	Peda	Present	Restrained, followed by children	Senior man
Nemetod (neophyte)	All red	Tamwa	Subnab	Gouria, hornbill, etc.	Pedasuh and oktek	Present	Energetic (one circuit only)	Neophyte
Sunset								
Kwanugwi (preceptor)	None	None	None	None	Peda	Bow and dummy arrow	Slow, very restrained (fires arrow)	Old man
Ipele (bowman)	Red and black designs	Ipele (miniature tamwa)	Subnab (dead-white immature material)	Ebata (cockatoo-down)	Penis bound with nab (kynodesme)	Red bow and ipele arrow	Slow, very restrained (fires arrow)	Intermediate

Source: Gell (1975), table 4.

when examining in particular the syntagmatic sequence of colors in the body painting (from the black of the *eli,* through the polychrome motifs of the Fish, to the red of the *ipele,* while the duration of "organic process time" moves from red to black), Gell concludes—using certain arguments derived from Edmund Leach concerning time structues—that the ritual is constructed according to an inversion of symbolic time in relation to profane time: "The fundamental mechanism whereby the 'regeneration of the total society' is achieved . . . is the inversion of time" (338). The author stresses that the *ipele* are, in relation to the *eli,* "endowed with characteristically 'cultural' attributes" and are associated with a certain "structural formality": he thus sees in the "red bowman" the figure of the Cassowary "metamorphosed into his nascent self" and in the conclusion of Ida more generally "a victory over 'entropy' " (338).

THE YAFAR YANGIS AS A RITUAL EXPRESSION OF ONTOGENESIS

The Yafar adopted the Ida cult (that is to say, the ritual and the mythology associated with it) from the Punda—probably as a result of their intermarriages with the latter—several generations earlier. As chapter 1 shows, it is the same ritual, although the Yafar renamed it Yangis.

Chapter 1 provides details of all the ethnographical elements—whether from observation, free commentary, or the secret exegesis of the Yafar—that have led me to interpret Yangis as the ritual enactment of the reproduction of the two moiety totems, the embodiment of the society. In it the *eli* are the "mothers" giving birth to the totemic "sons," enacted by the *ipele.* Mothers and sons are the personifications of both the male and female totemic species, but for each totemic line the process of reproduction proceeds from the mothers to the sons: the *sexual identity* of the moieties is thus independent of the *reproductive process* that links mothers to sons.

This analysis is based on two ideas: that of totem (which Gell does not use) and that of Oedipus complex (which he passes over in his monograph and which he seems to refute in this book). I use the notion of totemism only at the level of the moieties; the clan "emblems" painted on the *ogomô mesoog* masks do not seem to represent natural species that can be called totems, although for the groups concerned they may give rise to taboos concerning food. The fact that the Yafar define themselves, according to their moiety, as "children of the blood" of the male and female primordial sago palms (or of the male sago palm and the female coconut palm) is implicitly illustrated by a secret cosmogonic myth revealing that the red paint with which the *ipele* cover themselves represents the blood spilled by their mother from which they emerge after her death. Last, a Yafar exegesis reveals the meaning to be given to the behavior of the performers embodying the *ipele:* by first pointing their arrows at the body of the earth-mother, they signify the desire for matricial return (whose phallic expression recalls the notion of incest), whereas in finally pointing them at the sun (the metamorphosed original mother's breast), they appropriate the mother's feeding function as a transition toward socialization, and therefore to the replacement of the father; this emancipation from the umbilical link is possible only through the mediation of the "mother's brother" (guide or preceptor), who, in this context, replaces the natural father.

These suggestions, which will be developed in chapter 1, give a general idea of the extent to which the oedipal symbolic system is closely bound up with totemic structure, or how the latter is made more dynamic by the transition in the maternal register from an umbilical relation to a feeding relation and by the engagement that follows in the process of socialization. The social Subject is personified here in those whom the Yafar call "children of the blood," an expression they use elsewhere to designate themselves collectively, both moieties together.

As we shall see, the method (and the implicit reference to Freud) that I am proposing in order to understand Yangis has been based on the ethnographical material, above all on the exegetical commentaries provided by the interested parties themselves. This problem of the heuristic value to be given to the native exegesis probably accounts for the methodological divergence between Gell's interpretation and mine: indeed, this gives rise to the alternative of locating meaning, in the absence of exegesis, in the structure of signs (linguistic or nonverbal) and of the symbols that *constitute* the raw material of the public ritual, or as far as possible in local commentaries *about* the ritual in order to reveal something of its coherence. Whether or not such commentaries were forthcoming during our investigations determined, both for Gell and for me, but with different results, the method to be applied to the work of interpretation.

COMMENTARIES AND CRITICISMS: THE OTHER CONTRIBUTIONS

The subtlety of Gell's semiotic and structural approach on the one hand, and the insight provided by the new approach, on the other—which makes possible the Yafar exegesis and its psychoanalytical extension—led me to compare the two and to recognize their complementarity at the level both of interpretation and of method. This prompted me to present the two studies for the consideration of a number of anthropologists and psychoanalysts. Apart from Alfred Gell, who had opened the debate, none of the contributors has been involved in field research in West Sepik Province. However, Marilyn Strathern, Roy Wagner, Donald Tuzin, and Andrew Strathern are among the best specialists of New Guinea societies, and all have had considerable experience in the field; they have been joined by Richard Werbner, who, although he has not done research in Melanesia, has carried out field research elsewhere and is particularly interested in Melanesia, especially in Gell's research into the Umeda. On the side of the psychoanalysts, André Green has long been known for his contributions to the anthropological debate, through his work on mythology and Greek tragedy and his interventions in pluridisciplinary discussions at the seminar on identity directed by Claude Lévi-Strauss in 1974–75. As an alternative to André Green's contribution, François Manenti's text offers an interpretation more directly inspired by the theory of Jacques Lacan; it is probably one of the first Lacanian readings of a Melanesian ritual.

While the chapters by Tuzin and A. Strathern, and to a large degree the one by Gell, pose fundamental questions about method and thus offer epistemological commentaries on the analysis of Ida-Yangis and on the understanding of ritual in general, the diversity of the reconstructions offered by Marilyn Strathern, Wagner, and Werbner open up new interpretative approaches on the basis of Umeda and Yafar ethnographical material and of the two hermeneutics applied to them. Marilyn Strathern, in particular, brings to the discussion her theories, which have already been tested in other New Guinea societies, on the dialectic of gender and on the notion of androgynousness as revealed by the symbolic gift of a "detachable part" of the person. Roy Wagner, for his part, gives us an analysis of Yafar and Umeda material on the basis of his theory of the symbol, as he defined it in his *Symbols that Stand for Themselves,* while Richard Werbner develops a comparative discussion of the two interpretations of Ida and Yangis and explores meaning by taking into account differential cultural depths at the regional level.

So the ground, I hope, has been prepared. It only remains to invite the reader to exercise a little patience in the first stage, the analysis of the Yafar Yangis. The sometimes minute ethnographical details, the apparently insignificant role of certain ritual gestures may surprise; yet it is by a meticulous consideration of these elements and of the Yafar commentaries that one may be able to arrive at an interpretation moving in the direction of reestablishing a not immediately obvious meaning.

NOTES

1. The works available on the Border Mountains as such are, from north to south, those of A. G. Gell, B. Juillerat, P. B. Huber, and H. Peter (see main titles in References), and K. W. Galis (1956, 1956–57) for the formerly Dutch part of the region.

Bernard Juillerat

I "The Mother's Brother Is the Breast": Incest and Its Prohibition in the Yafar Yangis

This chapter is a detailed ethnographic account of the Yangis ritual of the Yafar people of West Sepik Province. As I have explained in the Introduction, Yangis is the Yafar equivalent of the Ida festival of the Umeda, analyzed by Alfred Gell in *Metamorphosis of the Cassowaries*. The aim of this chapter is not to comment further on Gell's notable book or to offer a detailed criticism of his method. Many points of his analysis of the Ida ritual among the Umeda are corroborated by my own field-work among the Yafar. As already noted, however, the evidence of a rich local exegesis calls for a reconsideration of Gell's interpretation of the Ida/Yangis ritual and of the structuralist-semiotic method he applied in his "observer's model," in that both are based on the postulated lack of native exegesis (Gell 1975:211–15). Because my own material is in most cases sufficient to rebuild the ritual coherence, I shall not compare each point discussed with my colleague's work but instead shall leave that to the initiative of the interested reader by giving the page references to relevant passages of *Metamorphosis of the Cassowaries* (hereafter referred to as *MC*).

The Yafar (200 people in three hamlets) and the Wamuru (about the same population) are the only Amanab speakers who perform the Yangis ritual.[1] One or two generations ago, the Potayneri (the Yafar's southern neighbors) performed it once or twice, with some fear of supernatural consequences, and then gave up after the death of the man responsible for organizing the ritual. The Wamuru, who have recently converted to Christianity, will probably never organize it again. The 1976 performance by the Yafar was the first after an interruption of ten or more years, and the ritual leaders were extremely afraid to allow the high sacredness involved in the calling of remote deities to surge again. I have already mentioned that the Yafar call Ida by another name, Yangis (henceforth, I shall use that name for the Yafar performance, and Ida for that of the Waina speakers: Punda, Umeda, Sowanda).[2] The name *ira* is also used in Yafar, but usually to refer to the women's dance style, in which they move their hips from side to side in order to swing their skirts (*efreeg ira* means "to wag its tail" [dog] or "to wriggle" [fish]). In myths, *ira* seems to mean simply "ritual" when following the ritual name (see *MC:*156).[3] The etymology for Yangis is not certain; in reference to the Amanab language, we may identify the segment *angô* (present also in Waina: *MC:*133–35, 148) as meaning both "female" and "peripheral." The ending *-is* might refer to the Amanab and Waina word for sago jelly, *yis,* which is also a basic reference in the ritual. The first phoneme of the word could, hypothetically, evoke the *yi* (*ii, iy*) pigeon—*Ptilinopus rivoli*—which is a mythical symbol for "man" (in opposition to the bird of paradise representing woman). "Yangis" would then be the aggregate of the meanings: "man," "woman," "sago jelly." We shall see that the sago jelly and its ritualized cooking process during Yangis refers to the fusion of both sexual principles in conception.

Together with the ceremony, the Yafar borrowed from the Umeda and Punda a body of esoteric knowledge that, as will be shown, is part of the exegetical material for Yangis. My informants often stated that the entire cult is roughly the same in Umeda, Punda, and Yafar and that its original place is Umeda, considered the "mother" group, with Punda and Yafar being its "daughters" (Juillerat 1986). Umeda is regarded as a maternal totemic place, where the original mother-coconut was to be found, while the (previously unique) Yafar village, Sahya, is the male totemic place, where the penis of the first god emerged out of the earth and changed into a sacred tree (which has since disappeared; see note 68). The myths about the primordial male sago palm are also supposed to have taken place in Sahya. From an exclusively maternal point of view, however, Umeda is associated with the original coconut, while the "daughters' " groups are said to have come out of its fallen flowers. The coconut inflorescence is the naturalistic representation of the unity of the local tribal groups (Waina and Northern Amanab), who follow the

scientific community of firsthand material. This is why I chose to publish the exegetical elements of Yangis in the present form without the numerous ritual names that are not crucial to our understanding. Furthermore, I have been induced to do so by the previous investigations undertaken by Gell. Should the reader ever work in the Amanab district, I trust that he or she will remember that secrecy is still a key element for the perpetuation of ritual life and social order in these societies.

I first provide all the necessary ethnographic material to support my general interpretation.

MYTHOLOGICAL AND CONCEPTUAL BACKGROUND

Sexual Totemism

Before entering into an analytical examination of Yangis, let us make clear the more general conceptual and social framework in which this ritual takes place. Alfred Gell has already given a comprehensive analysis of Umeda social structure in his second chapter, as I did for the Yafar elsewhere (Juillerat 1981, 1986). To understand Yangis, it is first necessary to become familiar with the representation both Yafar and Waina speakers share of their society as a part or a reflection of a sexualized cosmos. The two symbolically male and female moieties of the society (in Amanab: *Araneri* or *Aratuar,* and *Angwaneri* or *Angwatuar*) are associated with natural species.[7] More specifically, they are associated with the coconut, *sa,* which is often replaced by the sago palm of the *fenaw* subspecies (clone) for the female moiety, and the sago palm clone *afwêêg* for the male moiety.[8] Coconut and *afwêêg* sago palm are the moieties' main totems, and *Araneri* people secretly assert that they are the "children of the *afwêêg* blood," while *Angwaneri* say they are the "children of the coconut (flowers') blood"; this is shortened into the formulation *afwêêg taf, sa taf. Taf,* "blood," is referred to more generally as the original substance and serves also as a euphemistic form of semen. Yafar people as a whole designate themselves by the same term they use to qualify the *ifegê* [Waina: *ipele*] figures in Yangis: *taf na ruwar,* "the children [who originated out] of blood."[9] We shall understand later that Yangis (Ida) is the expression of that very relationship, the two *ifegê* being the totemic mothers' sons in their transformation into men.

The totemic pair is definitely to be seen as a parental couple. This is confirmed by the way a Punda man expressed it to me: "We used to say that our Mother is close to our house (the coconut palm), while our Father is away in the forest" (the *afur* [see note 8] sago palm). This is still more obvious when one considers the way the universe came into being out of the repeated copulations of a humanlike pair of deities, whose secret names I shall only refer to by initials. W . . . and B . . . were in empty space when there was no earth, no sky, and no sun. The first earth, quite small, was formed little by little out of their sexual fluids. The fire that eventually rushed out of their intercourse burned and strengthened the earth. W . . . put a little of his semen on the top of his head and pushed the celestial vault upward.[10] The *afwêêg* sago tree and the coconut are the naturalistic incarnations of W . . . and B. . . . Informants A and B said that sago palms, and *afwêêg* in particular, were like erect penes full of semen. In a complementary way, the coconut palm (in spite of its trunk, which is considered its male part, originally separated from its petiolar fiber sheets) is the basic maternal incarnation of Waina and Amanab cultures. Myths and numerous exegetical elements give the inflorescence or the hanging nuts as breasts; the fallen nut as the uterus in gestation (the origin of the amniotic liquid is the water of the mythical coconut); the germinated nut as the dying mother who just bore a son; and the coconut infrapetiolar fiber used in the fish masks in Yangis and Ida (*MC:*186) also as a female envelope out of which grow the new (male) leaves. More convincing evidence of the maternal connotation of the coconut palm is provided by the rite performed on a coconut tree a few months before Yangis, which is discussed below. For the ritual performance, where plant material is needed to make masks, the coconut, being the scarcest species (planted only in villages), cannot be felled nor its leaves cut. The only part collected is the infrapetiolar fiber, also used in daily life for sago washing. This peculiarity of coconut cultivation, contrasting with the omnipresence of wild and planted sago, is important. It leads to a new formulation of the totemic pair in the ritual context, with *afwêêg / fenaw*, the female sago clone being substituted for the coconut. This is why Yangis is basically dealing with sago reproduction, and only implicitly with that of the coconut. *Fenaw* appears thus as a substitution for the coconut. But in both views, the ritual is carried out (under the responsibility of their respective priests) by the men of the two moieties who are the social embodiment of both sexualized forces at work in nature. Totems and moieties (nature and society, male and female principles) are thus renewed in Yangis.

The words "totemism" and "totem" have not been dismissed here, in spite of the semantic weakening endured by those concepts through multiple cultural forms and theoretical interpretations (Lévi-Strauss 1963b), because of their clear sociological definitions provided by the sexualized moieties. (Clan totemism among the Yafar would be a much more uncertain notion, in spite of the existence of emblems and tabooed species at the clan level: see table 1.1). Moreover the term "sexual" has been preferred to "dual" (or "of moieties"), because—for the cultural area considered—sexual differentiation has primacy over dualism as such; meaning determines structure, not the reverse.

Hoofuk/Roofuk

In order to understand what natural reproduction and its social expression mean for the Yafar, a key concept in the representation of fertility must be explained: *hoofuk*.[11] The different levels of signification of that word are

1. Tuber flesh, sago, or banana pith, heart of all tree trunks.

2. Vital force situated in the body and associated with the digestive system in animal and man.

3. White substance supposedly present in the uterus and its reproductive power (also linked to the original coconut water).

4. Reproductive substance in plants, animals, and men (especially semen, sexual fluids, and menstrual blood) and also apparent in clay underground or in stone caves.

Moreover, this concept is often associated with the idea of origin, life source, exegetical knowledge, Western "cargo," and its alleged secret place of production (for instance, in the millenarian movement of 1981; Juillerat 1986, 1991a), and also with the color white (Juillerat 1978b; *MC*:314). In the first three levels of meaning, *hoofuk* is opposed to *roofuk*, "skin, bark, envelope, or sterile debris covering the soil in cultivation." A frequently recurring rite that opens many magical operations for improving fertility consists of spells and manipulations that evoke the "peeling off" (*roof*) of the soil, cultivars, planting sticks, or game. In magic, the word *hoofuk* is often related to the two totemic species and Yangis itself is seen as a complex enterprise to renew the *hoofuk* of the two sago clones already specified. This concept is valid for the reproductive powers of both sexes, but bears a dominantly female connotation. The word is used also to describe the proximity to fertility that characterizes Yangis dancers whose bodies are covered with paintings and decorated with perfumed ritual plants. They are said "to be the *hoofuk*." In more general terms, the communities who perform Ida or Yangis and keep the esoteric knowledge associated with this cult feel "in the *hoofuk*," in opposition to other groups deprived of similar power over fertility.

YANGIS

In the following section, I first give the chronology of ritual roles in the public performance, then describe the secondary rites practiced by priests and older men before the village festival takes place.[12] Gell discusses more roles for Ida than I observed for Yangis. But the main roles, particularly those appearing in pairs, were the same, with slight differences in the structure of masks and body paintings. The trumpet music was identical. Clan emblems have, as I was told, different designs than those of the Umeda fish masks. The names of masks or roles are often semantically different in Yafar and Umeda or Punda (Waina names provided by Gell are indicated in brackets).

Ritual Figures: Description and Exegesis

ERI (SABAGA) [ELI SABBRA], "THE TWO PERSONS" (PLATE 1)   The word *êri* [*eli, ed*] "human being" (in opposition to animal or even white man, pidgin *masta*); but it seems to have, in certain contexts, a male connotation.[13]

However, the basic local interpretation for the *êri* roles is that they represent the "mothers" (*MC*:179–82, 224) of the totemic sago palms, that is, the fading out female generation that must give way to the daughters' generation (see *yis* below).[14] But, when the two *êri* hold each other's hand, people say this is to express copulation. Some add that the swinging of the mask sago leaves during the dance is like the woman's skirts (*nay*) moving during intercourse. The contradiction is only apparent: the transmission of the *hoofuk* in the female line demands that, for both totemic species, mothers precede daughters; this is an all-female, or female-dominated representation. But if one envisions the symbolic gender of the two sago palms, the *êri sabaga* must be identified as the vegetal metaphor of the anthropomorphic original couple, W . . . and B . . . (see below: "Sexual identity, reproduction, and filiation"). Whatever the local interpretation, the *êri* are often designated as *afwêêg-ii fenaw-ii, afwêêg* and *fenaw* sago palms. Yafar informants did not identify them with cassowaries (*MC:*179–80, 243–45).

Masks (êri mesoog, "êri's *head*", [ageli]). The main elements are the sago leaves that dominate them. They have been cut off from *afwêêg* and *fenaw* clones (see also the ritual felling of the two species), by people from the *Araneri* (male) and *Angwaneri* (female) moieties, respectively (or perhaps with a gender inversion). The Yafar masks are slightly different from the Umeda *ageli* (*MC:*174–75), but I could not check their fabrication in detail. I was told that, as is the case for the fish masks, some raw sago—designated by a secret word—was placed at its center to represent the palm's *hoofuk*.

Body paintings. The basic design is black spotted with white. When the elders paint the two performers in the ritual enclosure, they recite about *afwêêg suhig* and *fenaw suhig* and use charcoal from the soft inner material of these sago species' petioles. The term *suhig,* central also for the plantation ritual in a new garden, refers to blackness as a sign of maturity at its peak. One may identify it also in the word for the blackened ritual phallocrypt *suh-wagmô* [*pedasuh*]. Black paint is the proper color for seniority, strength, and reproductivity.[15] People say it also refers to the dark green color of healthy plants, in contrast to yellowish dry leaves (Juillerat 1978b). For the *êri,* blackness recalls that the sago palm's "mothers" are simultaneously at the peak of their fecundity and about to lose it in favor of their "daughters." The white kaolinic splashes could refer to the white fluid (see above, definition 3 of *hoofuk*) supposedly present as the mark of the residual fecundity still at work in the old (black) mothers.

I was told that the *êri's* body bears secret designs (which I could not observe because I heard about it only months later). As will be discussed in more detail later, the original Mother (B . . . or the anthropomorphic Coconut deity) died in childbirth and her corpse was cut into pieces; her single breast became the sun. According to informant B, this severed breast is shown on the *Angwaneri* dancer's body with a white (kaolin and

Plate 1. *Eli* [Yafar *êri*] during a Punda Ida ritual (1986). Black body paint, *ageli* mask surmounted by sago leaves and *pedasuh* phallocrypt. (Photo D. Niles, Courtesy of Institute of Papua New Guinea Studies, Music Department)

sago) triangular design under the neck, and the severing operation itself is made apparent by a red (ochre) design for the shed blood. These paintings are made exclusively by the two priests and their aides with appropriate spells.

OTHER EXEGETICAL ELEMENTS   1. As in Umeda, the Yafar *êri* must dance without interruption until dawn, and should not sleep during the entire ceremony: if they did sleep, it is said that growth (sago palms, gardens, children) would stop.

2. The *êri* enter the dancing ground each with a bundle in his hand. The packages contain sago from the male and female totemic clones, respectively, taro and yam flesh from two sexualized clones of these species, and sexual fluids provided by the two moiety priests and their wives; all ingredients are here again called *hoofuk*. Through a prescribed inversion also noticed by Gell in another ritual context, the *Araneri* performer holds the female bundle and the *Angwaneri* performer the male one. This exchange of *hoofuk* stuff between the performers, the Master of the Sky and the Master of the Earth (and thus between both moieties of the society), expresses the denial of hierarchy and the complementariness of the sexes in that particular phase of Yangis. Upon entering the arena and before the music and songs begin, the performers violently fling their bundles to the ground; at the same time, and together with the priests, they shout respectively: "*afwêêg* (or *fenaw*) *hoofuk pupuu!*" The last word is not translatable, but it is also shouted ("*hoofuk pupuu!*") during the garden ritual when the cultivator plants his stick for the first time into the new swidden soil. This act, called *hoofuk fatik* ("to drop the *hoofuk*"), is said to provoke an "explosion" that can be heard in remote villages.[16] The complete silence during the hour preceding the beginning of the performance was said to be necessary for a clear and powerful "noise" of the *hoofuk fatik*. (This cross-sexual relationship argues in favor of an interpretation of the *êri*'s performance as the representation of divine copulation).

3. A shout "*hwig kwiyêêg!*" (long penis) is also head when the *êri* enter. (This is related to the *bêêbi—Calamus* sp.—liana used as the central axis of masks; see below).

4. Throughout the night, the dancers keep in their mouths a piece of cassowary meat given to them by the two moiety priests before their appearance. When they get out of the arena at dawn, the priests take

back the meat and put it into the mouths of the two *yis* dancers who are now replacing the *êri*.

5. Moreover, by the end of the night, before the first glimmerings of dawn, the two priests secretly give the *êri* performers (perhaps also the *rawsu-inaag*) some cooked wild fowl (*abi: Talegalla* sp.) egg to eat. A spell is said in a low voice evoking the "fat" parts of the body of the sago palms. My best informant related this way of nourishing the *êri* to the following myth (see Juillerat 1991a:chap. 2):

> Two brothers and two sisters live together. The elder brother has married the two sisters. He discovers that his younger brother is having sexual intercourse with the younger sister. He then lures his brother into the forest on the pretext of collecting *abi* eggs and grubs, and kills him in the *abi* nest. Next day, the elder brother asks his younger wife to come and help him to collect *abi* eggs. She discovers her lover's body. Her husband compels her to swallow the dead. She sits down on the nest (like a fowl) and does so; her husband leaves. She can't move and only after a long time is she helped by two little birds (which are invoked in spells in difficult childbirth) and she evacuates, as children, her lover's bones. They immediately turn into *ogomô* spirits (sago growth spirits; see below) and they go to a dance at a (Yangis) festival (called *ira* in the myth, which might suggest a Waina origin of the story), the trumpets of which are heard from a distant village. Their mother joins the feast later and feeds her sons with cooked *abi* eggs (the public version talks only of sago jelly). They are very tall now and she is quite small. Then the *abi* mother utters her call, thus announcing dawn after "a very long night."

Informant A said the myth is about *ogomô* spirits, but that only the *êri* (not the *ogomô* performers; see below) are ritually fed with eggs; he added that the *êri* may be generically designated by the word *ogomô*, while other Yafar men limited the designation to the black performers coming in the morning after the *yis*.

What is important here is the feeding by the mother, a recurrent theme that we shall have to discuss again concerning the *ifegê* [*ipele*] bowmen. Maternal food helps in growing up; it is the natural continuation of pregnancy and birth. The *abi* egg actually represents the breast and its milk.[17] The story of the Great Mother B . . . and her death says that the first *abi* egg appeared out of the blood lost from the amputation of her breast. The *abi* personage in the myth, in giving birth to a natural growth principle, conforms to a basic Yafar representation wherein the younger sibling, excluded from the central and socialized protagonists' unit (perpetuating itself through the elder sibling), is led to the natural world where he or she is involved in some nonhuman process (Juillerat 1991a).

The *êri* are fed by the end of the night and their feeding "provokes," as the myth explicitly shows, daybreak: light after darkness (long night, *siy kwiyêêg*), life (conception, birth, growth . . .) after the working of natural forces to promote it (sexual intercourse, pregnancy . . .).

The *abi* nest is, moreover, the place (*kebik*) of pregnancy where the reproductive transformation is in process. In reference to that myth, the village place during Yangis is actually called *abi kebik*. Later we shall briefly consider the *abi* as a ritual figure.

RAWSU-INAAG [MOLNA TAMWA]   The Yafar name is different from the Umeda "fish of the daughters" (*molna tamwa; MC:*182, 231), but the Punda term *yawsu-ina* was provided as the real name for this role (*molna tamwa* being given as a more descriptive form). The suffix *-inaag* means "inside." *Su* is short for *suwê*, "fire"; fire is frequently used metaphorically (especially in spells) for blood. *Raw* demands closer consideration. Informant B told me secretly that the word designated a double lateral part of the vagina that "falls down" during first intercourse (another day he said this occurred at first childbirth). Informant A said the word had no precise meaning but it was evident that he did not want to talk about it. The segment *raw* appears independently in a technical term, *raw feg* ("to do *raw*"), which designates the squeezing of cooked pandanus fruits in one's hands in order to filter them and separate the seeds. Because pandanus is bright red and considered similar to blood (special taboos rule its consumption), one may easily guess that *raw-suwê* refers to blood shed and that the pandanus preparation is implicitly compared to defloration. Thus "hymen" appears as a likely correct translation for *raw* [*yaw*]; *raw feg* should have the etymological meaning of "to deflower" or "to let bleed"; and *rawsu-inaag* is literally "in the blood of the hymen." This was, in fact, the translation provided by informant B. The latter gave a ritual name for it, which is shouted by elder men when the two performers enter the arena. Both informants stated that the two figures are also called *emwêêg taf*, "vagina blood"

(*Angwaneri* performer), and *hwig taf,* "penis blood" (*Araneri* performer), respectively, and that they represented the blood discarded by the *êri* during intercourse. B stated that a man also bleeds during first intercourse, because a small "skin" breaks on his penis.

In mythology, the blood lost during the divine copulation turned into *bana* fish, a river species (*Eleotridae* family) with little red spots (*MC:*258). Another way of expressing this connection was to relate that two *bana* fish were created out of the "water" (blood?) kept in two original *afwêêg* and *fenaw* stumps. Indeed, the *rawsu-inaag* are sometimes called *bana.*

Let us bear in mind (*MC:*182) that the *rawsu-inaag* masks are carried by adolescent boys who walk to and fro on the edge of the village place during the first night, while the *êri* dance with clicking phallocrypts in the center. The *rawsu-inaag* are all painted red and wear ordinary phallocrypts; their masks (Bwampi and Urêy *ogomô:* see below) are the fish masks, *ogomô mesoog* [*tamwa*], and they are accompanied by children and women who sing a repetitive melody without words, filling up the whole of the first night. Their peripheral position, their "slow walking pace" (*MC:*182) and the absence of the ritual penis gourd are features that adequately express their exclusion from the proper reproductive process, which is worked out by the *êri* (*MC:*233–34).

Thus, the first night of Yangis displays a ritual disguise, the founding bisexual fusion that gives birth to (or regenerates) the totemic species and moieties. It is spatially organized after a concentric dual pattern, where primary (strong) action is complemented by secondary (weak) action. The lateral production of fertile blood to be changed into *bana* fish is structurally close to the opposition mentioned above between elder and younger siblings in which the younger is absorbed into nature.

Alfred Gell's Umeda informants described the *molna tamwa* as the "daughters" of the *eli.* Scientifically, it would be critical to try to decide which is the "right" explanation. However, they are not contradictory: the shed blood might denote the origin of the totemic sago palms' daughters who—for the Yafar—will only appear at dawn with the *yis* performers. I would even claim that this lateral procreative process is a crucial representation; as I have already emphasized and will show again later, there is a "privilege" of lateral forces (lost semen or blood, umbilical cord, placenta, but also younger—sometimes elder—sibling) to create natural fertility principles personified in anthropomorphic deities.[18] Let us add that local and individual interpretations are sometimes really contradictory: some younger Yafar informants told me that the *rawsu-inaag* were the (maternal) "grandmothers" of the two sago palms. At any rate, the common idea is that not only sexuality but female filiation is crucial in the first night of Yangis.

YIS [ABA], "SAGO JELLY" (PLATE 2)   In both Amanab and Waina languages, *aba* means "sago" (raw or cooked) and *yis* means "sago jelly" (a mixture of one part raw sago to four to six parts boiling water). The Umeda use the term *aba* for the two masks appearing at dawn, right after the *êri*'s and *rawsu-inaag*'s exit, while the Yafar call them *yis*. They are also named *afwêêg hoofuk* and *sa (fenaw) hoofuk*. The *yis* dance is closely synchronized with the confection by the two moiety priests on the dancing ground of a ritual sago jelly. Along with the *êri*'s appearance and the shooting of the *ifegê*'s arrows at the conclusion of Yangis, this is the most significant and sacred moment of the entire festival.

   a. *The* yis *ceremony* (MC:*184–85, 251–52*). As Gell has shown for the Umeda, sago (*aba*) is the vegetal metaphor for semen.[19] But *yis* is something different: a transformation has occurred through the addition of water and cooking. For fresh sago flour (as opposed to sago that has been stored in forest ponds for several months), the Yafar add a beaten red bark, collected by women from the wild tree *wayif*.[20] They say the jelly would not solidify if this bark and its juice are not mixed with the sago previously diluted in the *limbum* container.[21] I never learned whether this corresponded to a real chemical process or was purely symbolic. In some Lower Sepik communities, people put a little bit of red ochre in their sago to transform it into firm jelly. Let us add that before the opening of Yangis, as we shall see below, all domestic *limbum* are ritually prepared for the confection of *yis* destined for consumption among relatives: men knowing the appropriate spells (about sago fertility and human conception) go into all houses and rub the inside of all containers with red ochre and magical plants.[22] My interpretation— implicitly confirmed by my informants—is that the crucial point is to mix something red for the female part in conception together with sago (for semen), and that the solidification of the jelly represents the coagulation of both sexual substances, that is, the formation of the embryo. The *yis* ceremony follows the performance of the *êri* as dawn replaces night and as conception is the result of intercourse.

   The first pieces of firewood used for the *yis* ceremony must be from *Pometia pinnata*. The two priests blow first through the pieces as if they

Plate 2. The two *aba* [Yafar *yis*] during a Punda Ida ritual just before dawn (1986). Body paint made of polychrome stripes, *ageli* mask, and *pedasuh* phallocrypt. (Photo D. Niles, Courtesy of Institute of Papua New Guinea Studies, Music Department)

were wooden trumpets, with spells about the "fire of the penis sago jelly, fire of the vagina sago jelly—of the *afwêêg* sago jelly—of the *fenaw* sago jelly," and then about the odors of the things symbolizing the *hoofuk* (possum's musk, grease, egg yolk). Then they put a bit of sago from both totemic species on the wood and again pronounce similar spells. The sago itself is brought by the two priests: *afwêêg* sago by the Master of the Sky, *fenaw* sago by the Master of the Earth (but again there could be an inversion here of sexual identities). The two types of sago are mixed up and the jelly is made, while the *yis* dancers walk around with their clicking phallocrypts and leap over the fire, muttering under their masks: "*Hoofuk* of the penis sago jelly, *hoofuk* of the vagina sago jelly—of the *afwêêg* sago jelly—of the *fenaw* sago jelly." Their leaping over the fire can be explained by the identification of the masks with the sago, which is undergoing its transformation into jelly through the action of fire, that is, their identification with the male and female *hoofuk* in their fusion. The two varieties of sago represent at the same time the two "totemic semens" and the complementary sexual principles.

Then the two moiety priests, helped by the two *yis* performers, carry the heavy *limbum* full of jelly through the dancing ground, and an assistant walks backward before the *yis* and throws upward pieces of jelly, while holding in his hand a magical bulb of *Acorus calamus* dedicated to the growth of sago palms.[23] This operation is called the *yis kofatik,* the "breaking-dropping of the sago jelly." Meanwhile, they shout spells, saying: "*yis* of Nip (a male celestial place), *yis* of Amop (a female chthonian place), *yis* of the penis, *yis* of the vagina, *yis* of the umbilical cord."[24] The throwing up of jelly is said to help the sago palms grow rapidly (*MC:*185). The totemic "embyros" of the sago palms (the solidified jelly) now have to grow and become two babies by the end of Yangis as the personification of the *ifegê.* The rest of the jelly will be deposited at the bottom of sago palms near the village.

In short, the *yis* ceremony displays the conception and the beginning of growth of the totemic palms as sons.

b. *The* yis *figures.* In contrast to the Umeda ritual, the Yafar *yis* did not wear the *êri*'s masks, but special masks that were also used by the *ware-inaag,* following the *yis* in the arena. The body paintings were similar to those in Umeda.

The *yis* are associated with the mythological figure of the young and fertile woman Oogango, the wild melon (*öög*) woman (in Waina, Tetagwa; *MC:*188). A myth relates that the girl was hiding in a wild cucurbit picked up by Wefroog, the trickster, one of the two culture heroes (see *MC:*347–48). She is beautiful because she has (like this melon) colored designs on her body, whereas her negative counterpart, Ahgoango—the *ahgo* toad (*Asterophrys robusta*) woman, all black, dies of trying to be decorated.[25] This reference does not provide a close relationship between ritual and myth: these two complementary realms of symbolic expression are the only two loci where certain key symbols may appear. The young and fertile woman, the daughter receiving the reproductive power from her mother, is one of them. Informant B gave some more details about Oogango's origin: she is alleged to be a child of the parental deities W . . . and B . . .. W . . . named and painted her with B . . .'s (menstrual?) blood. Even though one must approach "one-man information" with caution, this allows us to understand something of the meaning given by the culture to polychrome body paintings. Informant A asserted also that painted designs on the body of *yis* and Fish were the visual expression of *hoofuk* and maternal blood.

The *yis* figure is also sometimes related to the *abi* wildfowl mentioned earlier.

WARE-INAAG [TEH] (PLATE 3)   These two dancers appear one after the other after the exit of the *yis* whose masks they wear. Their body paintings are similar to the *yis* designs, but with diagonal instead of horizontal colored bands. The Umeda call them *teh* or *ulateh,* "firewood" or "fire-wood of the net bag," that is, first-quality firewood (*MC:*225). This seems connected to the ritual firewood used in the *yis* ceremony. The Yafar name means "in the *ware* canes."[26] A myth (Juillerat 1991a:chap. 3) tells of a man, wounded in the thigh by a jealous husband, who hides in the wild canes and is then discovered and cured by a mother and her daughter, who are hunting wild pig with their dog. A young *ware* sprout has grown through his wound and he is adopted by the women, who both want to marry him: the young couple wins over the old woman. However, I prefer another explanation: the possible association to the vast swamps planted with wild canes (*ware*) that constitute the western limit of the world (see also the discussion below concerning the *ifegê*); this is the place where many mythical personages go forever after their wordly existence has ended. It may be seen as the peripheral place in the world with no possible return. This idea of laterality is effectively confirmed by the term *yis na mingik,* "remains of sago jelly," which is what the *ware-inaag* roles are often called. Informant B added that these personages symbolize the residual blood at the "*yis* birth"; but the *yis,* as we have seen, is the newly formed embryo. Thus the residue in this case would be that of both sexual fluids discarded (unused) in conception. Here the idea of residue or waste (of blood, or of reproductive stuff) is again significant.[27] The residue of the divine conception would recall the cosmic residue lying "in the *ware*" of the margin of the world. The *ware-inaag* are peripheral to the *yis* as the *rawsu-inaag* were to the *êri: êri,* and *yis* appear as the active and productive personages, whereas *rawsu-inaag* and *ware-inaag* are their nonreproductive waste discarded during the reproductive process.

SAWÔG [TAMWA], "FISH"   The first series of black-painted dancers appears after the *ware-inaag*'s exit. They are progressively replaced by polychrome performers wearing the same emblematic masks (fish masks, *ogomô mesoog;* see below). Like the Umeda, both types are said to be "Fish" (*sawôg*), but the former are usually designated by the term *ogomô,* while the latter are the actual *sawôg* roles. Metaphorically, and secretly, one can call them *yis fut* (original sago jelly, for the black Fish) and *yis ab*(*uk*) or *awêg yis* (red or fresh sago jelly, for the colored Fish).

All Yafar informants made a clear distinction between the emblematic masks and the body paintings: the masks had to embody the *ogomô*'s presence, while the body colors alone were inspired by the patterns of fish. More especially for the polychrome Fish, the dancer had to be seen as the incarnation of a fish carrying an *ogomô.*

The Umeda opposition between *ahoragwa* and *tetagwa* (black and polychrome mythical women, or ritual "Fish") dancing successively in Ida is also present in Yangis. A contradiction appears only in the fact that the *yis,* as well as the polychrome Fish, are associated with Oogango (above). In any case, the complementary coupling of *ogomô* and *sawôg* (*MC:*188) is evident.

    a. *The* ogomô [ahoragwana] *(plate 4).* The Waina name refers to the black and mythical woman mentioned earlier under the Amanab name of Ahgoango, the Toad woman (*MC:*188). The Yafar word used for these black-painted performers, whose masks are decorated with the dancer's clan emblem, designates sago palm growth spirits, called more properly in the Amanab area *mwayfik.*[28]

The *ogomô* spirits are to be clearly distinguished from the socialized bush spirits, who are often spirits of the dead. The *ogomô* are supposed to come to Yangis from remote lands, allegedly occupied by some Yafar clans a long time ago. They are by nature dangerous and their presence

Plate 3. *Ware-inaag,* "in the wild canes." Mask made of fringes from the *hööb* pandanus, of a vertical axis decorated with *boof* fruits (*Rejoua aurantiaca*), purple amarant flowers (*Celosia argentea*), a crown of cut cassowary black feathers, white cockatoo, and *Paradisea minor* plumes. Body paintings are similar to *yis,* but with diagonal polychrome bands. Yafar Yangis 1976. (Photo Juillerat)

Table 1.1.

The Three Pairs of *Ogomô* and Their Clan Emblematic Species

Name of *Ogomô*	Clan Emblem	Name of Clan	Moiety
1. Bwampi	*Nank* insect	Bwasneri	*Angwaneri* (F)
Urey	*Bwerinaag* grub	Sumneri	*Araneri* (M)
2. Mwangwoy	Python (*ha*)	Amisneri	*Angwaneri* (F)
Wêy	*Wêy* nightbird	Ifêêg	*Araneri* (M)
3. Waruwô	*Yibus* pigeon[a]	Wiyneri	*Angwaneri* (F)
Bay (Wank)[b]	*Sêhêf* tree	Biyuneri	*Angwaneri* (F)
Kwoy	Young cassowary	Wamawneri	*Araneri* (M)

Note: The *ifegê* emblems are not associated to an *ogomô* or a specific clan and do not appear in the list.

a. *Ptilinopus rivoli* or *P. superbus.*

b. Wank is sometimes considered a separate *ogomô* without emblem and is absent in Yangis.

in the masks leads the dancers to fear a direct contact with them. To dream of an *ogomô* would be a bad omen, but an *ogomô* may sometimes give a huge pig to a hunter. The self (*sungwaag*) of the dancer may be endangered through its proximity and thus become ripe (*abuk*), that is, weakened and ill. This and other indications (their coming through underground roads, for instance) shows that they are related to the maternal realm, actually the male principle at work in the growth of the fetus. The number of *ogomô* coming to Yangis is normally seven (including the Cassowary, table 1.1). Each one has a name and a design painted on one mask only; this emblem represents a plant or an animal that is taboo to the members of the corresponding patriclan. There are more clans or immigrated segments in Yafar society than there are *ogomô*. Men affiliated to a group without any *ogomô* may wear the mask of a clan of their own moiety or semimoiety, or individually their mother's brother's or matrilateral cross-cousin's mask.

Informant B offered some mythical elements, with a few contradictions in the details, but seemingly trustworthy in their basic principles: the *ogomô* would be the (apparently male) children of B . . . , the origi-

Plate 4. Yangis *ogomô* (black Fish) in full *ogohyaag* dance, wearing bow and arrow, *suh-wagmô* phallocrypt, and the *ogomô mesoog* mask (fish mask) decorated with clan emblem. (Photo Juillerat)

nal Mother, while the *abi* appearing in the myth (above) may be considered in that role as a reduplication of the primordial maternal figure. Informant B ordered the *ogomô* in pairs, saying they were born as three sets of twins (table 1.1).

Informant A provided the same list, but in a slightly different order and not in pairs (he did not talk about twins or B . . .'s sons). The seventh *ogomô,* whose name in Yangis is Kwoy, Cassowary, as said by B to be the other's father.[29] He has a leading role as a dancer in the ritual, and his body paint is all red (of a rather dull hue contrasting with the *ifegê*'s bright paint), because the mythical father is said to have used his female companion's menstrual blood to anoint himself (B's information). At each of the childbirths, several plant or animal species (including two ancestral dogs) originated from the umbilical cords, amnions, and placentas.

b. *The* sawôg *(Fish)* [tetagwana tamwa] *(plates 5, 6).* The *sawôg* proper (with polychrome body painting) wear the same *ogomô* masks as the black Fish just described. One by one, they replace the *ogomô* dancers at about 9 a.m.; then the Fish stay on the scene until late in the afternoon, with new dancers, freshly painted, being substituted continually.[30] the cosmetic patterns (called *sawôg na genof,* "designs of the fish") are varied, but a certain number (about 10) are typical and allegedly correspond to fish species patterns (*MC:*199, fig. 30). New designs may be freely invented, sometimes inspired by articles manufactured in the West.

Information confirmed by several Yafar men provides vital insight into the *sawôg* roles. One or two generations ago, the polychrome dancers did not wear the emblematic masks: instead their head was wrapped in a net bag (*wura*) (plate 7) and their penis was naked, decorated only with a thin tie made of a piece of the *fut* vine, a young sago shoot leaf (*na yug*), and a ginger leaf. The sago shoot anticipates the future identity of the *ifegê:* thus the *sawôg* seem to be the *ifegê* in their fetal stage (see also the mythical origin of fish, note 47). They danced exclusively on the edge of the place, while the black *ogomô* remained in the center for the whole day with their clicking *suh-wagmô.* Adolescent boys played the *sawôg* parts and their real or classificatory mothers danced among them (in the female swinging style), holding wide open a large net bag "to catch their sons" and yelling: "My child, my fish!" The boys carefully avoided being "trapped," but they could also intentionally rub their arm on their mother's skin. The woman would then discreetly wipe off the paint

Plate 5. Yangis *sawôg* (Fish). Detail of body painting. (Photo Juillerat)

Plate 6. Yangis *sawôg* (Fish) dancing *ogohyaag* in file in the center of the place. Free body polychome designs and clan emblematic mask paintings. In the background, two dancing women and *fuf* players. (Photo Juillerat)

fearing notice by younger women.[31] Men say that these encounters between mothers and sons were the women's initiative and not ritually
obligatory. The tight physical contact with the net bag prepared as a
mask (and in which some real or symbolic semen was smeared) was
particularly feared, and many deaths were imputed to this practice. This
is the alleged reason why today the Fish dancers wear the *besa* masks
instead.

This now abandoned spatial distribution of both black *ogomô* and
colored Fish, their complementariness (black + central + phallocrypt
vs. colored + peripheral + naked) and the intervention of the mothers
allow a more coherent interpretation of the relationship between black
and polychrome performers. The opposition may be stressed in the way
shown in table 1.2.

The recurrent theme of the separation from the mother is evident on
both symbolic and social levels. In playing a Fish role for the first time,

Plate 7. Two boys with their heads wrapped in a net bag, during a Yafar curing ritual (1978) dedicated to the female *sawangô* spirits. In old times the *sawôg* in Yangis were masked in the same way instead of wearing the actual *ogomô mesoog* mask. (Photo Juillerat)

the boy distances himself from dependence on his mother, while she tries ritually to keep a kind of complicity with him. Informants A and B established a connection between the women's ritual attempt to catch their sons and a short myth that tells the story of children who have been treated badly by their parents. While the parents are absent, the children willingly metamorphose into fish. On their return, the desperate parents strive to capture their children-fish, the father upstream with bow and arrow, the mother downstream with a huge net bag. Unsuccessful, they decide to turn into a crocodile and the nightbird *koon*, respectively. This bird's call is said to echo the wailing of the inconsolable mother who cries: "My children! My fish!"

However, the new way of performing the *sawôg* dance, as well as that of the black *ogomô,* is described as the "work of the *hoofuk*"

Table 1.2.
Binary Oppositions between *Ogomô* and *Sawôg*

Black *Ogomô* Dancers	Polychrome Fish Dancers
Sago growth spirits	Fetus
Ogomô masks	Net bag mask (*wura*)=uterus (*wurag*)
Phallic dance style (growth)	No phallic dance style
Phallocrypt	Naked penis (=young sago shoot)
Blackness	Polychromy
Maleness-centrality	Femaleness-marginality

(*hoofuk na gafungô*), that is, gestation and the development of the fetus. Today, the uninterrupted vertical movement of the phallocrypts in the *ogohyaag* male dance performed in the center of the place expresses the central growth in height (or length), while the lateral movement of the women's hips and skirts (called *ira:* plate 8) as they dance at the periphery of the scene displays the female growth principle providing flesh to the child.

KOOR [KWOD]   Alfred Gell describes five sorts of "subsidiary figures" (*MC:*194–99) appearing successively during the dance of the Fish. The Yafar performance had only one such ritual type, the *koor,* corresponding roughly to the Umeda *kwod:* body entirely red, head concealed in yellow-dyed (*Curcuma*) *Gnetum gnemon* underbark, penis bound with a vegetal tie (*MC:*195). The only difference was that the two Yafar *koor* performers did not walk in "a semi-crounching, doubled-up position" and "in a slow, bobbing step" like their sole Umeda homologue, but appeared one after the other, rushing into the village directly from the bush (not through the theatrical screen used by all other performers)— such as the *yaut,* the Umeda fiend—and disappeared the same way after racing for half a minute through the hamlet, bow in hand. The effect was not "sinister" as for the *kwod,* and the Yafar public showed amusement with women laughing and running away in the silence imposed by the interruption of the *fuf* trumpets.

Koor is also a mythical flying figure with red eyes; he is dangerous but capable of friendship with men to whom he may give game. He appears as a good hunter with his red-eyed dog. But the Yangis figure

Plate 8. A group of Yafar women in the *ira* dance style at the periphery of the place. Decorations of net bags, *Paradisea minor* plumes and white cockatoo feathers at the bottom of their skirts (1976 Yangis). (Photo Juillerat)

seems rather to refer to *koor* as the Sowanda word for "ghost" (Amanab *ifaaf*).[32] In Amanab, *koorêk* is sometimes used for "rotten." Furthermore, informant B stated that the *koor* figure portrayed the *suweegik* (< *suweeg* "smoke" < *suwê* "fire"), the contaminating emanation from women during pregnancy or menstruation, and that its origin was actually B . . .'s *suweegik*. This polluting vapor is related to ghosts because they live in the bowels of the earth close to the cosmic procreative fluids. Like the *koor* actors, ghosts in the Amanab and Waina cultures are the object of some ridicule, probably because of their double proximity to the decaying corpse and to the cosmic and female fertility.

With only one "ogre" (Gell) or "ritual clown" (Werbner) in Yangis, it is hazardous to theorize on the social function of this kind of personage. His grotesque aspect and behavior provide fun and relief (*MC:*281), but also some disgust; it has actually been shown that, if the *koor* are grotesque because of their sudden appearance and oddity, these features embody the idea of pollution and portray an extremely marginal product in the procreative process.[33] Something that urgently needs to be dis-

Table 1.3.

Chronological List of Ritual Figures in Yangis

Name	Number	Mask Type	Body Paintings	Penis Treatment	Actor's Status	Other
êri (sabaga) [eli (sabbra)]	2	êri mesoog [ageli]	Black with white spots	suh-wagmô [pedasuh]	Older, married	Center of place
rawsu-inaag [molna tamwa]	2	ogomô mesoog [tamwa]	All red	wagmô [peda]	Young, bachelors	Periphery, followed by boys
yis [aba]	2	yis mesoog [ageli]	Horizontal polychrome bands	suh-wagmô	Senior, married	Leap over fire, hold sago jelly
ware-inaag [teh]	2	yis mesoog [ageli]	Diagonal polychrome bands	suh-wagmô	Married	
ogomô [ahoragwana tamwa]	6	ogomô mesoog	Black with white spots	suh-wagmô	Older bachelors, married men	Number varies during the course of the ritual
kwoy	1	ogomô mesoog	All red	suh-wagmô	Older bachelors, married men	Leading role
sawôg [tetagwana tamwa]	6	ogomô mesoog (Net bag)	Free polychrome designs	suh-wagmô (Naked)	Younger bachelors and married men	Number varies during the course of the ritual
koor [kwod]	2	Head concealed in yellow underbark	All red	Naked	Old men	Running through place
amof [amov]	2 or more	Head concealed in yellow underbark	Polychrome	wagmô or motionless suh-wagmô	Married	Followed by women and children
ifegê [ipele]	2	ifegê mesoog [ipele tamwa]	All bright red and black design on the back	Foreskin up and vegetal and plume decoration	Bachelors or young married men	Shoot arrow toward sun
anuwanam [kwanugwi]	1 (+1)	None	None	None	Older and married men	Must have performed ifegê in previous ritual

carded in order to proceed toward the end of pregnancy (*amof*). The physical aspect of the *koor* works as a caricature of pollution and thus provokes in the spectators—most of whom do not understand the mythical references and ignore the symbolic meaning conveyed by that role— the adequate feeling and attitude. This is, I would suggest, the social function of the *koor* figure: to transmit to the crowd the proper feeling without disclosing the religious message.

AMOF [AMOV], "TERMITES" (PLATES 9,10)   In the performance of Yangis that I observed, two *amof* came the first day at 4 p.m. and walked around the edge of the place for one hour. One wore an ordinary ovoid *wagmô* phallocrypt, the other a *suh-wagmô*, which the performer let hang motionless (except for the first steps). The public remained passive. The second day, both had only *wagmô*, their pace had more of a hopping style, and, as in Umeda, a retinue of children and women followed them, singing: "*Amof-eee! amof-eee!*"

The Yafar exegesis and my endeavor to interpret the significant elements of the *amof* paraphernalia (see *MC:*203–4) led me to conclude that these figures mark the end of pregnancy: the "work of the *hoofuk*," expressed by the Fish and their phallic dance, is over; the totemic sago "babies" are now ready to be born. It is this message that is brought by the Termites, inciting the public to a joyful demonstration. I would stress two features:

1. The absence of *suh-wagmô*, already mentioned, which confirms that the *ogohyaag* dance means growth at work (and not copulation).

2. The general color (yellow, orange, and red) that predominates in the *amof* decorations: yellow head (like that of the *koor*), and colorful leaves of crotons and *boof* [*subove*] fruits (*MC:*202). This species, *Rejoua aurantiaca,* is a wild or semicultivated tree, the numerous, bright orange fruits of which fall down before full ripeness. Unedible and light, they float in numbers at the surface of creeks where this tree often grows. In short, they are the perfect symbol of *ripeness* and *caducity.* This concept is a crucial one in Yafar and Waina symbolism: the self (*sungwaag*) of any human being may be endangered by early ripening through contamination during sleep with the maternal underworld and then be the easy victim of a human sorcerer (see Juillerat 1986, 1991a). The purpose of some aspects of hunting ritual is to let "ripen" the game's *sungwaag* to accelerate its death when wounded. The antidote to the early ripening of the individual's self is the ritual protection provided by

Plate 9. *Amof* (Termite) on the first day of the Yafar Yangis (1976). Head wrapped in an underbark cloth dyed with turmeric, collar of yellow ("ripe") croton leaves, headdress of cassowary and bird of paradise feathers; ritual phallocrypt worn in walking pace (no *ogohyaag* dance). In the background, a group of women dancing. (Photo Juillerat)

Plate 10. Two *amof* (Termites) on the second day of the Yafar Yangis. The performers run and play with the women and children. (Photo Juillerat)

the *gungwan* shrub (*Antiaropsis toxicaria* and *A. decipiens*), whose fruits "never rot nor fall down."[34] Let us add that the sorcery for provoking abortion uses sympathetic magic in reference to tree species losing their fruits before full ripeness. The following story (from informant B) refers to the *boof* caducity and tells also how the *amof* figure was created by the culture hero Wefroog:[35]

> Wefroog catches sight of a *boof* tree. He asks its fruits: "Will you stay, or will you fall? I need you to make a man." Nothing moves; he goes away, but hears a big noise. He turns back: all the *boof* fruits are on the ground. Wefroog uses sticks and roots from the *afwêêg* sago palm to make the limbs; then he decorates his new creature with the fruits. He utters spells "*kikikiki*" and the man comes to life. Wefroog gives him his two names:[36] *Boof* and *Amof.* Then he orders him to go to the [Yangis] festival: "You must dance at the periphery of the place, with the women."

Informant B added that the two names of the Termites were shouted in Yangis when they entered the arena: "*Boof-eee! Amof-eee!*"

That material gives a more accurate signification to the role, but does not explain why termites have been chosen as a natural symbol. Arguing from Umeda comments, Gell tried to relate the ridiculous aspect of this big-headed insect to the secret knowledge of women about procreation and the sanction produced on men who would have known too much about it (that is, have a head similar to a termite's; *MC*:278–79). I had no similar argument from the Yafar, but other associations were provided:

1. The termites often build their nests on sago palms. A sago trunk with termites is said to have a better *hoofuk*.

2. In order to cure swelling, one usually appeals to the sago growth spirits *mwayfik* and the spells talk about "wiping off termites" (and other insects) that cover the sago palm's or man's *hoofuk*, to have access to it and free some of it. Swollen limbs are due to an excess of *hoofuk* and determine the suppression of sago jelly and fish in the diet; the corresponding curing rite appeals to the sago spirits *mwayfik* and its spells first "wipe off" termites, ants, centipedes (that is, *roofuk*).

3. Informant A asserts that the *amof* roles in Yangis also evoke fishing with termite nests as bait thrown on the surface of a river. The fish surround and eat up the insects (giving the opportunity to shoot them with multipronged arrows) and the remaining termites may then adhere through gravitation to some floating *boof* fruits.

Informant A seems to have associated the *amof* roles with this fishing technique apparently because of the fish symbolism in Yangis and of the simultaneous presence on the dancing arena of Fish, Termites, and *boof* fruits. Without dismissing this connection, I feel more convinced by the first two points, which conform quite adequately to the *hoofuk/roofuk* polarity in Yafar thought about fertility: the *roofuk* (skin, bark, debris) must be wiped off to let the *hoofuk* free itself, to allow growth (gardens) or, here, birth. An important or thick *roofuk* is supposed to contain an abundant *hoofuk*. The presence of termites as a sign of fertility would provide the most adequate explanation to the *amof* roles. One could hypothesize that the *amof* dancers materially refer to the breaking of the amnion (as *roofuk*) announcing the imminence of birth.[37]

SAWÔG, ÊRI, AND YIS AGAIN   By the end of the second day of the performance, we witness the reappearance in the arena of the *êri, yis,* and *ware-inaag,* who dance in the middle of the stage with the *sawôg* until the end of the ceremony; the *amof* remain at the periphery. All these performers will leave only after the *ifegê* have fired their arrows and fled. Their concluding presence in the arena quite probably has no other signification than to recall their roles in the reproductive process; they appear as a summary of Yangis chronology, while the *ifegê* walk around the arena.

THE IFEGÊ [IPELE] AND THEIR ANUWANAM [KWANUGWI] (PLATES 11,12)

a. *The* ifegê. In Umeda, the *ipele* are preceded by the *nemetod* ("new men"; *MC:*203–4), neophytes for the *ipele* roles. In Yafar, there were only the two *ifegê* accompanied by their "preceptors" (*MC:*205), *anuwanam.* On each day, the *ifegê* appeared only once, going around the ritual arena one time. Informant A explained the absence of *nemetod* in Yafar saying that this was the privilege of Umeda as the mother of the Yafar daughter group (see above and Juillerat 1986).[38] Thus the role appeared taboo to the Yafar, but the reason remains obscure. However, it can be pragmatically explained by the fact that the Umeda *nemetod*'s role is performed (with the ritual and black phallocrypt) by the adolescent boy who has just received his first phallocrypt (ovoid and yellow gourd, for daily use) from a "mother's brother" (*MC:*203, 283), whereas the same rite of passage, now abandoned, was not associated to Yangis by the Yafar who organized that festival too rarely. Thus in Umeda the ritual *nemetod* and the boy newly assigned to adulthood is one and the same person, while the *ipele* who follows him a little later is a purely ritual reduplication of the *nemetod.* The Ida performance established here an interesting parallelism between the real and the symbolic initiate.

The word *ifegê* has the same mundane meaning as the Waina *ipele:* a three-pronged arrow used to shoot birds and small animals, especially lizards. This is the symbol of the neophyte hunter's toy bow. In Yangis, only the *ifegê* from the *Angwaneri* (female) moiety holds such an arrow; the *Araneri* (male moiety) *ifegê* has a *yuu* arrow, with one smooth rounded section head. A piece of sago sprout (*na yug*) is fixed within the base of the arrowhead together with some dried menstrual blood and magical roots. But the true etymology of *ifegê* is *ifêêg êri,* literally "original human being." This means that the arrow type has been named after that meaning, and not the reverse.[39]

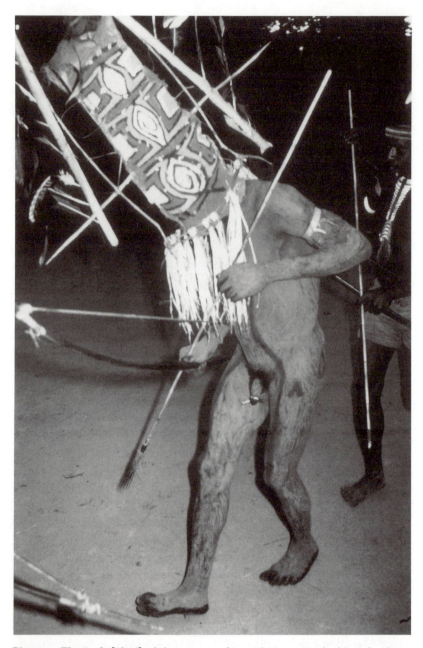

Plate 11. The *ipele* [*ifegê*] of the *angwatodna* moiety, covered with red ochre, arrow and sight directed toward the ground, "in search of the mother"; at the lower left corner, extremity of first "preceptor's" bow; following the *ipele*, second preceptor followed by the (not visible in the picture) *edtodna* moiety *ipele*. Punda Ida in 1986. (Photo D. Niles, Courtesy of Institute of Papua New Guinea Studies, Music Department)

Plate 12. The shooting of the arrow toward the sun by *kwanugwi* [Yafar *anuwanam*] and *ipele* [*ifegê*] at the 1986 Punda Ida ritual. (Photo D. Niles, Courtesy of Institute of Papua New Guinea Studies, Music Department)

The body paintings were all red for the *Araneri ifegê*. Those of the *Angwaneri* performer were red with some black stripes on the back representing (according to informant A) vines, *wesêk kekwareg,* coiled round the young *afwêêg* sago shoot.

The Yafar *ifegê*'s penis wore a special decoration, different from that described by Gell for the Umeda *ipele* (which corresponded to the Yafar *koor*'s penis). In Umeda, it was a short strip of the white *subnab* material, the same as that used to make Fish mask fringes (*MC:*205), that is, strips of the black palm *coeur de palmier* in its transformation into leaves. In Yafar, the *ifegê*'s mask fringes are actually made of that material, but their penis is the object of very significant treatment: the foreskin is pulled back, the glans covered with strips of *kêg* (? *Schefflera* sp.) leaves conceal-ing a little piece of *na yug abuk* (red sago shoot) and decorated with caudal plumes (*nay*) of the bird of paradise (*Paradisea minor*), a female symbol for the women's skirts (*nay,* made of young sago leaves twisted in plaited thin ropes), and the whole thing is tied up with strips from the *fut* vine.[40] I was told that the performers also smear their meatus with dried menstrual blood. The analogy between the *ifegê*'s penis and arrow, on the one hand, and between penis + arrow and sago shoot, on the other, is clear and explicitly acknowledged by Yafar men.

Normally, the two *ifegê* should remain seated under the shelter in the ritual enclosure hours before their time comes to appear. It is likely that this seclusion (*MC:*204) corresponds to the *ifegê*'s intrauterine life.

As they are painted with first-quality red ochre blended with betel juice and *Curcuma* mixed with lime (Juillerat 1978a), the Master of the Sky and the Master of the Earth, with some assistants, refer in their spells to the *afwêêg taf suwê* (fire blood of the *afwêêg* sago palm) for the *Araneri* dancer, and to the *sa taf suwê* (fire blood of the coconut) for the *Angwaneri* dancer.[41] Then the men who are about to act the *anuwanam* parts put the masks on the *ifegê*'s head, and the priests ritually mark the eyes with a Curcuma bubble on the masks' *besa* (coconut fiber) to be-come the holes through which the performers will see.[42] Both *ifegê* masks have the same design; they have not been worn by any other dancer before.

The conclusion to be drawn about the *ifegê*'s identity is that they are the totemic young sago (or sago and coconut) sprouts, which are all red when they come out of the freshly planted sucker; the ritual use of "red sago shoots" (*na yug abuk*) in association with the *ifegê* figures, their arrows or penes, is thus quite clear. The natural color of the palm's first shoot was a logically necessary condition to build up a convincing anal-ogy with the mythical *ifegê*'s blood and their mother's miscarriage (be-low): the *ifegê* are also called the "bloody sago shoots" (*na yug abuk taf-na*). Note that the *ifegê*'s penes are treated in a way similar to their whole body; in the ritual, as well as in the myth mentioned later, the penis is a reduplication of the entire person.

b. *The* anuwanam. This word designates any person who has already had a specific experience (in production, sex, hunting, killing, ritual); one says that he or she is *anuwanam* in that particular domain. This status is opposed to that of *asagyam,* the neophyte undergoing that experience for the first time and often being helped or ritually introduced to it by some *anuwanam.* In Yangis, the word designates the undecorated man who precedes the two *ifegê* as a guide, wearing an ordinary ovoid phallocrypt or even modern clothes and holding a headless arrow shaft (*waymero*) at hand, the tip of which is smeared—like that of the *ifegê*—with menstrual blood and magical stuff. In 1976, only one *anuwanam* walked with the two *ifegê,* but another one waited at the shooting site and (discreetly) fired another arrow before the second (*Araneri*) *ifegê.*[43] Logically, the *anuwanam* must have played the part of an *ifegê* (*asagyam*) in a previous ceremony. Gell writes that the *nemetod* is "accompanied by a 'mother's brother' of the opposite moiety," also undecorated. In Yafar, the *anuwanam* is said to portray the *ifegê*'s mother's brother (MB), but the men are not necessarily related as MB/ZS (sister's son) in reality. Some informants established another association between the two *anuwanam* and the culture heroes. The *anuwanam* who leads the two *ifegê* is said to be Wefroog, the trickster, the physically weak, "feminine," but creative hero, whereas the *anuwanam* standing by would be Abunung, the stupid and imaginationless hero. The relation between that mythical pair and the argument of Yangis is relatively clear; it could have some relation to the Promethean role ascribed to these figures and discussed in the last section of this study. The *anuwanam* are the socialized totems, which have become men, and for this reason as well as their initiatory role they are related to the culture heroes.[44]

Before going ahead to analyze the walking style, the meaningful position given to bow and arrow, and the firing of the arrows in the late afternoon of the second day, let us pause in order to discuss the mythical elements indispensable to the understanding of the Yangis finale.

The Great Mother's Miscarriage and Death

I referred previously to an original divine couple, W . . . and B . . .. They were described as anthropomorphic but monstrous in size. We shall see later that this anthropomorphism could conceal a hypothetical pair of cassowaries, at the origin of the universe. The transformation of these original parents into other natural species is probably the most sacred part of their mythology. According to informant B, B . . . gave birth to the *ogomô*, as already described, in three consecutive twin pregnancies. She then became pregnant again, but expelled only blood and died. Two flows of blood ran separately from her and out of these two streams arose the two *ifegê*. A comment specifies that the blood ran into an iron tree (*Intsia palembanica*) and that the *ifegê* appeared out of the blood spurted around the tree shaken by the wind.[45] Their father (or mother's brother) saw them and made two toy bows for them out of the leaf ribs of the *wana* black palm and arrows out of the bark of sago plam petioles (*na pepa*). He also gave them their name.

He then began to dismember B . . .'s body, cutting it piece by piece, bone by bone, organ by organ. He planted the different parts in the ground or put them in other places of the universe. These parts then turned into vegetal and animal species, or heavenly bodies. The first part to be severed was B . . .'s single and central breast, called the "neck breast" (*uneg tot*).[46] With the aid of a rope or of a long log, the god climbed to heaven and put the breast where it was to become the sun.[47] From the blood shed during the amputation originated the egg of an *abi*, the black wildfowl *Talegalla* with red legs and red eggshell (see section "*Eri*, Other Exegetical Elements," and *MC:*281–82).

The male actor of this myth, manipulating the female *materia* and naming the new species thus created, should be W. . . . Informant B, however, said he was the original cassowary called, with some uncertainty, Yafa (see Waina *yapa* for a male cassowary; *MC:*225; there could be a possible relation to Yafar < *Yafa êri*). This point supports the idea of an original cassowary pair. My interlocutor gave the following details: after his female companion's death, Yafa considered his penis too long (useless) and shortened it. The semen flowed in two directions and generated two new magical plants. Yafa planted the cut-off piece that became the *bêêbi*, the highest liana of the forest (*Calamus sp.*) used as one of the main mask elements in Yangis (see below).[48] The large quantity of water absorbed by that species is supposed to be Yafa's semen. Later he would have gone up in the sky, from where he pours down his nocturnal semen in the form of mist and dew.

The myth continues: the newborn babies' penes were all bloody (*taf mungwô*, "only blood") and had no skin. Their father took some *kêg* (?

Schefflera sp.) and *saasa* (*Cycas circinalis* palm) leaves from the dead mother's skirt and tied his sons' penes up with a bandage.[49] Then the *ifegê* felt hungry and began their search for the maternal breast. They sought on the ground and shot some small lizards.[50] But their father (maternal uncle in the ritual sequence) told them not to seek downward and showed them that the sun was the coveted breast.

We might note that the birth out of the mother's blood is a form of parthenogenesis. The *ifegê* lack some of the father's stuff and actually have a bloody and weak penis, but they receive his postpartum care (bandage, bow and arrow, name).[51]

In the last pages of the present analysis, we shall consider the proposition that Yangis represents the emancipation of man out of maternalized nature, the beginning of society and culture. In this perspective, the *ifegê*'s birth out of their mother's blood reminds the Yafar and Waina of the alleged blood relationship between their two totemic palm trees and their moieties (see above, "Sexual Totemism"). My informants did not explicate that link, but we might see, through the *ifegê*'s birth, the appearance of man out of the natural species from the "blood" out of which they declare themselves to have emerged as "children of the blood." This poses the question of the Great Mother's mythical identity: does she represent the single ancestral anthropomorphic deity or the double (male and female totemic lines) ancestral vegetal mothers? The exegesis does make this distinction and suggests that the idea of a single original maternal figure appears in mythology under varied forms and incarnations (see below: "Sexual Identity, Reproduction, and Filiation").

We may now return to Yangis and the *ifegê*'s epiphany.

The Search for the Mother

As already specified, the *anuwanam* are presented as the *ifegê*'s mother's brothers, not as their fathers. More esoteric material would be necessary to explain this apparent contradiction. The tie between *anuwanam* and *asagyam,* initiated and neophyte, is valid here in both ritual and social domains. The ideal initiator in many Melanesian societies is the maternal uncle. The mother's brother is in a privileged kinship position to be a guide leading to the maternal breast and a mediator between son and mother. Yafar patrilineal culture considers the wife's brother a provider of female fecundity for the husband to establish his descent, that is, as the provider of a mother in her procreative function, while later he becomes for his nephews and nieces the provider of a mother in her feeding function. The uncle is the social equivalent of the biological father; he is the socializing part of *the* father (Lévi-Strauss 1958; Green 1977).

During their walk around the place, the *anuwanam* repeatedly mutter the words *mara taf,* "blood of the iron tree" (see above). The *ifegê* follow them repeating mentally the word *tot,* "breast." Informants specify that they "search for their mother" (*afaagêm isegê*) or that they "come and search for the breast" (*totom isegê bô*).

The two *ifegê* and their guide (their two guides in Umeda) walk at a different pace than all the other actors already described: "The dance of the *ipele* is intensely controlled: the dancer leans forward placing his weight with each pace deliberately on his leading foot. The effect is of a slow, measured, loping step, reminiscent of a slow bowler or a javelin thrower beginning his run-up; power held on a tight leash. Until the last moments of the dance the bow is held low, with the arrow pointed at the ground. Menacingly, the bow is tensed and relaxed in time with the dance. The dance of the preceptors is similar" (*MC:*206). Gell's remarkable observation gives in these few lines the ritualized attitude of the sacred "children of the blood" (*taf na ruwar*) seeking the breast of their lost mother (plate 11). The only detail that is lacking for the Yafar performance is that throughout the dance the *ifegê* alternatively turn their glance from one side to the other and that the ready arrow is not a threat but indicates the hunter's eagerness to catch the prey: small lizards or the mother's breast, depending at what level one puts the interpretation.

"The arrow pointed at the ground" was spontaneously emphasized to me by my informants and opposed to the subsequent inversion of the shaft toward the sun. The just-born *ifegê* look at where they have come from: the mother's belly represented by the earth. Informant B told me that the Yafar experts used to comment that "the *ifegê*'s arrow was like their penis: looking downward for the mother"; but this was "bad" and eventually their father or uncle told them: "No, you must not seek for your mother downward, she is dead and rotting," and he showed them her breast up above. This meant, in my interlocutors' explanation, that the mother's brother's role was to prevent his nephews from returning to their mother's womb, and to teach them that the only part of her person they had right to was her breast. The search for the mother's breast toward the earth is identified here with the pre-incestuous instinct of the return to the womb. The mother's brother's role is then to divert his nephews from doing so and thus to differentiate between the mother's two successive but antagonistic functions.

Now the inversion of the *anuwanam*'s headless arrow takes all its significance. The lack of an arrowhead (see also *MC:*206) means that the brother has no right to his sister's milk (see, however, another interpretation in the Epilogue, "Castration and Phallic Regeneration"). He is only a mediator. Might we see in the menstrual blood smeared at the arrow tip a metaphorical "fire" showing more clearly to the *ifegê* where the still unpierced breast of their mother (perhaps a "dark sun") is, like a tracer bullet in the night preceding the effective firing toward the target? Following the example of their uncle, the *ifegê* actually shoot their own arrows, which do have arrowheads, to catch or break open the breast; in "looking at the sun" (*akba noofuk*), the performers mutter again under their masks the word *tot,* "breast," which must be understood now as the secret name for the sun (plate 12).

At this point a brief comment needs to be made about the three kinds of arrowheads used in this particular sequence: headless shaft for the *anuwanam* (MB), three-pronged arrow (*ifegê*) for the *Angwaneri ifegê,* single-tipped arrow (*yuu*) for the *Araneri ifegê.* The arrows are fired in that same order: headless just to show the mother's breast or sun; three-pronged to express perhaps the ambivalence of that son/mother relationship, the totemic son of the female moiety being marked with a stronger tie to the Mother (as the *Angwaneri* moiety's totem), and as such with a higher incestuous risk—single-headed for the male moiety's *ifegê* who shoots last and has the last say, that provided by his totemic affiliation and his stronger identification with the Father (as his moiety totem); but they both constitute one unique but split entity, *the* Son-Nephew.

In the myth summarized above, the day breaks when the *abi* (wildfowl) mother has fed her sons. The emission of milk provokes the breaking of light. When the *ifegê* perforate the heavenly breast, one may guess in a quite Bachelardian spirit (although this was not told to me explicitly), that the milk flows out, inundating the universe with light.

Before firing their arrows from the western side of the arena, the *ifegê* and their preceptor aim at the Orient while they walk on the eastern side of the place. This uncompleted gesture is accomplished briefly with the meaning of mistaken intention of the *ifegê* searching for their mother in the wrong direction (for a further interpretation, see below, "Sociology of Yangis").

When eventually released to the west, the arrows fall behind the houses and will be later picked up by older men who will plant the arrowheads at the bottom of *fenaw* and *afwêêg* sago palms and mix the menstrual blood into a dog's sago jelly to help it see game (a common magic for dogs). However, the cosmological imagery tells that both of the *ifegê*'s arrows are grabbed by the sun, one in each of its hands. The sun then slowly sinks backward to the horizon and plants the arrows, heads upward toward the east, in the swampy grassland (called *Api fwog*) that characterizes the western limits of the world (see above: "*Ware-inaag*") before sinking into its underground road back to the east (Juillerat 1986).[52] The two planted arrows are called *sa bangra* (coconut twig) or *sa fut* (original coconut) for the *Angwaneri* arrow, and *afwêêg bangra* or *afwêêg fut* for the *Araneri* arrow. It is also stated that if the sun does not catch the arrows or if the performers do not aim straight at the sun, the shafts will be lost in the ocean (*kêfutuk buu,* "strong water," made of the original divine blood and semen), and the reproduction of the two totemic species will not be ensured: their *hoofuk* will be lost in the cosmic *hoofuk*.

Furthermore, in a private conversation, the Master of the Earth told me that the two "real" *ifegê* (not the performers) endeavor to keep captive the arrows in their *besag* (the sago palm equivalent of the coconut fiber, *besa*), that is, within the "womb." This is again an allusion to the difficulty of the mother/son separation. In order to free the palms' sprouts from their maternal envelope, the *ifegê* dancers should mentally say before firing their arrows: "*Sa besag rararara*" (*Angwaneri*) and "*afwêêg besag rararara*" (*Araneri*), that is, "to tear open [verbalized in that onomatopeic form] the coconut or sago palm womb." Otherwise the arrows would fall short "and the women would see them." My interlocutor then evoked both *ifegê,* in the shape of sago shoots, sitting in the *Api fwog* swamp, looking eastward with their respective arrows planted at their sides and "the breast" (sun) between them. Here they are again called *sa afwêêg* (or *fenaw afwêêg*). This is a beautiful fantasy about the phallic promotion of the totems as sons, through the mediation of the mother's breast.

The festival ends with the exit of the *ifegê* and after them all the other figures, mostly Fish, still dancing. Long harmonic notes of *fuf* trumpets accompany their departure. But a last and puzzling ritual behavior has to be examined. Just after firing their arrows, the *ifegê* successively run hastily out and drop their bows "as if," as Gell suggestively describes, "their lives depended on it" (*MC:*207). In 1976, I was informed of that in advance by several young men; this indicates that it is quite an expected and symbolically significant attitude. I asked for explanations and received what I would call popular comments: the dancers are afraid to have their bodies seen (especially their penis) by the women who are about to come back after their disappearance during the *ifegê* sequence; the dancers would be afraid of the action of the menstrual blood of the arrows; they would fear a return of their arrow toward them as a boomerang. One may note that those explanations put forward a fear on the part of the performers themselves, not a ritualized panic of the mythical figures. But they all talk about fright. In fact, it is indicative of a panic or guilt attributed to the ancestral *ifegê* when they pierced their mother's breast. This ritual attitude could then have something to do with the hypothesis proposed above concerning the sudden flow of milk (light). But, as we shall see later, that explanation must be distinguished from a psychoanalytical interpretaion that would call forth the idea of transgression due to this quasi-incestuous relationship to the mother (arrow = penis).

Such a high density of meaning and sacredness can only keep women apart. Just before the entrance of the *ifegê,* the *fuf* players interrupt their regular music to give the staccato harmonic rhythm, the immediate effect of which is to let the women depart and conceal themselves behind or in the houses (*MC:*206). In so doing, the *fuf* players pronounce mentally the two words: "*Af-eee, tot-eee!*", "mother, breast!" The reasons given for that prohibition applied to women were that they must not see the *ifegê*'s stripped penes. Also, it was believed that, should the women see the shooting of the arrows, these arrows would fall short of their destination (an image of a female-induced castration). They would fall in front of the houses or at the bowmen's feet, or they might even turn around and strike the breasts of women who had had intercourse during the preparatory period of Yangis. The latter point confirms the idea of breast as the target.

What about Cassowaries?

Alfred Gell's interpretation of Ida is mainly based on the figure of the Cassowary, whose successive metamorphoses would lead from the *eli* of the first night to their regeneration into the *ipele* of the last day. The *eli sabbra* (two men) roles of the first night are said in Umeda to be cassowaries and, according to Gell, the Umeda secret name of the cassowary is "man."

My own information about the position and relevance of the Cassowary figure in Yangis is still confused, despite the fact that it is frequently mentioned in spells and is also the subject of myths in which it is identified with a maternal feeding figure and with the sun.

As specified earlier, the myth about the Great Mother's death presents the male god who cuts up the maternal body as the primordial cassowary, Yafa. This same original figure is supposed to appear in the Yangis sequence of the black Fish (*ogomô*) as the only performer painted in red and dancing at the head of the black *ogomô,* supposedly his sons.[53] This red *ogomô* was the only figure in Yangis to be explicitly called Cassowary (*kwoy*). The dancing *êri* and *ifegê* were never related to this bird, and my suggestion, made with Gell's book in mind, was turned down. Both the myth of the Great Mother and this ritual role give the cassowary a male identity. This is also the case when Yafar men of both moieties cut the *bêêbi* (see below) liana in the ritual enclosure.

Another myth shows a hybrid creature, half cassowary (legs and lower body parts) half coconut (*besa* fiber and leaves) traveling in an eternal night from village to village, especially from Umeda to Sahya (old Yafar village) through other places, and distributing eggs or coconuts (or some hybrid form of both) to the villagers: "Where they received that food people were happy, but when the cassowary moved to some other place they were starving." Slowly the coconut palm lost its leaves and *besa* fibers (shared between villages), and the cassowary's head appeared. Two heroes, one from Umeda and one from Sahya, each opened successively one eye in the *besa* cassowary-coconut's head. Eventually, the creature was stoned to death in Umeda, because people were tired of being alternately fed and hungry (see elements of that myth in *MC:*226); its body was shared between the different tribes of the region. One egg remained, out of which originated the first natural cassowary after it was fertilized by one of the human heroes. One of the bird's eyes is sometimes said to have become the sun.[54] Its blood and other body parts were shared between Yafar and Umeda people and kept in a net bag hung in a sacred house built by some ancestor with the bird's bones. This supposedly same net bag is today the trophy of the Masters of the Sun (*akba na awaag;* Juillerat 1986) of the northern Amanab and Waina groups and is called either "net bag of the cassowary" (*kwoy na wura*) or "net bag of the sun" (*akba na wura*). The Umeda received the cassowary's head or tongue, whereas the Yafar got the lower parts (allusions are made in spells both to its penis and vagina).

The feeding function of the cassowary-coconut gives it a maternal role, and the association with the sun is explained in the alternate presence and absence of the mythical bird in the night (successively feeding and abandoning its "children"), exactly as the sun is alternately present and absent, warm and cold, in the succession of days and nights.[55] This image is perfectly consistent with the heavenly breast and calls forth the Freudian notion of *fort/da* (absent–bad mother/present–good mother). The opening of eyes in the *besa* (head) of the cassowary-coconut would give some evidence of the identification of the *ageli* in Umeda with a cassowary mask or head (*MC:*236). Similarly, the two *ifegê*'s masks hanging under the ritual shelter and waiting for their public appearance are called *kwoy bong-wa,* "the cassowaries at the hook," and both *ifegê* dancers sitting underneath are called *kwoy fut,* "original cassowaries," but also *na yug, sa yug,* "sago shoot, coconut shoot" (sago petioles are planted at their sides). Moreover, when the *ifegê* performers are being painted, spells refer to the "original fire (blood) of the cassowary." Also the ritual enclosure, normally called the "fish pond," is referred to in spells as the "place of the cassowary's blood" (*kwoy taf kebik*) when the spot is cleared in the bush, but also as the *afwêêg taf kebik* and *sa taf kebik* (the place of the two totemic bloods).

The appearance of the cassowary out of the coconut crown might be interpreted as the emergence of a phallic symbol out of a female entity (see the example of the turkey in Jones 1916). The sun would consequently be a female symbol endowed with a phallic connotation (B . . .'s single breast).

Thus a relationship—which with my present knowledge cannot be understood with certainty—exists between the cassowary figure and the totemic palms, especially the coconut. On the other hand, the cassowary is male and/or female, or is androgynous (see the Epilogue; Gardner 1984), or should be taken as a divine couple.[56] It is difficult in these conditions to know whether we are dealing with a multiple symbol used at different levels of Yangis and in other contexts as well, or whether we are lacking an exegetical piece that would make everything clear. The idea of breaking open the Cassowary's head or penis when cutting the *bêêbi* liana and facing the east (below) was explained as a way to release growth, as if the Cassowary kept the growth principle captive within itself and must be broken to free it.

Table 1.4.
Some Symbolic Equivalences on the Cassowary
Theme in Yafar Culture

Cassowary	Primordial black coconut Sun Mother (nursing role) Mobility, alternance
Cassowary's neck-head	Phallic symbol Growth Fish (*ogomô mesoog*) mask
Cassowary's penis	Phallic regeneration Growth *Bêêbi* (*Calamus*) liana Celestial road of the sun
Cassowary's semen	*Bêêbi* liana's water Morning mist and dew
Cassowary's eye opening	Daybreak (see *sangêk* songs below) Life
Cassowary's egg	Mother's breast and milk
Cassowary's wattle	Original mother's central breast (see the Epilogue)

Table 1.4 shows a few of the analogies revealed by this material.

In summary, the cassowary is certainly a permanent basic symbol in Yangis, present throughout the story of the regeneration of the two totemic palms. It provides a thematic reference rather than an active figure. But—as suggested earlier—it could also be the most secret identity in the creation myth (see the Epilogue).

Space, Time, and Color

Gell has analyzed in detail the chronology of body paintings in Ida and I shall not discuss it here again at length. I want to stress only one aspect revealed by the ancient way of playing the Fish parts, with the black *ogomô* in the center and the colored Fish at the periphery (see above, "*Sawôg*"). The point is that—if one takes this fact into account—all black roles are central, whereas all colored ones are peripheral. The opposition is, of course, more perceptible when both types of figures are present simultaneously on the village place: *êri/rawsu-inaag* and *ogomô/ sawôg* (ancient style). But it is also confirmed with the *yis* (they only come to the center to throw the sago jelly up) turning around the fire situated on the side, with the *koor,* with the Termites who must walk with the women, and with the *ifegê*. None of the colored personages, except the pair *yis/ware-inaag* (and the *sawôg* modern-style), wear the ritual phallocrypt, whereas the two kinds of black figures do. The vertical *ogohyaag* movement is thus associated with blackness and centrality and "produces" lateral colored figures. Black paint and *suh-wagmô* are the relevant features of active central agents in the reproductive process (*êri, ogomô*), while red and polychrome designs characterize the resulting lateral products: discarded blood or fluids (*rawsu-inaag, ware-inaag*), renewed *hoofuk* or embryo (*yis*), growing fetus (*sawôg*), polluting emanation (*koor*), anticipation of newborn babies (*amof*), totemic babies (*ifegê*) (figure 1.1). Two principles are involved, one active, the other passive; they are linked by a causal relationship and by a centrifugal movement. This transformation from black to color is, as clearly perceived by Gell, that of regeneration, of the passage from one generation to the next, from active seniority to immature youth.

There is not much to add to Gell's general analysis of color symbolism in Ida.[57] The color sequence is definitely white-red-black, and the significations may be summarized as follows:

White: Life *in statu nascendi,* like maternal *hoofuk* and semen. Gell is surprised not to find a completely white figure in Ida (*MC:*330). We could suggest that white is present in the ritual sago jelly (conception), and perhaps implicitly evoked in the cosmic milk as light (after the "perforation" of the sun). Because it is particularly sacred (it is the very color of the original *hoofuk*), white could be the object of a taboo on its representation.

Red: Blood, life in its growing sequence, the *hoofuk* in its transformation into being.

Black: Life in its achieved maturity, strength, reproductivity.

The course of symbolic reproduction, as it is expressed in Yangis, is not reversed (*MC:*335, 344) compared with the "organic process of

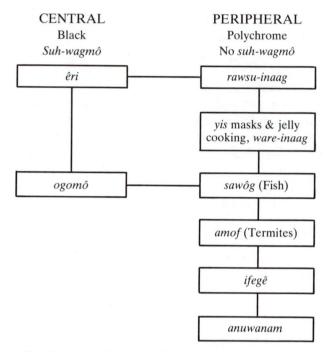

Figure 1.1. The division of ritual roles into central-black-producer and peripheral-colored-produced.

time." Red to black corresponds to the growth sequence, whereas black to red corresponds to the reproduction sequence; they show an inversion in color symbolism, not in time process. The ritual begins with the older generation and ends with the renewed younger one: in this sense, Yangis is a symbolic rite of passage.

THE MUSICAL BACKGROUND

The Sangêk [Awsego] Songs

The second night of Yangis is filled with sacred songs (*MC*:199–201)—*Yangis sangêk*—chanted by a group of undecorated senior men walking to and fro on the empty and dark place. Nobody watches, people sleep in their houses, but the sacred texts must be sung until dawn in a prescribed order. Each song is repeated 6 to 10 times. The whole series is not necessarily produced, but men say that it should at least be completed in two consecutive Yangis festivals. In 1976, only a part of the *sangêk* was sung and the Yafar said that the rest would be performed at the next opportunity. The word *sangêk* may be translated by "sacred songs" and is not a term specific to Yangis. Other rituals have their own *sangêk*. The *Yangis sangêk* are also called *hoofuk sangêk*.

I taped all the songs, but then discovered that the singers themselves were sometimes unable or unwilling to give a clear translation, asserting that the text was partly in Waina language (with many ritual words or names) and remained obscure to them. However, different themes did emerge. I shall try to restore them here in their uncertain chronology (I never heard the end of the series):

1. A first series of songs names the recently dead men (from any clan) and asks their *sungwaag* (self of the living person becoming *itaaf,* "ghost," after death) not to come up. *Sungwaag* and *ifaaf* are often used as synonyms, but here they refer to the ghosts living in the deep underground, near the cosmic *hoofuk;* they are associated with decay and vegetal regeneration. As custodians of the cultivated plants, they "give back" the cultivars' *hoofuk* in planting, but should not come up themselves; they remain desocialized and dangerous, in opposition to the *nabasa,* who are the guardians of the game and who issued from the blood and bones of the dead. These opening songs must be understood as a defensive device against ghosts, while the underground roads have been opened to let come up the telluric forces for the festival.

2. Then a long series of songs evokes natural species in their environment. I heard songs about the following:

a. *amof-nam,* "of the termites": this song alludes to the termites walking very slowly and building up their nest made of leaves (see above: *amof* roles).

b. *kwoy teta,* "cassowary, wild pig": "the cassowary is standing in the night, the cassowary is standing in the sun. . . ."

c. wild breadfruit tree (*ubra*): the song tells about its branches, trunk, leaves, and heavy fruits.

d. "The cassowary is looking at the mountain far away. . . ."

e. "The possum *wage* sits in the hole of a *ews* tree. . . . Its eyes are [like] the fire. . . ."

f. A song about the bird of paradise.

g. "The *pitpit* (*ware*) cane of the river Fse, . . . of the river Sum, . . ."

h. *Sawgego* [*awror*], "palm cackatoo" (*Probosciger aterrimus*): "it sits on the *ay* (*Canarium* sp.) tree for its fruits, it knocks the fruits with its beak, with the lower part of its beak, with its jaw, with its mouth. . . ."

i. "The yam (*Dioscorea esculenta*) of the river Anuwa, . . . of the river Sim . . . ; it is growing, yam, yam. . . ."

j. "The wallaby at the river Anuwa, the wallaby at the river Sawaye, the wallaby at the river Tof, . . ."

k. "The *fuwô* bird at the river Sim, . . . at the river Anuwa. . . . The good word, the nice call [of that bird]. . . ."

l. "Samway, Amway" [two mythical women].

m. At the first gleam of dawn, a *sangêk* tells about the "eyes" that are opened in the cassowary's head (or *besa*); this is expressed by the ritual word *kya, kyawe, kyaô,* and the Waina word *poko,* "to come out, to appear."

n. Then a *sangêk* would allude to all creatures of nature, animals and plants, to the process of flowering and to frogs multiplying in abundance.

o. When the sky is clear and the *kwibi* (*Centropus menbeki*) birds make their call heard, a last song, called "*mosuwô*" ("umbilical cord") is chanted: "umbilical cord, egg of the umbilical cord [?], to tie [it], umbilical cord of the *afwêêg* (sago palm), . . . of the *akwaga* (sago palm)." Informant A explained that the song meant that "when the newborn opens its eyes, its cord is not yet dry."

p. When the sun rises, the *sangêk* are closed with a rapid and meaningless *reere reere reere. . . .*"

In some of those songs, we may recognize the allusion, already discussed for the Termites performers, to the "container" in which the embryo develops: the termites make their nest in order to provide protection to the growing fetus. Some other *sangêk* refer metaphorically to growth or to animals and plants situated in tree holes, at rivers, or in the soil. The song in (b) could refer to the totemic pair in its zoomorphic shape (as noted above, the cassowary is related to the coconut and the pig to the sago palm). The umbilical symbolism is rather clear: the broken tie to the mother is associated to the opening of the baby's eyes and consequently to light and daybreak (life).

During the second night, the two *êri* who had performed the first night (painted again for the occasion) made a short appearance and were followed a little before dawn by a new ritual figure: the *abi* wildfowl (red leg *Talegalla*). Because I had not been informed that they were coming out, I did not watch them. For Umeda, Gell (*MC*:201) says that they wear the fish mask with the Cassowary emblem and that the young dancers are unpainted, wear ritual phallocrypts, and walk "keeping close to the ground," while the songs stop for a while in order that *fuf* staccato may be heard. Yafar informant B said that they were all painted red and were coming directly from and going back to the forest (not from the ritual enclosure); they would wear special fish masks painted in a hidden place in the forest by men of a particular clan of the *Araneri* moiety. In 1976, only one *abi* was said to have come out, the role being performed by a man from the *Araneri* moiety. In the ancient times, several *abi* figures would dance in the arena in the daytime. It must be remembered here what has been said above about the feeding of the *êri* performers with *abi* egg. As on the first night, the *Talegalla* wildfowl's presence (food or mask) seems to announce the end of the "long night" to which the myth already quoted alludes.

The Fuf *Trumpets*

During the first night and the two whole days, men play wooden trumpets without interruption. Any man, even adolescent boys, may play. Visitors from other villages are invited to play also, and players freely replace each other.[58] The basic orchestra is composed of five *fuf* that are held in one hand and blown through while walking around the place. Two longer bass trumpets, called *sawye-fuf*, may at certain moments be played by adolescent boys on the edge of the place to accompany the five other players.

The five *fuf* trumpets are played successively (in the beginning of each

Table 1.5.
Order of *Fuf* Trumpets and Symbolic References

Fuf Trumpets				Yangis Roles
fufuk [fufwi]}		(1)	[2]	*êri* (sexual inter-course or
	fufuk [*fufwi sabya*]			"mothers")
samag [karar]}		(2)	[3]	*êri* (sexual inter-course or "mothers")
engigêk [fuk-gapatray]		(3)	[4]	*yis* (?) (concep-tion)
pêpôk [sapôkeney]		(4)	[5]	*sawôg* (fetus)
tööfuk [agway]		(5)	[1]	*ifegê* (growing baby)
(2–3 *sawye-fuf [ruref]*, optional)		(6)	[−1]	full growth(?)

Note: (1) . . . Order in which they are played. [1] = lowest note; [5] = highest note. [*fufwi*] = Waina names (collected in Punda).

musical piece) in the order shown in Table 1.5. The first two *fufuk* (*samag* and *fufuk* proper–"husband" and "wife," respectively) are blown first and respond back and forth. They represent the male-female opposition that is basic to the ritual. *Engigêk,* from *engêk,* literally "second," is played next (plate 13). *Pêpôk* proceeds from *pêpi,* the name of a tiny toad and of a mythical young boy (Juillerat 1991a) portraying the new vegetal shoot. *Tööfuk,* from *tööf,* "sago petiole," evokes the growing palm leaves and is blown in long blasts. The whole set of five *fuf* trumpets thus appears as a symbolization of the vegetal (and by extension, human) growth process, starting with the musical enunciation of the sexual polarity and dialogue, and ending with the image of the growth in full process. The *sawye-fuf* bass trumpets might be seen as the musical intimation of accomplished growth (plate 14).

The *fuf* sequence in five stages is strikingly similar to the successive phases of the Yangis ritual (table 1.5). This music in general refers directly to vegetal fertility and growth in agriculture; only during the

Plate 13. *Er fuf,* players of the *fuf* trumpets (here the two *fufuk* walking in front followed by the *engigêk*) of the group of five, in the Yafar Yangis (1976). (Photo Juillerat)

Plate 14. *Er fuf,* two sitting players of *sawye-fuf* trumpets during the Yafar Yangis (1976). (Photo Juillerat)

growth period of gardens (approximately from October to April) is it played out of a ritual context. Blowing into the trumpets is similar to the act of inflating and, by lexical connection, to *fufwêy,* "wind, air"; *hefafôg,* "to breathe"; *fôfô,* "a whistle"; *fuföög,* "to swell up"; and also perhaps *hoofuk* (see above, "*Hoofuk/roofuk*").

In October 1986—by which time this text had already been completed—the Punda performed an Ida ritual. I could not myself see it, although I had been in the area some time before, but Don Niles (head of the Music Department of the Institute of Papua New Guinea Studies) was present. He commented:

> Although there are some *fuf* compositions which are inspired by specific bird songs, such pieces are not played during Ida. Instead, the players improvise based on a rhythm established by the *fufuk* and interlock their parts according to the idealized order of entry of the individual instruments. Greatest rhythmic complexity occurs in the two *fufuk* parts and lessens in the other

parts. The bass instruments produce a rhythmic pulse.[59] In addition to the musical variety resulting from different rhythms and combination of pitches, individual ingenuity, and changing performers, players vary the style by performing pieces either fast, loud and with greater rhythmic variation (*kekag-nam*) or slower, somewhat softer, and with more sustained pitches (*auwauwi-nam*). Specific *fuf* patterns are played at the arrival of visitors and of certain masked dancers, especially the *ifegê*. In the latter case, the music is an aural cue for the women to turn their backs to the dancing ground or seclude themselves so they do not see the *ifegê*. (D. Niles, personal communication; the vernacular words are in Amanab.)

New sets of *fuf* are made by a specialist—assisted by other men of his clan or village—who transmits his skill to his sons. The trumpets are periodically anointed (especially in ritual context) with animal blood. They are sacred instruments in the sense that they must not be taken away from the village (except those that are new and have never been played in a ritual). But they are not manipulated with special care, or stored in special places, or hidden from women's and children's sight. They are said to have originated from the Great Mother's bones.

The Suh-wagmô [Pedasuh] *or Ritual Phallocrypts (plates 1,2,4,5,6)*

Wagmô is the botanical name for gourds (*Lagenaria* sp., planted in gardens) and also the name for the everyday yellow and ovoid phallocrypt (Gell 1971). At the same time, *suhêg* connotes fertility, vegetal health (dark leaves), and blackness. The elongated gourds used for the ritual phallocrypts are stored uncovered under the roof of the house in the smoke to keep them black with soot. The complementary element of the *suh-wagmô* is the *kwoy-kêg*, "bone of cassowary" [*oktek (MC:*180)]: a belt worn on the abdomen and made of bone and sago seeds on which the *suh-wagmô* clicks in the *ogohyaag* dance. We have seen that this vertical movement is thought by the Yafar to show fetal development, *hoofuk na gafungô*, "the work of fertility."

The mythical origin of the *suh-wagmô* is the clattering call of the *horteta* bird (not identified), whose name can't be pronounced in the magical spells said by elders over the dancer's phallocrypt in the ritual enclosure. One may only say: "*afwêêg kêg wesigif! Sa kêg wesigif! Bêêbi kêg wesigif!*" That is, "let the *afwêêg* sago palm bone click! Let the coconut bone click! Let the *Calamus* liana bone click!" Bone alludes here to the hardwood of sacred species, particularly of the two totemic palms. Thus the hard material of the gourd and belt and the noise made by their percussion evoke also the natural production of firm wood in growth, and—we might add—strong bones in human fetal development.

A rite is also needed to prevent the phallocrypt from slipping off during the dance (plate 3): this would bring shame to the performer, but also would be a sign of the loss of the totemic *hoofuk;* that is why the spell refers to the hook (used in houses to hang objects) of the mythical celestial and chthonian places. To protect themselves from such incidents, the dancers should not eat viscous animals, like fish or frogs.

YANGIS: THE NONPUBLIC RITES

Alfred Gell based his analysis of Ida mainly on the public performance, and gave the old men's verbal "magical 'frills' " a very low status in comparison with the public ritual material. He considered Umeda ritual to be "primarily non-verbal, and also primarily non-esoteric." For him, "Ida is a public, non-verbal spectacle, whose meaning is also public and non-verbal, and is not given separate existence in the exegetical homilies of 'ritual specialists' or 'doctors'—of whom there were none in Umeda" (*MC*:212).

Gell's failure to perceive verbal and esoteric aspects of Ida reveals the degree to which those societies may present the outsider a facade of naivete concerning religious matters. This is done in order better to conceal not only the symbolic coherence of the nonpublic rites and verbal corpus (myths or spells) and their relationship to the public performance, but also the very existence of specialized inherited religious duties (see above and Juillerat 1986). The Yangis public performance is like the visible tip of the iceberg; it is the elaborated ritual product emerging out of a totalizing complex of images about nature, reproduction, and society. The spells uttered by the men responsible for the ritual during the preparatory phases, some of them months before the performance (and in spite of their repetitive or even "obsessional" verbalized form), provided on many occasions, when explained by informants, the link between some aspects of the public ritual (masks, colors, botanical species) and the esoteric stock of knowledge to which it referred.[60]

The nonpublic rites, performed out of women's sight, bear the whole weight of the verbal side of Yangis, while the public festival is totally free from loud magical speech. Nonpublic verbal rites have the important function of sacralizing the materials and men who are to appear in the public arena, calling the natural or spiritual forces, establishing the contact with the divine and thus giving to the public ritual its meaning and efficacy, preparing and protecting the village and the community from the excess of that sacredness. Without this preliminary ritual speech, Yangis would have no religious value or reality.

I do not intend to treat separately the verbal aspects of ritual. Instead I will deal successively with nonpublic ritual moments, some of which were apparently not known or could not be observed by Gell.[61] The main reason for analyzing them now is that they provide more evidence about some crucial representations, such as "closed" or "open" fertility, sexual totemism, nursing symbolism, meaning of the ritual enclosure.

With a duration of about the length of a human gestation, the preparatory period of Yangis is materially necessary and marked by some significant rites. Mineral pigments must be stored in large quantities; massive amounts of sago have to be processed and stored in forest waterholes or special racks; provisions of firewood must be collected by women; game meat has to be smoked and kept for distribution and consumption at the festival; new adornments must be made. We shall see below that a hunting period is ritually opened and closed, and two totemic sago palms felled. But we need first to understand the meaning of the restraint and control that characterize this preparatory time.

Prohibition on Fertility

The opposition already defined between *hoofuk* and *roofuk* (true substance, vital principle, inside versus outside, skin or protection) must be kept in mind in order to understand the Umeda or Yafar people's attitudes during the 8–10 months preceding the public performance.[62] Gell notes that after a last musical night of *fuf* trumpets ([*huf smav*]; *MC:*158–60) inaugurating the preparatory period, certain taboos are prescribed, for instance against collecting coconuts or coconut intrapetiolar fiber for sago processing (used as painting supports in the fish masks), allowing important gathering of people, being noisy (shouting, singing, playing any music including the *fuf* orchestra, which will be heard again only at the opening of Ida).[63] Moreover, a mutual segregation of the moieties is encouraged by the relative prohibition for people of one moiety to enter the other's territory. This expresses a symbolic segregation of the sexes before their violent encounter in Ida. To those general attitudes, one must add the more specific taboos (especially about sex and food) placed on performers (*MC:*168–70) whose identities are secretly chosen at the beginning of the preliminary period. These prohibitions are also respected in Yafar.[64]

But the most conspicuous of all—which was often emphasized by my interlocutors—was that the village area must not be weeded or cleared of pigs' excreta and debris.[65] People must no longer cut their hair (the modern hairstyle is to shave the peripheral area of the head); in the old days men were forbidden to shave their face as well and bathing was restricted as much as possible. House building is still forbidden because it would necessitate the felling of high trees, especially iron trees for the main posts (this would anger the *ogomô*). The soil must not be turned over, dug, or leveled. Most of these taboos will be ritually broken during the last days before the public performance (see below). As Gell rightly remarks: "One has the impression that the behaviour enjoined during the period of preparation is the antithesis of that enjoined during the performance itself" (*MC:*160). This very opposition is expressed precisely by the *roofuk/hoofuk* polarity. The period of preparation for Yangis puts the emphasis on the *roofuk:* the *hoofuk* or reproductive power is kept enclosed within its natural container (weeds, hair, dirt). Anything evoking fertility and growth, such as sexuality, bright colors, music, noise, or social collective activities is banned. Words that recall the totems' *hoofuk* or reproductive process are prohibited. The strict control over fertility is necessary for months, in order to give it its maximal power at the performance. Life forces are to be kept under pressure so that they burst (remember the *êri*'s two bundles thrown to the ground and "exploding" noisily) more abruptly and with a greater efficacy when ritually released. The passage between silence and unrestrained noise, songs, and music is most striking—as has been already stated—during the hour that precedes the *êri*'s appearance. Not the slightest loud voice is heard, shadows are slipping in the dark, and only some men whisper, expecting the moment when the *êri* will be led by the priests out of the backstage and the *hoofuk fatik* performed. At that point, the ceremony starts with all its suddenly discharged expression of collective joy through the crowd's song, *fuf* music and clicking phallocrypts. Darkness and light are corollaries of silence and noise: as the *êri*'s dance will end with dawn, it has to begin in complete obscurity. No light or fire is to be lighted until the performance has reached its regular course.[66]

Felling of the Two Totemic Sago Palms

Approximately four months before the ceremony, in order to mark the inauguration of the period of intensive sago processing, one *afwêêg* and one *fenaw* sago palm are felled simultaneously by men of the opposite moiety of that of the sago clones. Spells are uttered invoking the *ogomô*. Both trees must fall at the same moment and the simultaneity of this double operation is ensured by intermediate men transmitting the calls of the two groups (working on lands belonging to their respective moieties). These sagos will be processed and a meal with game meat will be taken only by men in the village. Men of the *Araneri* (male) moiety eat the *fenaw* (female) sago jelly, and *Angwaneri* men eat the *afwêêg* sago. The remainder of the two sagos are stored until the festival. They will be used for the ritual bundles thrown to the ground at the opening of Yangis (*hoofuk fatik*) and for the ritual sago jelly confected at dawn on the first day.

Thus the cooperation of both moieties is stressed as well as the indivisible duality of the sexual principles, portrayed here by the totemic sago clones. The synchronization of the felling is significant of the aim to couple the totems as an equal pair free from sexual hierarchy.

Inauguration of the Hunting Period: A Prayer to the Mother-Coconut

Some time later, an intensive hunting period is opened by a ritual on a flowering coconut tree in the hamlet. To hunt intensively appears as a breach of the restraint imposed during the preparatory period, hence the necessity of marking it ritually. All women and children are sent to the forest to work and the men gather at the bottom of two coconut trees— one for each moiety—where they cook the meat of some small game. With their bodies scantily painted, the two designated *ifegê* performers climb their respective palm, saying: "Mother, give me!" (*naya, ka fay!*). Among the men standing below are the designated *êri* and *yis* performers, also scantily decorated. All the assembled men look downward and keep their hands open over their heads. Then the two *ifegê* cut open the spadix spathe, saying: "Break open the possum children, break open the cassowary children," and so on. They shake the inflorescence, and flowers fall; the Yafar exegesis sees the coconut flowers as maternal milk. In doing so, the two men say: *Naya na tot o-fefe!* (Mother's breast is doing), *kwoy ruwar na wan pe* (the cassowary's children fall together), and *ogomô* are named. Men who get a flower into their hands are said to be "in Mother's net bag" (*naya na wura-inaag*), that is, in her womb, or actually in her net bag like a baby (in both cases, fed by her). Men who do not get any flower will say: *Naya ka waha na* (Mother abandoned me). When the two designated *ifegê* performers climb down, they are ritually welcomed and verbally associated with the Mother's milk as well as with game; they are invited to share the meal being prepared, in which animal hearts and blood are mixed with magical rhizomes and with the coconut flowers received by some of the participants. When they stir this food, men speak ritually of the "eating of blood [from] Mother's milk" (*naya na tot taf o-nehya*). Dogs are also fed.[67]

After this ritual, men hunt intensively for one or two months, until they have smoked enough meat for the festival. This includes the construction of pig traps (*awra*) by small groups of men in different parts of the territory (Juillerat 1986). To conclude the hunt, a small rite is performed: the two *ifegê* again climb the same coconut and bind the flowering spadix, saying: "To bind (detain) the possum children, to bind the cassowary children," and so on.

The coconut is the basic symbol of motherhood (*say afar mwig*, literally "coconut mother original") as well as the main *Angwaneri* totem. It is the vegetal form of the Mother-Earth. Her role as game procreator refers to a myth (see below, " 'The Mother's Brother Is the Breast': The Avoidance of Incest") in which all the animals were kept by a jealous father within the underground, under a *Ficus* tree (which appears to be a coconut in the esoteric version, or even a monstrous cosmic woman). Wild animals are also symbolically associated with children in sexual rites performed by young married couples in order to conceive (Juillerat 1986). Flowers as milk are a promise of blood for the elected hunter; but milk also makes the child become an adult man and a hunter. Inversely, the mythical *ifegê* were born out of their mother's blood before searching for her breast. Milk and blood refer alternately to the two maternal functions so often polarized in Yafar symbolism: procreation and nutrition. To open, and then close, the maternal milky flow is thus, in this context, the metaphor for having or not having access to blood, that is, for opening and concluding the hunt. It is also significant that the future performers of the *ifegê* roles climb the coconut (mother) to reach its inflorescence (breast), anticipating in that way their firing of arrows toward the sun at the end of Yangis.

Pigments and Personal Decoration

Once the hunt has been closed, colored pigments (Juillerat 1978a) are collected in the following order, according to informant B: *Curcuma* rhizomes, red ochre, yellow earth (*geege*), certain soft woods (*ko* tree and sago petioles stripped from their bark) for charcoal, and kaolinic earth from certain caves. *Curcuma* and *geege* earth are smoked, red ochre nodules are burnt for their oxidation, woods are charred and white clay is dried. All of this magical stuff is stored secretly from women in bachelors' houses or garden shelters (see also Forge 1962).

Three weeks before the public ritual, men make new armbands and women new skirts and net bags or other male ornaments (*MC:*170). Each man prepares his own personal decoration, such as plumes or possum furs.

Chronology during the Last Five Days

I give here briefly the day-to-day chronology of activities that led to the opening of the 1976 performance. It appears rather different from that described by Gell for Umeda (*MC:*170–74).

April 12: The sago stored for several months is brought to the village by women and placed on special flat racks erected by men before each house.

April 13: Women collect breadfruit leaves for the first preparation of domestic sago jelly and pieces of *Pometia pinnata* firewood, which is also used ritually for their first fire in order to heat the stones (to boil the water). The Master of the Earth (*bete na awaag*) accompanies them. He collects the first leaf and piece of wood for each woman.

April 14: All women and children are sent to collect large ordinary leaves to pack individual portions of sago jelly and bring back food from gardens. No woman or child is present in the village. This allows the men to engage in two ritual operations: the cleaning and leveling of the village ground, and the collection of coconut fiber for the fish masks (see details below). When the women return, everyone cuts their hair and the men shave.

April 15: In the morning, there is the ritual inauguration of the sago jelly fabrication. The men of knowledge (*aynaag*) go into each house and perform a rite on the *limbum* container and on the *Pometia pinnata* firewood (brought in two days before). These men thus enter the houses of their own moiety and, if possible, submoieties. In each house, they first place on the piece of wood some raw sago and magical *Acorus calamus* rhizome for sago production, saying spells about growth and invoking the garden guardian. Then they unpack the first bundle of sago with spells evoking the "peeling off" (*roof*) of the sago *hoofuk*. After that, they utter ritual words on the *limbum* and rub its inside with a magical plant (*Homalomena* sp.). It is significant that the latter spells allude also to hunting and procreation, because the *limbum* is the container of the future jelly that represents the embryo, as we have seen for the *yis* ceremony. The head of the family, as a hunter, may also profit by the rite, through the identification between sago, child, and game. This domestic ritual ends by dropping a bit of sago into the *limbum*.

The whole day, women will prepare large provisions of sago jelly for consumption and distribution during the public festival. The fetching of water at the river for the jelly is also accompanied by minor rites.

In the afternoon, the moieties meet at the place where the ritual is to be held, and the men clear the enclosure. In the afternoon, they work in the enclosure and paint the coconut fibers for the fish masks (see details below).

April 16: In the morning, vegetal materials are gathered and prepared secretly in the forest by all the men (*êr tofa*), and then brought with songs to the enclosure. A meal is taken in the family houses in the afternoon.

At about 5 p.m., *fuf* trumpets are played in the enclosure, while a rite is performed on the *Calamus* liana (see below) and mask structures are constructed. Young men prepare colors for the body paintings. The *êri* and *rawsu-inaag* performers are painted when it is night. At about 9 p.m., the public ritual is opened.

Let us examine in more detail the most crucial moments just mentioned.

The End of Restraint on Fertility: Village Cleaning and Coconut Fiber Collection

Keeping the village ground dirty and unweeded since the opening of the preparatory period has been defined as a retention of *hoofuk* under its natural "skin," or *roofuk*. Two days before the public opening of Yangis, men ritually remove the first weed in the absence of women and children. Elders gather at the center of the place and uproot one particular type of grass, using a stick of sago palm wood (*nabik*). They chew betel with *Acorus calamus* root (from a magical clone for sago) and also tie two leaves of that same species to the stick. Spells are said while all the men endeavor to hold the stick, or place one hand on the other men's hands. According to informant B, this widespread kind of weed is the equivalent of the original female deity's pubic hair. The operation is considered dangerous and great tension prevails: the *roofuk* is being removed and the earth dug for the first time in many months; the *hoofuk* of the Mother-Earth will be uncovered, underground roads will be open through which the *ogomô* spirits will come to dance. In order to prevent the earth from becoming too "soft," the Master of the Sky (from the *Araneri* moiety) strengthens it by letting his penis touch the ground. He is thus repeating the primordial sexual intercourse of W . . . , the original god, who made firm the small and fragile primordial earth by repeated copulations with his female companion B . . . , and then tested its solidity with his penis (Juillerat 1986).[68]

Once the preliminary rite is over, the younger men weed the whole village using modern tools (in old times only flat sago sticks) and make the dancing ground flat. When the women are called back, they do the main work of cleaning.

But before that, pieces of coconut fiber, *besa* [*wata*], have to be collected from the tops of palms. I did not notice any particular rite for this operation, which is carried out by the main performers in Yangis and in a certain order, beginning with the *ifegê*. To cut off the *besa* is to free the base of the coconut leaves, to release and accelerate the upward movement of growth, to liberate the phallic principle from its maternal gangue.[69] The *besa* will later be sewn together in pairs and painted on both sides (*MC*:186) apparently to represent the maternal womb marked with the colors of fertility.[70] In the meantime, they will be kept hidden from women's sight.

As already specified, at the end of the same day, men, women, and children cut their hair and shave the periphery of their heads. In times past, men shaved and people washed for the first time since the opening of the preparatory period.

Meeting of the Moieties and Clearing of the Ritual Enclosure

The day before the opening of Yangis, men adorn themselves, take their bows and arrows, and gather in the village place; in a ritualized excitement marked with war cries, demonstrations of pseudo-agressiveness and mock aiming with arrows, *Araneri* and *Angwaneri* men face each other in two groups. After some peliminary minor rites, both moieties collectively "provoke" each other in a face-to-face threatening behavior, arrows upward at the ready and bows drawn. Such a ritualized attitude will be repeated several times during the next two days.[71] Then the *Angwaneri* (female) moiety runs once around the place with war cries and goes down to the river into the secondary bush. Following them, the *Araneri* (male moiety) do the same. This is the most conspicuous moment emphasizing the priority of the female moiety over the male one. This was crudely explained by informant A through the analogy with sexual intercourse in which the woman lies down first. This establishes a direct equivalence between the encounter of the moieties in the ritual enclosure and copulation. However, the primacy of femaleness is to be explained also by women's dominant role in procreation and, as Gell himself suggests (*MC:*172–73), by the expression of a "straightforward inversion (in ritual and myth) of the mundane truth." It is at the same time a way to recall that women were performing Yangis in the mythical times, white men were segregated in the forest, until they killed all the women and stole the masks and pigments (*MC:*250; Juillerat 1986, 1988, 1991a).

The ritual enclosure is only a cleared space in the secondary growth, separated from the river by a natural screen of vegetation, with only a hole (called *sawôg na meeg*, "the hole of the fish") to allow access to the water. This space is named "place of the fish," *sawôg na kebik,* or "swamp of the fish," *sawôg na bogo* (*MC:*171). Fish, with their particular designs, are actually supposed to come into the painted dancers. For that reason, fishing is prohibited for a time after the ceremony. The performers, in washing off the paint after their dance, are said to give back their designs to the fish and the first, in turn, are supposed to wear the dancers' motifs for the following days. On the upper side, a path is cleared leading to the village place, to which performers have access through a low screened door opened in a fence, *pepag* (*MC:*173).[72]

Once in the "place of the fish," *Araneri* men occupy the upstream area, while the *Angwaneri* men clear the downstream space. Throughout all the activities that take place over the next few days, the men will respect this subdivision. The clearing of the enclosure is accompanied by spells about the "peeling off," *roof*, of the Mother-Earth, and with special *sangêk* songs evoking the appearance of the totemic *hoofuk* and "bloods" (secretly called "cassowary's blood") at the surface of the ground.

Then each moiety plants in its area a stick of sago petiole, *na bero* ([*napeda*]; *MC:*171), on which the roots of sacred plants and sexual fluids are rubbed. This is to mark the two extremities of the ritual shelter that is about to be built. The *na bero* are secretly called *afwêêg kêg* and *fenaw kêg*, "bone" of the two totemic sago trees; it is alleged that if they were uprooted all people would die, which clearly means that the two totems are the embodiment of the society whose permanence is conceived as depending on sexual complementarity. As they plant it, all the men of the corresponding moiety hold the *na bero*, or some other man's arm, to participate to the action. Spells and songs are said during the operation. One spell in particular names the "mouth" or "jaw hole" (*Araneri*) and the "vagina" or "rectum" (*Angwaneri*). Songs refer to hunting and are similar to those chanted for a neophyte performing for the first time a role in a ceremony dedicated to socialized bush spirits and animal guardians (Juillerat 1978b, 1986).

Informant B declared that the ritual shelter represents the Great Mother's body. It is divided into an upper part, which goes to the *Araneri* moiety, and a lower part, which goes to the *Angwaneri* moiety. The body polarity between mouth and vagina is expressed by the unifying term "*am-mesoog*" (that is, *emwêêg-mesoog*, "vagina-head"). It is likely that it refers here to the diety's corpse and that the two opposed body orifices are seen as the locations through which fertility can realize itself out of the maternal *materia*. The *na bero* are thus supposed to grow out of the two orifices of the Great Mother's corpse, calling forth the images of the clitoris and of the uvula, respectively.

The shelter is then erected without any special rite between the two *na bero*.

Main Operations Carried Out in the Enclosure

I shall mention here only a few aspects of the preparation of materials
and colors that help us to better understand Yangis symbolism. The
collection of vegetal materials for the masks (April 16) will be examined
afterward.[73]

On April 15, at midday, the *besa* were brought to the enclosure
and distributed to the different clan members. Ritual leaders se-
lect them depending on their size and quality, and mutter the
corresponding *ogomô*'s names. Each *besa* is scratched with the
fingernails "to take off the blood" (of the Great Mother's childbirths, according to informant B), and then sewn in pairs. The
painting is then carried out, while the *besa* are kept lying on top
of mounds of food: sago jelly (the first portions made by women
in the morning), tubers, bananas, and smoked meat. Each
mound belongs to a clan having an *ogomô* emblem (only the
ancient Yafar clans; see table 1.2); they are lined up in their
respective moiety area in the enclosure. The *besa*—and also the
beaten *Gnetum gnemon* underbark (*masiy senk* [*ehov sog*];
MC:202) used for the *koor* and *amof* roles—are first anointed
with *Curcuma* on both sides, while all the men shout a spell.[74]
    Before painting the clan designs, a technical and ritual process
must be carried out: the fabrication of black paint, called
snebuk-yis (charcoal-sago jelly), a mixture of liquid raw sago,
breadfruit latex and the juice of *abeger* (*Schefflera* sp.) leafless
stems with *ko* tree charcoal. For this operation, older men of
both moieties join in, while all other participants stand with their
moiety in a face-to-face warlike confrontation as already described. The spells shouted by all are based on the analogy between sago jelly fabrication and conception. The homogeneous
paint is secretly named "black semen" (that is, original or divine
semen).[75] The other paints are prepared with less magical care.
    The painting process can then begin over the mounds of food.
Men work in small groups of three or four. A leading painter
first draws the design in black, then the younger men fill in the
surfaces with red and yellow, or align white dots along the black
outline (for more details, see Juillerat 1978a). I heard that some
raw sago is placed on the center of the surface before the colors.
The whole work is synchronized, with all the participants beginning a new stage at the same time. The songs related to the

different colors are quite similar to those chanted for a neophyte in rituals dedicated to hunting (Juillerat 1978b). When the *besa* have been painted, they receive a transversal stick (to which a "tail" will be attached later) and they are fitted over some performer's head. An elder marks with a *Curcuma* root the location of the eyes and pierces the holes. This is accompanied by spells referring to the "breaking of the cassowary's eye" (see above, "What about Cassowaries?") as well as other animals' eyes. Then the *besa* are hung up under the shelter and all the men share the meal.

The identification of the painted *besa* with the original Mother's uterus along with the fact that the different *ogomô* are individually named for each mask suggests that, through the mediation of the *ogomô* (the male growth principle proceeding from the Mother) and his emblem, each clan ensures its own relationship to the natural fecundity embodied in the maternal divinity. The mask material and the paints belong to the maternal and natural domains, while the design is the differentiated sign of a constituted social unity. Assigned to a rather weak status in the social system, the patriclan finds here a way to better establish its identity.

Among other minor rites performed within the enclosure, a "cross" is stuck into the ground in each of the moiety areas. It is made of two *ay* (*Canarium* sp.) sticks tied together with a string taken from a woman's underskirt. Men ritually say that "they tie in the blood—in the vagina blood—in the penis blood." The cross represents the standing and strong body (or skeleton) of the Great Mother B . . . , in opposition to the shelter representing her recumbent corpse. Actually, the vertical *ay* stick (about 1-meter high) is said to be her spine (*rumuri-kêg*), and the horizontal stick her shoulder transversal axis (*ôbu kêg*).[76] The whole structure is called *riruwag*, probably derived from *rii*, "tree, vertical stem," and *ruwag*, "to hang." The declared function of the *riruwag* is to strengthen the performers in their dance and protect them from death. I noticed that some masks were held over it for a short while and given spells before being worn by a dancer.

Another conspicuous rite worth mentioning deals with the *Calamus* (*bêêbi*) liana. This vine of the *Palmae* family absorbs an impressive quantity of water and is thus symbolically connected with rain, but also with semen. Yafar cosmology imagines it as the "road of the moon and the sun," having its root in the west

and its "head" in the east (Juillerat 1986). Another exegesis situates it as the perimeter of the "solid water," that is, the ocean.
In Yangis, the *bêêbi* constitutes the vertical axis of certain masks,
particularly the *êri,* the *yis* and the *ware-inaag;* its lower part is
split and some raw sago is placed in the fork.

On April 16, the two pieces of *bêêbi* collected by the two
moieties were sacralized and cut. They were first held up toward
the east and spells were recited about growth and its male principle and spirit, about erection and, metaphorically, about a
small snake whose peculiarity is to stand up when approached.
The *Araneri* men hold the vine high and obliquely, the
Angwaneri men low and more horizontally. Each moiety will
then cut its *bêêbi* into convenient pieces for the masks; they have
to use a stone adze and shout spells referring again to the cassowary. It was explained to me that to cut the liana is to break the
cassowary's head or its penis (or testicles). To cut open the bird's
head is to free the growth principle. To break its penis is to have
access to the *hoofuk* and allow the reproductive process to occur.[77] During this loud shouting of the spells, allegedly to prevent
the women from hearing them from the village, the younger men
play *fuf* trumpets and walk around the ritual area.

Those are the main operations performed in the "fish pond" enclosure before the opening of the public feast. But between the painting of
the *besa* and the *riruwag* and *bêêbi* sequences, men go for an entire
morning into a primary forest area to collect all the vegetal material
necessary for the construction of the masks (*MC*:173–74). This is called
the *êr tofa,* the "gathering of the persons," the latter being the masks
and the spiritual entities they embody. The proceeding gives much importance to the dual division of labor between moieties. Men have a
gathering place where the collected material is prepared (more particularly, the mask fringes bound in long girdles). But for the collection
itself, men split into *Araneri* and *Angwaneri* groups and disappear into
the surrounding forest to find the desired species. These are mainly:

- *sööbi* [*sob*] black palm, from which *Araneri* men draw out the
  immature fronds from the crown (fish masks) (plate 15)

- *hööbi* [*hub*] wild pandanus, from which *Angwaneri* men draw out
  immature leaves (*êri, yis, ware-inaag* masks)

Plate 15. Group of Yafar men of the *Araneri* (male) moiety, during the *êr tofa,* collecting *sööb naabi* [*subnab*], the white immature fronds (*naabi*) from the crown of a black palm subspecies (*sööb*) that are used to make the fringes of the *ogomô* and *sawôg* masks. (Photo Juillerat)

- leaves from some *afwêêg* and *fenaw* sago palms collected by *Araneri* and *Angwaneri* men (*êri* masks), respectively

- *bêêbi* lianas, other vines, and minor material are collected by both moieties.

Many series of magical words about growth and regeneration are recited during the collection. As the men bring back all the material to the "fish pond" enclosure, their songs (*MC:*173), called *sawôg sangêk*, refer to "bringing back fish species," "cassowary children" and "W . . . and B . . .'s children." The whole operation is marked by great excitement; much betel is chewed and periodically the moieties oppose each other in the way already described. Before returning to the village, all men must wash. The designated dancers do so with coconut water before eating its flesh.[78] As they do so, they sing: "Let B . . .'s blood come up! Let W . . .'s blood come up! Let the children of the penis blood come up! Let the children of the womb come up! Let the children of the amnion come up! . . . Mother, mother eee!" Then another chant refers to the men's beauty and seductive power, once their bodies are purified and anointed with perfumes, for the women coming to the ceremony from other tribes.

The end of that last day of preparation is dedicated to the construction of masks, the mixture of colors for body paintings, to the preparation of bows, ceremonial arrows and personal decorations, and to the testing of *suh-wagmô* phallocrypts.

After the Public Performance

I was told later that right after all the masks have disappeared out of the arena, when *fuf* trumpets have sounded their long harmonic tones, a group of elders discreetly perform behind the dancers' steps a short Gungwan rite (see note 34 and below, "Gungwan: The Closing of the Mother-Earth") in order to close the underground roads through which the *ogomô* came and went, to isolate the community from the maternal-chthonian powers now gone back to their own place, and to cut the supernatural world away from the mundane domain and society. A stone is buried to strengthen the earth and the Gunwan spells are recited. One of them refers to the disappearance of the divine parental couple who have been present during Yangis: "Where is [now] W . . .'s trail? Where is B . . .'s trail?"

On April 19, men and women assembled at a collective meal in two separate groups on the central village place (an unusual site for eating). The men were still wearing their personal decorations. This was asserted to have no religious meaning: they ate the remaining sago jelly and meat.

On April 21, the village site was cleaned by the women of all the debris left by the crowd, while men shared fresh small game meat and sago in the ritual enclosure and decorated their faces with scant nonritual designs (similar to those of women during the performance). Then they went up to the hamlet and played *fuf* trumpets, walking around for the entire day and taking turns at playing. The food racks and the ritual leaf screen were demolished. That was the "official" conclusion of Yangis. From then on, no one would walk through the enclosure until the next ceremony.

Alfred Gell (*MC:*208) writes that the Umeda go hunting again to obtain blood to anoint themselves at a river site. My Yafar informants confirmed this practice and explained that this helps them to find game in the future. Actually, this rite restores the hunters to their full efficiency because it cleanses their persons of the excess of *hoofuk* acquired during their participation in Yangis, which could hinder their success in hunting. In this case, the antithesis *hoofuk/taf* (blood) is the relevant duality.

MYTH AND RITUAL

The old problem of the connection of ritual and myth is posed again with Yangis. I think it is first of all necessary to discard the question of the anteriority of one on the other, in spite of the statement made by my best informant that one must perform rites not to forget the sacred stories; this statement poses ritual as an opportunity to recall the myths and takes for granted a semantic link between them. The secret knowledge to which Yangis refers is composed of isolated symbolic analogies as well as of longer or shorter excerpts from myths, but also of whole symbolic systems otherwise autonomous from Yangis, including, for instance, the notion of self, the conception of fertility and sociocosmological representation.[79] What appears clearly is that myth and ritual (and this is also valid for other Yafar rites) do not correspond to each other in a way that allows one to see them as exact equivalents. The whole "story" acted in Yangis is not the ritualized form of one particular myth. But in spite of that, we can ascertain that all ritual figures and most symbolic elements in Yangis have their cultural explanation in local mythology and cosmology. Both ritual and myth take their materials out of the same system of representations, of which they are two different realizations: acted drama and verbalized story. But each chooses its proper elements and organizes them differently. Any comparison between myth and ritual has to take into account the common stock of knowledge and imagery. The whole of that general view on the world is present neither in myth nor in rituals, because these are only contingent and partial expressions of it. The local exegetical comments both on rituals and myths lead back separately to the fundamental set of ideas and images, but in so doing, they may also establish parallelisms between stories and rites.

Myth and ritual use the same symbolic material, but—as we shall demonstrate later in comparing the ritual and mythical expressions of incest—they differ in that they have distinct functions. In Umeda-Yafar culture, myth appears as the free expression of fantasies, without any caution about moral issues or efficiency; it is pure imagery. Whereas ritual has a social aim, it is more dangerous and must be handled with care because it is efficacious and is supposed to have an effect on reality. It is meaning put into symbolic action for a power over man. For these reasons, ritual is morally oriented. It is the bearer of a precise message, about life in most cases, and sometimes about death.

I hope the present analysis of Yangis will have made clear that the elaboration of the worldview into stories, ritual, or multiple symbols only appears inextricable and contradictory, whereas, in fact, the basic system is rather coherent, being supported by universal mental representations about sexuality and filiation as will be shown in greater detail in the following pages.

SOCIOLOGY OF YANGIS

Sociology of Ritual or Symbolization of Society

Recent trends in anthropology have stressed the sociological and even economic or environmental factors determining ritual. Consequently its cultural content has been somewhat neglected. Much has been won by way of comprehension of the social aspects of ritual process, but at the same time the study of symbolic systems and culture as such has been considered rather old-fashioned and nonheuristic. Some authors—like Geertz (1973), Sahlins (1976), Wagner (1972, 1984), and Jorgensen (1981b)—have, however, brought attention back to the limits of an all-sociological method and to the necessity of taking into account cultural systems in their semantic dimensions.

These are the normal fluctuating orientations of anthropological theory. Outside of them, however, human societies show much variability in the importance they assign to actual social differentiation or to the elaboration of symbolic systems. This (that is, the object of study and not only the anthropologist's theoretical choice) also directs the investigation with more or less emphasis upon social categories, or upon cultural values. But it must be stressed that cultural categories also may allow a valuable insight into the ethnosociological models. Ritual and myth, after they have been explicated by local exegesis, provide sociological clues, even if these deal more with mental representations than with social praxis. What can be said about the Yafar-Umeda case in this respect?

The most striking fact about Yangis, aside from its complex exegesis, is its very low level in practical sociological implications. It is, moreover, a general feature of the societies of that area (Border Mountains), which seem to strive more for the elaboration of a total representation of the society within the cosmos and for a permanent control over natural fertility, than for the building up of social hierarchies and competitions, or for the recognition of political statuses through economic strategies. In the latter sense, one may say that Yangis (Ida) is neither the locus of political tactics, nor the occasion to "make adult men" through initiation, even if the fact of performing a ritual role for the first time implies the completion of a further informal step toward manhood. We shall see, however, that the *ifegê* and *anuwanam* roles may be seen as the symbolic realization of such a step. The dancer's age and social status (married/bachelor) for each role—a feature that Gell carefully took notice of—participate more in the semantics of the ritual figure than in the access to social status. This is clear, for instance, with the *koor* performed by "old men," who have already procreated, because of its relation to female contamination; and inversely for the *rawsu-inaag,* performed by adolescent boys, who have to introduce the sago palms' "daughters" (*yis*), which appear at dawn out of that lost virginal blood.[80] In Yafar, all the other roles may be acted for the first time by adult men, married or not, and—as Yangis is much more rarely performed than the Ida of Punda and Umeda—most old Yafar men played a ritual personage only once or twice in their life.[81]

One must acknowledge, however, that the organization of this festival is the occasion for any middle-aged man to prove his ability to exercise ritual responsibility in helping (and having each time a growing influence) in the nonpublic rites. Interestingly, this shows that prestige is obtainable not so much in the public arena but behind the scene. The dual priesthood associated with the moieties in their cosmic and sexualized nature is inherited, but each man has the potential to achieve a higher though informal status through his mastery of secret lore and ritual practice (Juillerat 1986, 1991b). Secrecy, as we have seen, deals with inherited religious duties and the corresponding individual identities as well as with the content of knowledge; and we understand here that prestige is finally perceptible on the public scene—as this is its inherent raison d'être—but that it has first to be won in the background of ritual life. In this respect, small communities of this type do not function in the same way as larger societies where big men's political enterprises are carried out relatively openly.[82] The care taken to conceal from the public the competitive forces in action corroborates the ethical endeavor to exhibit to the outer world the image of a flawless social unity.

So far, we have considered social differentiation within the male-dominated domain. The sexual discrimination on which the men's monopoly of esoteric knowledge and ritual depends is realized at two levels: in reality, through the natural categories of sex, and culturally through the reduplication of those categories in the moieties. Dual organization is the sociosymbolic framework in which Yangis (Ida) can be performed; Gell's informants and my own agree on the fact that the moieties are operative only on the occasion of that ritual and have no other social function. Sexual totemism, as it has been analyzed in this text, has shown, however, that the very "function" of moieties, in and outside Yangis, is to incorporate society within nature, in its reproductive process, to build up a global representation of the universe, and to ensure the group's formal unity.

In Yafar and neighboring Amanab groups, each clan definitely belongs to one moiety; I had not one example in which a whole agnatic group would have been transferred to the opposite moiety in order to compensate a demographic unbalance (MC:35–36). Such disproportion is corrected by the temporary assignment of isolated men from one moiety to the other. This arrangement is valid only during the ceremonial period and the transfer is operated from families having several sons; then only one on two is transferred to the opposite moiety following in alternation the birth order.

As we may see, the repercussion of Yangis on the actual social organization is quite limited. Its relation to dual organization is crucial, but dualism itself has almost no sociological consequences in practice. However, sociology of religion is not only the study of how the religious system is managed by sociopolitical forces; it deals also with the images of society or interindividual relationships as they are expressed by religious ideas. Semantics of religion contain something of a mental picture of basic social principles. There is little doubt that the investigation of the secret lore can facilitate an understanding of the social system; to this end, knowledge of local exegesis is an essential component of the ethnographic inquiry and a basis for interpretation.[83]

The revelation of important exegetical material may lead us to discover the genuine significance of a ritual (myth, cosmology, and so on) and help in the elaboration of a more scientific interpretation. The following example will make more explicit these three levels (public, exegetical, interpretative):

a. Yangis public performance and comments present the *ifegê* as "new men" or "original men"; the structuralist interpretation of color symbolism can lead to the same conclusion by seeing their red body paint as a sign of regeneration (in comparison to the black *êri*); the arrow they shoot into the bush may be considered a symbolic act to improve natural growth.

b. The exegetical material adds, however, that the *ifegê* are seen as being in search of their divine and dead mother and that they fire their arrow toward her naturalized breast, the sun, with the help of their mother's brother.

c. All anthropological and psychoanalytical interpretation will have to take into account the emphasis on the mother/son relationship, on an implicit incest, and on the mother's role; it will also help to interpret hunting symbolism and to understand that nature is not only anthropomorphized, but becomes the locus of projective images about filiation and oedipal fantasies.

The latter conclusion would not have been possible without the enlightenment provided by local exegesis. The result is not just better knowledge of the symbolism; it also leads to crucial insight into how basic social (or infrasocial) relationships are fantasized in culture.[84] The sociological elements present in ritual or mythical analysis are, however, too close to psychology to be distinguished from universal psychoanalytical material. We are here at the limits of psychoanalysis and sociology, as if the latter were in part the further elaboration of the former, or could not free itself completely from the former.

Secrecy: Politics or Meaning

The notion of exegesis implies social control in the distribution of knowledge and, consequently, secrecy. Many authors who observed initiation rites in New Guinea have emphasized that secrecy is mainly a stratagem to keep the distance necessary to transform sex categories and age groups into discrete social groups. This is politics with restricted cultural meaning. But for Yangis, where performers are not initiates or novices, or initiators, and have temporarily lost their social identity to play a part in a symbolic or "canonical" (Rappaport 1974:182) drama, ritual becomes "enacted meaning" without much politics at stake. The political management of secret knowledge is then located outside the meaning of ritual; it works in a more global system in which selective transmission of knowledge produces secrecy (Barth 1987; Juillerat 1986, 1990; see also the critique of Brunton's position in Jorgensen 1981b). But in such canonical rituals, where the ostensible aspect of initiation rites—that is, the direct social function—is canceled out, there must be some genuine meaning to be transmitted. This backstage management of knowledge deals not only with the secret signification of symbols such as cassowary, coconut, or sun, but with the more universal truths of which they are the encoded language. The public performance corresponds then to the manifest level of ritual for which exegetical commentaries reveal a latent level of meaning, appearing rather comparable to the latent signification of dreams as opposed to their manifest scenario: the individually repressed meaning in a dream is disclosed through analysis, whereas the first step toward the disclosure of the socially repressed meaning of ritual is exegesis, and the next step is provided by anthropological interpretation.[85] Holders of esoteric knowledge are in some way the custodians of the socially repressed part of culture. It is repressed partly for properly sociological reasons (such as male dominance over women), but also because its deepest meaning is close to universal unconscious symbolization in man.

Thus, there could be significant opposition between the function of alleged secrets allowing differentiation within the initiatory hierarchy and the genuine secrets supporting symbolic rituals—seen as encoded nonverbal language—and giving them their raison d'être. When ritual has no direct sociological result, it must be endowed with more meaning to be perpetuated. In other words, the classical initiation ritual finds its main function in the promotion of individual status and the elaboration of hierarchy; thus, it does not need much esoteric meaning, whereas the canonical type of ritual is rooted in a worldview and is devoid of any crucial efficacy on the existing social order. But, as we shall consider later, Yangis bears some collective initiatory message, even if no particular individuals are to be initiated.

This distinction is schematic, but might provide some clue to indicate why in certain societies esoteric knowledge is important, whereas in others it is not the subject of much concern.

Sexual Identity, Reproduction, and Filiation

The Yafar comments provided on the ritual figures of the first night and dawn made evident a double and, in purely logical terms, contradictory local interpretation. The two *êri* were seen as mothers of the sago palms, but at the same time as portraying a sexualized pair, which the exegesis identified with the original divine couple, W . . . and B . . . and with the totemic species. Similarly, the *yis* masks were simultaneously the *êri*'s daughters (young fecund female and rejuvenated *hoofuk*) and the totemic sagos were simultaneously the two sexual fluids (from male and female moieties) brought into conception and the two totemic semens (*yis* ceremony). The *ifegê* reproduced again something of that ambivalence, in appearing as two newborn sago palm sons, reduplicating on a male version the *êri* duo, but also as the male and female regenerated totemic species. That apparent contradiction in sexual identities is in fact the result of two superimposed representations: one, synchronic, about reproductive sexuality, the other, diachronic, about filiation (figure 1.2; see also Green 1977).

The totemic palms, male and female, undergo the same reproductive evolution, the successive stages of which are identified with a respective

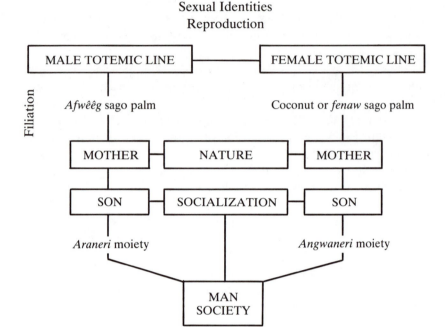

Figure 1.2. Synchrony of sexuality and diachrony of filiation in Yangis.

generational position and sexual identity: the old generation is that of mothers, the younger that of sons. In between, there is the indication of a daughters level (*rawsu-inaag* [*molna tamwa*] in Umeda, *yis* in Yafar) that appears only as the figuration of the mothers' renewed fecundity (*hoofuk*). This three-generation chain may be subdivided into two sections:

a. A mother/daughter section expresses the reduplication and transmission of female reproductive power, the uterine filiation with its basically biological function. This process deals more with self-regeneration or rejuvenation than with reproduction.

b. A mother/son section (the basic filiative link of the whole ritual) expresses the real generational shift, the transformation of female into male, or, better, the reproduction of father to son through the female reproductive process.

The production of the same (regeneration) or of the different (repro-duction) is one of the dialectical points taken into account in the view on life process among these cultures. But in both cases, the producer is female. The all-female reference of the first section puts the emphasis on the procreative maternal role in its self-perpetuation (the daughter *is* her rejuvenated mother) and poses the unity of the mother/daughter pair in its biological role. The second section recalls that males can only be produced by females and, in a subsequent theme carried out in the *ifegê* scene, that the son is the privileged partner of the mother in her nursing role. Roughly summarized, Yangis is saying here that daughters redupli-cate their mother through the continuity of the *hoofuk* transmission, and that sons receive their male strength from the father's semen, but then lose it during gestation only to recover it from their mother's milk and their socializing father's or mother's brother's intervention.[86] Being the copy of her mother, the daughter is passive in receiving the maternal fecundity, whereas the son has to strive to find the breast using in that aim his "innate" hunting faculty and his mother's brother mediation. We shall see later how the absence of the biological father's figure in the Yangis finale, and apparently of paternal filiation, is to be explained.

The attention on filiation leads to a vertical reading of Yangis. But simulanteously, a horizontal reading has to be proposed. At almost ev-ery level of the filiative double line, bisexualized pairs "cooperate' and exchange their male and female substances. Table 1.6 shows the series of dual figures, where the three pairs *êri, yis,* and *ifegê* are the leading roles. The two first ones have their "by-standers," that is, *rawsu-inaag* and *ware-inaag* who have been identified with discarded substances (blood and *hoofuk*), whereas the *ifegê* are guided by their preceptors. The *ogomô* and *sawôg,* although there are several of each, may be seen as constituting two pairs, following the distribution of the clan emblems in the two moieties. At the same time, the ancient dance style— described earlier—of the black and colored Fish estabished another duality that today is only perceptible successively (see above, "*Sawôg*"). As for the Termite roles, they were only two in Yafar, but could have been more numerous (as in Umeda and Punda). They enter the arena chronologically between the *sawôg* and the *ifegê.* They represent simulta-neously the termination of pregnancy and the completed fetus ready for birth: thus their duality is optional.

Sexual polarity is also stressed by two specific ritual actions that correspond to the crucial moments in procreation:

Table 1.6.
Correspondences between Different Sequences of Time in Yangis

Real Time	Ritual Figures	Main Specific Ritual Actions	Totemic References	Reproductive Process	Filiation and Kinship	Mythical References
Night	èri	hoofuk fatik	2 totemic species (male/female)	Sexual intercourse	Mothers	W . . ./B . . . divine couple; hierogamy; Afwêêg/fenaw sago palms (sago palm/coconut)
	rawsu-inaag		Their bloods	Virginal bloods		Their bloods
Dawn	yis	yis ceremony	Fusion of their sexual fluids	Conception	Daughters (Umeda)	Oogango (young fertile woman)
					Daughters (regenerated mothers)	
	ware-inaag			Discarded fluids		Western swamps in cosmology(?)
Morning	ogomô		Gestation of regenerating totemic sp.	Fetus growth		B . . .'s sons (?) and sago growth spirits
Whole day	sawôg		idem	idem		Fish as child
Afternoon	koor		idem	Emanations from pregnancy		Emanations from B . . .'s pregnancy
End of afternoon	amof		End of gestation	End of pregnancy	Male fetus	Association to boof fruits and ripeness
Before sunset	anuwanam				"Mother's brothers"	Culture heroes
	ifegê	Arrows shooting	Totemic species regenerated	Childbirth; Search for mother's breast	Sons born; nursing relationship; incest taboo	B . . .'s death in miscarriage; her body dismembered; her breast as sun

a. the *hoofuk fatik* (see above: "*Eri*") that marks the engagement (in the arena and with each other) of both totemic parents and their sexual stuffs, and the opening of Yangis

b. the *yis* ceremony displaying the fusion of male and female *hoofuk* into conception.

The next decisive moment would be birth, but—as far as I know—it is only acted by the coming of the *ifegê* out of their seclusion in the "fish pond" to the public place, and by the spell pronounced in a low voice by the preceptor(s): "Blood, blood, blood . . . placenta blood, umbilical blood." But immediately the word *taf,* "blood," gives place to the word *tot,* "breast," muttered by the *ifegê* performers. Birth leads without transition to suckling, which definitely cancels out the new forbidden uterine bond. Actually, since pregnancy, reproductive interaction has ceased and has been replaced by the new mother/son pair. Opened with a call for both sexual principles, Yangis ends with a "desexualized" genealogical tie: sexuality has allowed filiation.

Sexual confrontation, conception and birth-nursing: those three moments are ritually acted out at three significant times—night, dawn, and sunset. Night is for sexual antagonism striving for fusion; dawn—a promise of sunrise—accompanies the neutralization of sexual polarity into life. The hour before sunset evokes the postprocreative time, the mother in her second function while her reproductive role is fading out.[87] The mock firing of the *ifegê*'s arrows to the eastern sky (see above, "The Search for the Mother") reveals that shooting toward the east is prohibited. Informants explained that this was because the *ifegê* were first tempted to look for their mother in the east. Even if the *anuwanam* has the same attitude, the mother's brother is supposed to deter them from doing so and lead them to the western side of the arena. As in some myths, here a mistake is ritually expressed as a preventable possibility. What does east mean in this particular context? Its designation by the locution *yis mesoog,* "head (source) of sago jelly," makes this cardinal direction a space-time term for conception and pregnancy, in conformity with the ritual chronology analyzed above (the *yis* ceremony at dawn). Thus aiming at the east is similar to aiming at the earth; after the earth/sky and downward/upward opposition, the *ifegê* must face now an east/west alternative. As they look to the east, they express something about their past link to the mother and the irreversibility of time, as well as their restrained desire to "go back."

"The Mother's Brother is the Breast": The Avoidance of Incest

Actually, this regression/progression alternative is of the utmost importance for the general understanding of Yangis. The ritual ends with the *ifegê*'s victory over the temptation of a return to the uterus (that is, in sexual terms of incest) thanks to the replacement of the biological father by the mother's brother. As a public fertility undertaking endowed with a certain efficacy, Yangis had to express life. In psychoanalytical terms, life is the accomplishment of the separation from the mother, the victory over death instincts and over the incestuous annihilation of the self, and the neutralization of the castration complex. That is what Yangis discloses: to leave the womb for the breast is envisaged as the first phallic enterprise undertaken by the child and the oblique shooting of the *ifegê*'s arrows (a symbolic erection) is its ritual realization.

Incest may be prevented by the father's prohibition or sanction, but it can also be committed because of and against the father, as the myth summarized below illustrates:

> A father brings back pigs and cassowaries to his family. His three elder sons do not find any game.[88] They send their younger brother to spy on their father. The boy sees him catch a pig in an underground opening; he relates what he has watched to his brothers. The three young men go there, kill much game and then leave the door open. The animals spread out into the forest. The father sees them and guesses about his sons' treachery. He traps them in a gallery he has dug in the village ground and shuts the entrance for ever. In his anger, he has also dispatched into the earth sago palms, houses, and all cultural items.
>
> The secret version of the myth substitutes for the underground a supernatural monstrous woman, the father's wife: he catches his preys in her womb, is spied by his younger son and sends into that same place his guilty elder sons and his possessions. The cargoist extension of the story tells that all the European wealth, then under these Yafar ancestors' control, was thus lost because of that "bad father's" mistaken fury, and that the three sons were the white man's ancestors.

This myth could not have been included in a ritual, as ritual is primarily a defensive device.[89] Incest can be realized only in the pure imagery

Table 1.7

Conceptual Pairs between the Oedipal Myth and the Yangis Scenario

Myth	Yangis
Mother/son incest committed	Mother/son incest avoided
Father's sanction (castration)	MB's help (phallic enhancement)
=sons sent back to mother's womb	=sons diverted from mother's womb
Fusion	Separation
Death and possible rebirth in nature	Life and growth
Desocialization	Socialization

of myth free of any practical effect, while ritual has to display man's triumph over death. The opposition between the two scenarios is instructive, however, because together they express the alternatives inherent in the mother/son relationship and put forward some conceptual pairs (table 1.7)

We may understand better now why the father is absent in Yangis finale: his presence would have supposed his castrating intervention to prevent or punish incest, his imposition of the paternal law over his sons. In contradiction, the mother's brother—as an "antifather"—is not engaged in any competition with his nephews, to whom he provided a mother in the person of his sister.[90] "The mother's brother is the breast" (*nonoog ba tot ogwa*) are the words spoken for the benefit of young bachelors in order to remind them that they must honor their uncle with pig meat to pay for their mother's milk and care. If the mother's brother is fantasized as the guardian of the breast, the father—as the myth shows— is the guardian of the womb.[91] Consequently, father and mother's brother cannot both be present because of the incompatibility of the two corresponding maternal functions (pregnancy and nursing); they may also be seen as the two optional faces of the same male personage whose mediative roles between mother and son are mutually exclusive. But they also propose two different modalities of the œdipal triangle. As a dissuasion from incest, the one involves the threat of castration (desocialization), the other introduces the idea of guidance and initiation (socialization). The former remains captive of the biological family cell, whereas the latter, in bringing in the "fourth element" (Green 1977) represented by the mother's brother, breaks open the oversaturated triadic relationship and allows the subject's progression toward culture. The triangle subsists, but is displaced (figure 1.3).

The myth puts the Oedipus complex mainly on the side of the father, who incites his sons to deceive him because of his own egoistic behavior (concerning hunting at the manifest level of signification, but in fact reproduction and sexuality), and then castrates and desocializes them in the most definitive manner: through an irreversible return to their origin, that is, death, or, better, annihilation. The paternal punishment is equivalent to the total (symbolical) realization of the three sons' incestuous impulses. In keeping for himself the knowledge about procreation, the "bad father" denies filiation to his sons and unwittingly obliges them to transgress his implicit prohibition.[92] After the sanction has been carried out, he proposes to his younger son (who has been protected by his mother during the father's wrath) to "marry his sister," a solution rejected by the boy, who goes to another group and exchanges his sister for a wife. The younger son chooses the correct route toward manhood and autonomy, after having been taken under his mother's protection in an implicitly nursing relationship.

On this point, the myth contains the positive alternative of the incestuous scenario, as Yangis reveals the incestuous alternative of a positive scenario. The oedipal status of the *ifegê*—perceptively suspected by Gell (*MC*:293)—is thus clearly established.

What has just been analyzed has a further sociological extension. It can be detected through the initiatory relationship between *anuwanam* and *ifegê*. A man may act the part of the former only after having assumed the latter role and should normally do so in two consecutive festivals. I ignore whether the Waina, who performed their Ida each year in each village, believe it is important for a man to perform these roles at least once in his life. This would give a social efficacy to the symbolic meaning of the separation from the mother, first learned by the *ifegê*, and later taught by the *anuwanam*. At any rate, even in Yafar, one may give, according to one's own liking, a variable degree of relevance both to the individual experience of the performer in his idiosyncratic development and to the way the male community may socially integrate this initiatory aspect of Yangis and may consider having enacted at each ritual its collective liberation from the maternal ascendency and from nature.

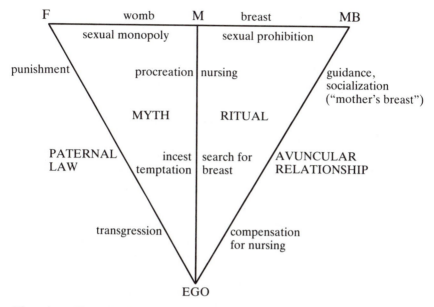

Figure 1.3. The reduplication of the oedipal triangle through the splitting of the paternal figure (F/MB).

The avoidance of incest, which is ensured by the *ifegê,* may be seen as a founding act; it establishes the social order over nature, in a similar way as—in the myth briefly quoted above ("The Meeting of the Moieties and the Clearing of the Ritual Enclosure")—the killing of women and the confiscation of their masks by men definitely establishes male domination (Gillison 1980; Juillerat 1988). The avoidance of incest and the annihilation of the women's secret are the double validation of the new order, the one based on filiation, the other on sexual opposition.[93]

In order to understand how these cultures see society as freed from the natural realm, it is imperative to consider the two conditions for the imposition of a new society: male control over fertility, and the sublimation of the Oedipus complex (Green 1980). This brings us also to the idea of passage or mutation: the Yangis finale actually leads the ritual hero from nature to culture; and the hero is the incarnation of the male subject, both individual and collective: the *ifegê-anuwanam* is the ritual impersonation of Society mediated by the totemic species. The undecorated *anuwanam* is the already socialized figure (ex-*ifegê*) coming back to guide the still unsocialized *ifegê* (future *anuwanam*). Masks and paints are the signs of nature and, in this respect, all decorated performers portray natural forces; in contrast, the *anuwanam* alone—the one who knows, the initiated—is a *man* and as such the representative of the society. More than the *ifegê*, he is the ultimate figure of Yangis. In this sense, the festival may be seen as an alternative to initiation (see Keesing 1982; Schieffelin 1982). But the initiatory efficacy works only in a purely symbolic way; there are no individuals to be initiated, no opposition between novices and initiators as such or as age groups. The performers do not participate as social persons, but as anonymous actors, as the bearers of symbols (even if they do not know the exact meaning of their roles). And *ifegê* and *anuwanam,* as initiand and initiator, act in the name of the totems, that is, of the whole society. In this respect, Yangis is in a clear-cut opposition to classical initiation rites or even to rituals in which the performers keep their social identity and act in their own and their group's name.

We may now fully grasp the mother's brother symbolism: as the only personage to have reached his full humanity, he uproots the "new man" (the initiand, the novice) from his natural and maternal environment; he saves him both from incest and from castration or parricide. But as a mediator between son and mother, he "initiates" his nephews in their father's name and is thus also a mediator between son and father. Like the breast, he is the temporary stage leading to full emancipation, while the (biological) father—insofar as he is seen as his son's rival—is considered unlikely to ensure his socialization.

These considerations lead us back to sexual totemism. We had first seen that sexual polarity was closely connected to filiation and that moiety totems had to be understood as a representation of the parental couple. At the conclusion of this study, we may understand that Yafar-Umeda totemism is even more than that: it includes the mother's brother's position as the link between the totemic (or divine) father and mother and society and inscribes within its own limits the dialectic of the Oedipus complex. In this sense, Yangis could be defined as a "totemic drama" (with a less tragic ending than that imagined by Freud in *Totem and Taboo!*), in which life impulses are acted out and man is saved.

But a problem still arises from the fact that the normal space of time that separates the infant's demand for the breast and his confrontation with the oedipal dilemma is not respected in the ritual chronology. Yangis actually shows the *ifegê* guided to the maternal breast, while in doing so they appear to be sublimating the Oedipus complex. That apparent contradiction could offer an argument to those who would have some difficulty integrating the latter idea: they could say there is no evidence that the oedipal scheme is actually the proper explanation and meaning of the "breast searching" sequence. However, Jacques Lacan, in one of his first texts, helps us to resolve that contradiction when he explains first that the unaccepted trauma of weaning gives to the "weaning complex" (*complexe du sevrage*) its positive value, that is, the perpetuation of the imago of the suckling relationship; and second, that the latter is dependent on the weaning complex only through its reshaping (*remaniement*) into the Oedipus complex (Lacan 1984 [1938]: 30). Lacan adds that the trauma of birth (followed directly by the first sucking experience) cannot turn into a mental representation (as the ego is not yet formed), and that this first separation can only be reactualized in the weaning ordeal. The finale of Yangis thus offers a condensation of the birth trauma, the weaning frustration, and the Oedipus complex.

These connections may explain the anachrony of the ending of the festival. The resolution of the complex—and with it the establishment of society—is thus inserted between birth and first sucking. What is then to be thought of a ritual whose conclusion opens on the beginning of the nursing tie and on the father's absence? That ambiguity is perhaps not innocent: it may be understood as a happy ending, leaving the spectator to imagine the future emancipation of the heroes through the next stages of their destiny; or it may, on the contrary, be perceived as the implicit recognition of that indelible tie, of that lifelong persistent nostalgia. A question I prefer to leave open at the moment is whether the very emphasis put on the fantasy of breast-feeding in Yangis actually argues in favor of the persistence of such an imago in the individual's unconscious.

The Promethean exaltation of the son as the promoter of Society appears as Yangis's ultimate aim. But the son is here the obligatory figure of the œdipal drama. He is the one who has to be severed from the mother. In opposition to uterine filiation, the mother/son relationship is in itself the start of emancipation, the promise of progression. The M/S cleavage appears as the splitting point that leaves—for those societies— the female with its natural power, and pushes the male up toward the restrictions of society.[94] Sociogenesis is described in terms of male ontogenesis.

To summarize, the establishment of culture against and out of nature, and the autonomy of maleness from femaleness, are expressed in Yangis at different levels, beginning with botanical morphology and leading to an encompassing picture of Society. The following are some specific examples of these different levels of expression:

sago and coconut shoots (totemism and ritual)

cassowary originating out of coconut tree (myth)

ifegê's birth (myth and ritual)

their penis treatment (ritual)

their arrows fired up (ritual)

autonomy of the male individual from his mother (ontogenesis, socialization)

autonomy of society out of nature (sociogenesis or ethnosociology).

Gungwan: The Closing of the Mother-Earth

Two weeks after Yangis, the Yafar performed their Gungwan festival (see Juillerat 1986), the main purpose of which is to strengthen the earth, to shut the invisible roads leading down to the cosmic bowels, to stop the people's uncontrolled self (*sungwaag*) from escaping during sleep down to the mother-earth. The effect of such a regression would be the precocious ripening of the self and later its death by the magical arrow of a sorcerer. After this protective rite of "closing the roads," the ritual proceeds with public masquerades and ends with a procession of masks as an image of social order and male dominance (plate 16). Gungwan corroborates the Yangis finale, but its practical aim is to protect the society—especially the Yangis performers' *sungwaag*—from any further contact with the maternal forces now dismissed. This is not the place to comment on the interpretation of Yafar sorcery to which these comments could lead (see Juillerat 1991a:chap. 7): a paternal sanction after the violation of the maternal womb, a fantasy about castration. But the cosmological system that sustains this representation of the Oedipus complex at the level of society deliberately situates humanity in that precarious middle zone between earth and heaven, between the danger of being absorbed into the underground or drowned in a surging flow, and the menace of a sanction coming from above in the form of the original stone adze brandished by a powerful male

Plate 16. Last phase of the Yafar Gungwan ritual. The procession of *agig*
masks coming out of the ritual enclosure; the first performer is the *ogosôk,*
"the one who goes first," a personification of the young adult male and an
incarnation of the whole community; as a neophyte in this role, he is assisted
by two maternal relatives and receives the bow from an elder, a symbol of
maleness and autonomy. (Photo Juillerat)

divinity. Those are metaphysical fears with not much room for actual individual emotion; but they express clearly the dilemma of double filiation. To repeat, a third solution had to be found: the Yafar-Umeda cultures have seen it in the relationship between the sun as a maternal breast far above the earth in a male heaven and the mother's brother as the male representative of the maternal clan. That made it possible at the same time to transform the procreative role of the primordial parental couple into a social role; the feeding breast appears then as a transitional object (Winnicott) leading to male autonomy.

CONCLUSION

The results presented in this essay should further the ongoing discussion on the heuristic value of exegesis. A second and more difficult problem is that of the etiology and function of Ida-Yangis. Is the etiology of ritual unavoidably to be discussed in terms of functions? And is it scientifically valid to define a hierarchy of functions and/or causes, or to give the primacy to one of them in particular? If we discard all kinds of materialistic functionalisms (like those of Malinowski or, more recently, Marvin Harris or Rappaport),[95] which, as the evidence presented here makes clear, do not fit the case of Ida-Yangis (in the sense that its performance has no long-term consequence for material life), we remain with a sociologically oriented explanation (which, despite limitations discussed earlier, could perhaps still be convincingly upheld against a more psychoanalytical conclusion), or with the idea defended in this text, according to which Ida-Yangis expresses the desire to enhance social identity and autonomy using to this end universal mental images about sexuality and "family complexes." One of the crucial points of the following comments concerns the use of individual psychology (and particularly the œdipal imagery) in sociological arguments: are the M/S incest prohibition and the desire to see the male child freed from his mother major determinants of Ida-Yangis, or are they only an optional means, a mediative language or even a mere symbol that says something else about social order and male domination (Godelier 1986)? If this ritual, when enacting physical reproduction and early childhood, is actually talking about the "social body," then the idea of "physical experience of the body" (Douglas 1973: 93) should be broadened into that of a more general individual experience, corporeal *and* mental.

I would personally propose, in the context of a debate on this point, that one must distinguish clearly between the original individual fantasies kept in the unconscious but permanently—out of any particular historical time—inoculated into culture, and the actual psychological feelings of particular individuals performing the ritual. The founding emotional process that is at the origin of ritual must be distinguished from the emotion induced as in a feedback on the individual. Only the former level has been taken into account here. Closer to Barth's (1975) interpretation of the Baktaman initiation rites, Ida-Yangis could be seen mainly as an act of social communication in a nonverbal language, or— in a complementary manner—the nonverbal facet of the controlled verbal transmission of an esoteric corpus of knowledge (here deprived of any initiation stages). But Barth favors the idea of communication because—unlike, for the same region, Poole (1982) and Jorgensen (1981b)—he considers "native explanations" as providing "a number of excellent insights," which unfortunately "can *not* be used as data on the contents of their [the informants'] cultural tradition" (1975:225). Thus, instead of "communication," I would privilege "meaning" in a definition of ritual and adhere to Turner's idea (1967) that "ritual has the 'performative' function of transcending thought's verbal and categorical boundaries by enacting meanings that are interstitial to them" (Wagner's formulation: 1984, p. 145). The case of Yangis shows that exegetical meanings have a cumulative effect equivalent to the syntagmatic series of symbolical items and attitudes of the public performance.

An older problem in the evolution of anthropological theory that the Ida-Yangis ethnography supplies with some new material is that of totemism. One may doubt that this aspect of social structure and ritual might still be able to ignite modern anthropological debate with passion. But who knows? Both moiety totems are here the male and female facets of Man in its reproductive and socializing process. As such they are more than the alleged origin of the moieties: they are the double and unified symbol of nature in its transformation into society. In this sense, Ida-Yangis could definitely be considered a "totemic festival," displaying ritually the birth of humanity and society out of natural species. Totemism appears here not so much as the *identification* through classification of man with nature as the expression of their radical and definitive *separation*.

More current to modern anthropological discussion are the copious material and theories on gender differentiation, both at the symbolic and social levels. Aside from the role that Ida-Yangis may have in keeping women apart from men, still more interesting is the relationship that brings together quite obviously the theme of male emancipation from maternal feminity, on the one hand, and the more general project of ensuring social reproduction and establishing the nature/culture separation (precisely through totemism), on the other hand. This point—as has already been mentioned—provides an opportunity to approach the problem of sexual discrimination through the filiative (and not only the properly sexual) bias. This view could provide a clue that argues for the idea of an atemporal origin of sexual discrimination out of the production and perpetuation of unconscious images; this would situate on another level of ritual function the sociological explanation based on a validation of male domination that the rite would provide retroactively. Put differently, does Ida-Yangis serve an already established male ideology, or is it—together with the social structure—the cultural product of a basic mental picture about sexuality, procreation, and filiation? Is it the a posteriori effect of a male dominance that still awaits its explanation, or is a symbolical construct made of the mental imagery at the core of the problem? Or, still more simply, is it a product of ideology or a by-product of ideology's cause? In both perspectives, however, it could be the expression of a defensive process; and Melanesian ethnography (among others) leads to the conclusion that the latter is basically a male reaction against something in woman that is difficult for men to cope with, something related to motherhood both in the biological and psychological meanings. We are thus brought back to an already well-documented fantasy in Melanesian as well as other cultures. Now, with the question of the recurrence or universality of imagery and meaning in the cosmologies of Melanesia and elsewhere standing open, I pass the pen to the other contributors.

NOTES

1. The ethnographic data discussed below are based only on one actual observation of Yangis in Yafar society (April 1976), but also on five periods of field research in that group and their neighbors since 1970 (total: 32 months). I thank Alfred Gell for his suggestion that the Yafar were one of the best groups in the area for a study.

2. Amanab and Waina are the two southernmost languages of the Waris family, Border Stock (Laycock 1975; Wurm and Haltori 1981).

3. Amanab *iraag* designates the amarant (*Celosia argentea*) with purple flowers cultivated in the gardens: people displaying that plant would usually hold a flowering twig in their hand and swing it rhythmically as if in a dance.

4. *Umeda* (in Amanab *umêrê*) is phonetically close to *Wamuru*. Both probably stem from Amanab *wamurog*, "coconut spadix," or its (unknown to me) Waina equivalent.

5. There are other inherited religious offices, but they do not play any role in Yangis or Ida (for more details, see Juillerat 1986, 1991b).

6. It must be remembered that there is no collective initiation in this area.

7. The *-tuar* form is a variant of the Waina *-tod* (*Edtod(na)*, *Angwatod(na)*); *-neri* < *na êri* means "people (descendants) of." See also *MC:*33–35, 133–35.

8. *Afwêêg* (Waina *afur* or *avul; MC:*139) and *fenaw* are considered the two original sago clones out of 30-named clones (sago palm is cultivated in that area by the transplantation of suckers).

9. From now on, I shall place all Waina (Umeda) words within brackets when comparing them with Amanab.

10. For the origin of the sun and moon, see below, the Great Mother's myth, and also note 19 and Juillerat (1986).

11. For more details, see Juillerat (1986). The Waina equivalent of *hoofuk* provided to me by some Punda men is *hufur,* or *hofoy.* The pair *hoofuk/roofuk* was formulated *hofoy/tofoy.*

12. For a detailed description of ritual items (masks, paints, and so on) and for the comparable chronology of Ida in Umeda, see *MC:*chap. 4.

13. Gender opposition is expressed in Amanab by the "father/mother" (*awaag/afaag*) pair, sometimes by the "husband/wife" (*regaag/angwaag*) pair; "woman" is separately translatable into *angwafik.*

14. The *êri* are sometimes called *angwafik aynaag,* "big (old) women," or *ruwar na afaag,* "children's mothers."

15. Two white hairs of a ritual master are to be mixed with the charcoal paint in the container. In 1976, the Master of the Earth (*bete na awaag, Angwaneri* moiety) provided them from his own head. He died suddenly one year later and his death was imputed by certain men to that perilous contribution. In general, white hair has a sacred connotation.

16. The association of supernatural sexual fusion with noise or explosion (expressed verbally by the onomatopoeia *boow!*) is also ascertained in myths.

17. In other contexts, the egg may also represent the sexualized female (yolk) and male (white) substances. The same double signification characterizes the coconut.

18. And we know that the placenta, in many mythologies, is seen as a "younger" twin sibling.

19. The designation *aba* seems logically more adequate as the masks portray the two kinds of sago before their blending. Amanab *aba* also means (1) dawn (*aba-gêm*, "at dawn"); and (2) a cleared place in the forest. Sago is symbolically related to the moon (as in Umeda, a full container of sago packed for storage is called "full moon"); the secret mythical origin of the moon is a coconut embryo anointed with *fenaw* sago (female clone).

20. Three identifications came out of my specimens: *Glochidion* sp., *Caesaria* sp., and *Grewia* sp. (Division of Botany, Department of Forests, Lae).

21. Pidgin word meaning "black palm" and also its leaf sheath, of which multifunctional containers are made.

22. This does not explain why the bark is used only with fresh sago. In Yangis, fermented sago is used both in domestic groups and in the ceremony, but red ochre is used in both cases.

23. I have not seen that the dancers' hands were plunged into the hot *yis,* as Gell observed in Umeda (*MC:*185). But when the priests join the performers with the *limbum,* they are supposed to say to them in ritual words: "Take, take, take." In both cases, the aim seems to be the identification of the dancers with the sago jelly.

24. The same spells are shouted when one plants a first sago sucker in a new garden.

25. Oogango is also symmetrically naturalized into the *ow* frog (*Xenobatrachus* sp.), a beautiful species with a black stripe on its pale

back. The myth describes Oogango painting, or scarifying, Ahgoango, who repeatedly faints out of pain. The myths about Oogango are too long to be analyzed here (Juillerat 1991a:chap. 4 and 6). These stories are unrelated to Yangis, except for the polarity between black and colored.

26. *Pitpit* is the pidgin word for *Saccharum edule,* a cultivated dry cane with edible inflorescence. In the forest, one finds wild *ware* cane thickets or "wild pitpit" (with no edible product) where wild pigs find a refuge during the day.

27. *Yis* is also a metaphor for the blood and water discarded in childbirth (a large quantity of it is called *yis bogo,* "sago jelly swamp").

28. *Ogomô* would be derived from Waina *ogomapur.*

29. The Cassowary appears here as an incarnation of W . . . (see also the discussion below about the cassowary symbolism). However, for reasons unknown the mask design is said to represent a "young cassowary."

30. Sweat washes off the body paint, and the dancer must be replaced before his skin could be visible to women (men's comment).

31. We detect here a discrimination between older and younger women concerning secrecy.

32. In Punda, "ghost" was translated by *yawt.*

33. There were no mudmen in Yafar. Werbner sees in the Umeda Fish appearing with mud on their feet a transformation of the hero into a clown (Werbner 1984: 272). The explanation is perhaps more simple: the aim is to show that fish came out of the river into the dancers and had to walk in the mud of the bank.

34. The Gungwan ceremony refers to that species; it is performed in most of the Amanab area and has as its main purpose the prevention of the individual self from going into the underground world (see "Gungwan: The Closing of the Mother-Earth"; and Juillerat 1986, 1991a).

35. Wefroog is the Amanab homologue of the Umeda Pul-tod (*MC:*34–35 and Appendix). A Yafar origin myth has the *boof* tree originating from some of the Great Mother B . . .'s menstrual blood: the analogy is in color and caducity. A huge *boof* tree is also said to mark the entrance of the deep underground, where spirits of the dead—if they go beyond it—become ghosts for ever (Juillerat 1986).

36. All Yafar men and women receive a "name of the right" and a "name of the left."

37. See below, the *sangêk* song alluding to termites making their nest slowly.

38. The Umeda Ida is called by Yafar men *afaag-na*, "of the mother," whereas their own (Yangis) is *röögunguk-na*, "of the daughter."

39. For hunting, the Yafar use also a four-pronged arrow, called *tit*. It should not be given to the *ifegê* performers, for fear it would fall short, because of its "heavier" weight. This gives special significance to the number three (see note 88).
Gell finds the etymology of Waina *ipele* in *ip* "breadfruit" (*MC*:284–85). The most usual word in Waina (Punda information) is, however, *ruwô* (Amanab *guwô*) and *ip* (*if*) was related to me with *ifêr* (*ivil, evil, efid,* also names of Umeda and Punda hamlets: *MC*:49, fig. 4) with the same meaning as Amanab *ifêêg* (*ifyêêg, iviêg*), that is, "having come first, earlier, former, anterior, 'elder.' " It is opposed to and often coupled with Waina *asera* (*asila*) or Amanab *sumneri* (Juillerat 1986:chap. 2); both words signify "having come after, posterior, 'younger.' " Thus we deal with a kind of elder/younger or anterior/posterior pair (the words are, however, not valid for kinship terminology) used in Waina to designate "hamlet moieties" (*MC*:84–90). To come back to the *ifegê* [*ipele*] figures, and accepting the relationship established by Gell between *-ele* and *-eli*, "man, people," the exact translation would be thus "first, original man," a meaning close to "new man," the literal translation of *nemetod*, and one of the names given to the Yafar *ifegê*. *Ifegê* is the Amanab pronunciation of Waina *iferê* (transcribed by Gell *ipele*). Thus, the three-pronged arrow is called *ifegê*, "original man," because it is ideally the young boy's arrow to catch his first preys and the cultural symbol of his phallic capacity to break his original link to his mother and proceed to the breast as a mediative object (see also note 50).
Ip (*if*) as "breadfruit" appears as a term with a metaphorical origin due to the primordial status of this species in mythology.

40. See also above for the *sawôg* roles in ancient times. This botanical species has not been identified, but the word *fut* means more generally "primordial, of the original times," and is a synonym for *ifêêg* [*ifêr, ivil*]: see note 39. For instance, *fut yis* designates the very ancient stands of sago palms far from the village. When seated in the ritual shelter waiting for their time to appear in public, the *ifegê* are also named *fut*, as they portray the original sago shoots.

41. Or also *afwêêg-* and *sa mwig suwê*, the "original fire (blood)" of the totemic species. We remember that the Yafar moieties allege to have proceeded from these species' blood.

42. The same operation has been performed on the *ogomô*'s masks, each *ogomô* spirit being named by the priests.

43. Chris Owen's film *The Red Bowmen* shows in a Punda Ida festival the two *ipele* preceded first by one, and later by two *kwanugwi*. These shots are incorporated in my own film *Le sang du sagou*. In the 1976 Yafar performance, both *anuwanam* belonged to the *Araneri* moiety, which seems to be an anomaly.

44. Informant A said that in old times the Waina groups had in their Ida two performers appearing in the morning, all black and wearing a fish mask with a black (no design) emblem made of a single *besa:* the Yafar called them "Wefroog and Abunung."

45. Some of that "blood," designated by the Waina term *mara tof* ("blood of the iron tree"), is periodically sought by hunters for ritual purposes (it is chewed with magical *Acorus calamus* rhizomes in order to animate the hunter's—in old times also the fighter's—heart). I brought back some specimens in the form of bright red discoidal spots appearing on undergrowth leaves, as if they had been actually spinkled with blood. Mrs. M. J. Charpentié, in Professor Ch. Zambettakis's Laboratory in the Museum National d'Histoire Naturelle (Paris), examined the specimens: they appeared to be an asexualized form of an Ascomycete fungus, *Polystigma*. Since no spores were visible, this identification was postulated from the knowledge of a similar fungus present in Europe, the asexualized form of which is identical in color and shape.

46. This phallic characteristic and the fact that her body was covered with hairs gives the Great Mother a rather terrifying aspect. The way my informants talked about her showed that her image provoked reluctance and fright.

47. Other specific organs mentioned by informant B were the eyes (morning and evening star), the skin of the skull (celestial vault), the teeth (stars), the tongue (*wabik* pandanus), the kneecap (tortoise), the clitoris (dwarf pandanus), the pubic hair (a kind of weed); other parts of the genitals and her heart, which became magical cultivated plants (certain clones of *Acorus calamus, Curcuma longa, Homalomena,* ginger . . .); the uterus thrown into the river quivered and turned into fishes, which the male god took and painted differently (but some species originated from the ribs); the body skin also abandoned to the river became the water spirits *angor;* the base of the sternum was kept and later shared between the Umeda, Punda, Yafar, and other groups that nowadays allegedly chew its scratched powder with betel and magical roots in

hunting ritual; the intestine was used to mark the village periphery. The cosmic destination of other body parts were designated, but with less certainty and sometimes contradictions. The remaining flesh went into the already existing earth and gave it its present size.

48. In certain spells the *bêêbi* is called "cassowary's penis" and the words "long penis," already mentioned, shouted when the *êri* enter the arena, would refer to that liana incorporated in their masks.

49. These two species are closely associated to the *ifegê* and would be their secret names. Their contact is feared. The fact that the deity used those species whereas the Yafar women make their skirts with young sago leaves, is indicative (if one puts some logic into mythology) that sago palms were not supposed to exist yet, and that the *ifegê* may be considered the two original sago palms.

50. During the little boy's first hunt, the search for lizards with a toy bow (called precisely *tumwi fango,* "small lizards bow," also another name for the *ifegê*'s weapon) is often seen in Yafar esoteric interpretation as the quest for the maternal breast. This may explain why the *ifegê* performers hold such an arrow (see note 39): this is the proper weapon for the young hunter to kill his prey. In psychoanalytical terms, the arrow and the hunting activity are the equivalent of the first object relationship (breast). The breast as an object to be caught is symbolized as game (for a boy), whereas the breast as dispenser of milk is figured as coconuts or coconut flowers, or egg.

51. The notion of parthenogenesis calls for that of autochthony. C. Lévi-Strauss in "The Structure of Myths" notes that among the Pueblo Indians mythical ancestors who came out of the earth often bear names like Bloody Foot, Soft Foot, or Wounded Foot. This makes them limp. I would personally see in such attributes of autochthony the stigma of the mother(-earth), the natural and original castration she puts on the son's phallus. The Pueblo ancestor's bloody foot appears as equivalent to the Yafar and Umeda original man's (*ifegê*) bloody penis. In the Pueblo mythology as well as in the Yafar and Umeda, the blood would be that of the mother, not that of the "injured" first man.

52. Api is the name of a river flowing from the northwestern Amanab territory toward West New Guinea; *fwog* designates a pile of trunks and branches obstructing the river but through which the water finds its way. Here *Api fwog* alludes to the canes and bamboos of this western swamp inhabited by ancient divinities and culture heroes.

53. Cassowary roles also appear in curing rituals dedicated to the female bush spirits (*sawangô*) and ending also with the firing of arrows toward the sun by two *ifegê* performers (whose masks are however different from the ones worn by the Yangis "children of the blood" and whose bodies are not so carefully painted). The *sawangô* cult exists in the whole Amanab linguistic area (except perhaps the extreme southeast); it is thus interesting to note that the *ifegê* figures and the shooting of arrows to the sun is not specific to the Ida-Yangis cult (see also the Epilogue).

54. This is a minor version for the creation of the sun. A third one gives the male god W . . .'s semen and B . . .'s menstrual blood as its origin.

55. This is the right moment to evoke the inaugurating ritual for the religious duty of "Master of the Sun" (*akba na awaag*), which consists in pointing an arrow toward the sun for an entire day. The charge of that priest, from a founding clan of the *Araneri* (male) moiety, is to care that the sun remains in its orbit, keeps its regular course and its normal heath: a way to ensure the society a well-balanced relationship to the cosmic breast.

56. Another way to situate the cassowary symbol is to see it as one unit of the pair wild pig/cassowary. A myth has the *afwêêg* sago palm growing out of blood falling from a pig's head hanging on a hook after butchering. Thus the double pair sago palm/pig and coconut/cassowary has some relevance, but this is not really useful for the understanding of Yangis. Pig and cassowary are also the zoomorphic realization of coconuts—black (cassowary) and red (pig)—and these are in other mythical contexts metaphors for the mother's two breasts. The same plant and animal duality is at the basis of the dual totemism of the Marind-Anim of West New Guinea (van Baal 1966).

57. However, the exegesis provides the origins of the pigments used in paintings; they refer again to the partition of the original Mother's body or to fluids emanating from the living divine pair. White clays originated from B . . .'s uterine *hoofuk,* latex from W . . .'s semen; red ochre is some of B . . .'s blood shed at the *ogomô*'s birth (she is the custodian of ochre and provides it to men who she finds to her liking); black paint is obtained from different tree species, especially from *ko* (which grew first out of some "black blood" fallen from one of the *ogomô*'s umbilical cord) and from *wabi* (*Alstonia scholaris*) the origin of which is the greasy flesh of B . . .'s loins.

58. Only Waina speakers and Yafar know how to play with five trumpets; the other Amanab groups have only the basic pair of *fuf* (*fufuk*) for their hunting rituals dedicated to their bush spirits. In other such rituals, Yafar, too, use only the two *fufuk*.

59. See, for explanation, the transcription in Sanger and Sorrell (1975).

60. More generally, magical spells (which the Yafar utter clearly, mutter, shout, or sing, depending on the context) greatly helped me to understand local religion. In a society where "ritually" (carried out with a rite) is translated by "with words" (*mô-na*), the verbal aspect of ritual cannot be dismissed.

61. Very probably—as Gell notes himself—because of his young age and "bachelor-hunter status" (*MC:*211; and Gell 1980).

62. In 1976, the Yafar had started the preparatory period five or six months before, but declared that this should be "at least eight moons."

63. Gell situates the *huf smav* in the beginning of the rainy season (October–November: see above about *fuf* music); that would bring the performance date up to July–August in the "dry" season. I heard that the Yafar actually performed their last Yangis in August 1984, but the Punda performed one in December of the same year and again in October 1986, and—as already mentioned—the Yafar 1976 ceremony was in April.

64. I would add: taboos of all red foods (Pandanus, red spotted fish, and the like) and of breadfruit (considered the "original sago jelly"), taboo of red or brightly colored clothes, a prohibition against pronouncing loudly the ritual roles names, the totems' names, and the names of plant species used in mask confection.

65. In 1976, the Yafar asked me to explain to a dissatisfied Australian patrol officer the ritual reason for the badly kept village.

66. The first lighting of a fire or torch during rituals was assigned to a particular patrilineage of the *Angwaneri* moiety (Juillerat 1986).

67. I never saw this ritual. This material was obtained from informant B. Informant A confirmed the performance and the dropping of the flowers. Two Punda men said the same ritual was performed among the Waina speakers.

68. The same rite is also performed after an earthquake, which is considered the result of a softening of the earth: the female earth has to be solidified by male intervention. This practice was related, by informant B, to a now-abandoned rite performed by the elders of certain clans who

periodically held together and gave spells to a dry tree (not belonging to any known species and supposed to be W . . .'s penis emerged from the earth) standing at the entrance of a cave with mineral white flows on its ceiling, near the ancestral Sahya village site.

69. Like the net bag, the *besa* symbolizes the uterus, and also the foreskin, called *hwig* (penis) *besag.* A myth, given by informant B, says the *besa* originated from a net bag placed over a growing coconut by the Great Mother B. . . . "If it breaks, everybody will die": the integrity of the original womb ensures life.

70. Another version (besides that given in the beginning of this study) of creation shows one single male god circumcising himself. His foreskin turns into coconut *besa,* and he paints it and copulates into it, bringing thus into life the primordial female divinity.

71. Even if a real excitement and a certain violence prevail due to the circumstances and the intensive consumption of betel, that fierce encounter and the repeated demonstrations of simulated violence between moieties are totally conventional and express the contradiction of sexual identities (in response to Huyghe's argument, 1982).

72. The enclosure is thus situated between two opposite openings: one giving on the river and through which the fish, as symbols of fertility, come in, the other giving access to the mundane world and through which performers appear metamorphosed into natural entities. One allows man to take the necessary powers from nature, the other restitutes that power to the society. The enclosure is thus the locus of mutation of natural into socialized powers, and one of the functions of the festival as a whole is to "introject" into society the natural forces that would otherwise definitely escape from it.

73. I was allowed to attend all operations in the enclosure and during the collection of materials, but I could not be present at all of them. I was, however, not allowed to photograph the painting of the *besa.*

74. All surfaces to be painted, including the human body, are previously anointed with *Curcuma* (Juillerat 1978a).

75. But also "solid" (*kêfutuk*): whereas white color alludes to sago, dawn, and anything *in statu nascendi,* black refers to seniority and strength. The divine semen proceeds from both qualities.

76. The origin of the *ay* (informant B) is B . . .'s nasal bone, a vertical and phallic symbol. A relation with the fish masks is that their *besa* are said to press strongly on the performers' nose (to counteract that effect,

dancers do not eat parrots' flesh during the ceremonial period). But a flattened or broken nose is also the mark of castration: when the spirit of the dead misses the underground way leading to the villages of socialized bush spirits, he (she) enters into the deep underworld and, at its entrance, is striken on the nose by a male guardian. That category of ghosts is called the "crushed noses" (Juillerat 1986).

The *riruwag* device should thus help the performers avoid being gravely contaminated by their close contact with the *besa* and becoming similar to castrated ghosts.

77. The *Calamus* liana appears here as the vegetal euphemization of the cassowary. Exegetical elements concerning cosmology assert that nocturnal mist and dew are the celestial cassowary's semen falling on the earth and going up again in daytime. But the *Calamus* was also described as the metaphor for the sago shoot, whose "way" is thus ritually opened. The *bêêbi* ritual is a cosmological rite also because it establishes a relationship between sago reproduction on the one hand, and the cosmic cassowary, the celestial vine, and sunrise on the other hand.

78. During the public performance, women also scantily wash with coconut water, before painting their faces with nonritual designs.

79. I have incorporated in this text only the mythical material having a direct relationship to some aspect of Yangis and left aside many other pieces of oral literature with only secondary connections with the ritual. I could not reconstitute a complete and coherent creation myth, as I had hoped when I first received the main exegetical elements (Juillerat 1980). But I know also that the Yafar did not disclose all they have to say about Yangis, and will probably never do so. For an analysis of the Yafar mythology as a whole, see Juillerat (1991a).

80. The performers' age can also have meteorological connotations: the *ogomô* parts, it is stated, must not be played by men who are too young, because the morning fog could cover them and later impede them from seeing game.

81. Informant A gave this ideal view: a man sees Yangis for the first time as a child, then he may participate at the second and/or third performance, before passively attending a fourth one again in old age.

82. Small- and large-scale criteria obviously have a quite insufficient relevance and are to be taken here as one of the possible determinant factors.

83. In a reply to my letter published in *Man* (Juillerat 1980), Gell suggested that I was only interested in mythology and exegesis as such and that my analysis would stop at the limits of the local gloss (Gell 1980). I hope the present study will provide sufficient evidence to refute this assertion.

84. This is why the discussion, already mentioned (*Man* 1980), about the value of local exegesis in opposition to a sociological approach ("My problem was never ritual exegesis but sociological interpretation": Gell in *Man* 1980) seems quite beside the point. See also Jorgensen (1981b).

85. To continue with the same parallelism, we might say that local exegesis corresponds to what the individual under analysis himself provides to explicate his dream, whereas the anthropologist (like the analyst) should be able to go further into the interpretative process. I do not refer here to psychoanalysis as a therapeutic technique, but only as a mode of research able to detect meaning at both the individual and cultural levels.

I am, however, aware of the limits of that analogy: the manifest material of dreams has limited interest, because it is purely symbolic and idiosyncratic, whereas actual social or even ritual behavior is endowed with a collective value and is the result of cultural history.

86. Male strength is represented in the procreative process by semen. But I had no evidence of an explicit analogy between milk and semen (see Godelier 1986).

87. In Yafar cosmology, west is related to femaleness or male old age ("father") and "low," east to maleness, youth ("son"), and "high": see "Socio-Cosmologie du Village," in Juillerat (1986). The sago jelly ritual as conception is thus chronologically linked to actual growth displayed by the Fish's entrance while the sun is rising from the horizon. For a similar opposition between night and day, see also the Polynesian notions of *Po* and *Ao* (Bausch 1978).

88. The number three that calls forth the œdipal triangle is also present in the *ifegê*'s three-pronged arrow. The latter, as the attribute of the oedipal figure of Yangis, recalls the three incestuous sons of the myth.

89. For a complete version and analysis of this myth, see Juillerat (1991a), chap. 1.

90. He is situated outside the reproductive family cell, neither the procreator nor the fruit of procreation. As such, he appears in the festival deprived of decoration and equipped with a pseudo-arrow.

91. A negative confirmation of this duality may be detected in a mythical episode in which a father cuts off the breasts of his murdered wife and

eats them with sago, leaving his new-born son hungry and obliged to hunt small lizards. But a different version shows him hanging the dead mother's breasts on a branch for his son (see Juillerat 1991a:chap. 5).

92. I found no figuration in Yafar culture of the actual murder of the father by the son(s). But the father's replacement by the mother's brother in Yangis could be interpreted as the avoidance of a representation of parricide. For the Hindu culture, G. Obeyesekere (1990) has noted that parricide never happens in myths, in contrast to filicide.

93. In my analysis of Yafar mythology (1991a), I came to the conclusion, however, that the annihilation of that all-female community represented the fantasized murder of a collective phallic mother.

94. Some anthropologists have reacted against such an opposition (see Strathern 1980). The point is to distinguish clearly the imaginary from the social domains. I would suggest, however, that such basic mental representation should be given some room among the factors responsible for male domination in mundane life.

95. See, however, the Epilogue of the new edition of *Pigs for the Ancestors* (1984), and also Sahlins (1976: 77).

Alfred Gell

2 Under the Sign of the Cassowary

Let me apologize at the outset for the inadequate nature of these brief comments on Juillerat's admirable and original essay. In a sense, I am the last person who ought to comment on my colleague's work, since I have expounded my views on the Yangis/Ida ritual at length elsewhere and on the methodological issues that have separated us in the past (which were aired in the correspondence columns of *Man* [1980]). It is now up to our colleagues to arrive at a verdict. I wish I could claim to possess a fund of local knowledge that might clarify some of the fascinating problems raised in Juillerat's text, but, except for a few tantalizing fragments, which I will detail below, I have nothing of ethnographic importance to add to what I have already published. But I am nonetheless delighted to participate in this enterprise, which seems to reflect exactly the correct attitude that ought to govern academic debate, which should be neither an exchange of mutual praise within a restricted clique nor a barrage of biting criticism between avowed enemies.

For my part, I welcome the end of the period, of almost 10 years, during which *Metamorphosis of the Cassowaries* occupied an almost hegemonic status in the ethnography of the Border Mountains cultural region (excluding the earlier papers in French by Juillerat and a couple of interesting articles by Huber). All this has changed, not only by virtue of the publication of the text presented in chapter 1, but also through the appearance of Juillerat's extensive cultural account of the Yafar (1986). I should have liked to integrate my response to the latter work into these comments, but I fear that to do so would mean writing well into next year and beyond. I can do no more at this juncture than recommend it to the attention of all my colleagues.

Before addressing specific points, let me first congratulate Juillerat on an important achievement in the research on Melanesian symbolism, cosmology, and ritual. This speciality is currently passing through a dynamic phase as a result of publications by such scholars as Tuzin, Poole, Lewis, Gillison, Herdt, and Mosco and the expected monographs from ethnographers of whom we have heard much but seen little, such as Jorgensen and Mimica. The text by Juillerat under discussion certainly deserves to be included in the works of this illustrious company. If its appearance is going to dull some of the shine on my monograph on Umeda—which has already been quite sufficiently praised—then so be it. I would be the last person to feel miffed on this account, since I can reasonably claim to have abetted this outcome.

After all, it was I who encouraged Juillerat to investigate Yafar in the first place. More important, by publishing my thesis, with its unequivocal interpretation of *Ida* as speedily as I did, I think I can claim to have established a precedent in Melanesian studies, namely, that you could be bold interpretatively and get away with it. This is what I see as futile about the position taken by Brunton (1980a), who holds up M. MacArthur's timid and disjointed ethnographic notes on Kunimaipa ritual as models of methodological purity. Truth value they may have, but they afford no inspiration whatsoever. On the other hand, when I read the more recent literature on Melanesian ritual, even though this literature is often informed by a theoretical stance opposed to my own and sometimes incorporates explicit criticisms of my work (as does the work of Lewis), I come away inwardly satisfied that the Umeda Cassowaries and I, their mouthpiece, have caused the rupture that makes this discourse possible.

If I was able to be, as I claim, "bold," it was not just because I had absorbed the lessons of Turner, Lévi-Strauss, Bateson, and Forge, but because Umeda thought itself tends toward a Nietzschean "reevaluation of all values." Once I had accepted the Cassowaries as my theme—not a difficult decision, under the circumstances—then those Cassowaries started to do their uniquely subversive work, only on an expanded cultural stage. I was still very green when I first set eyes on those prancing men, veiled in night, but I latched onto them immediately as an image of idealized adulthood. I identified with them. This identification between green (or red) youth and black Cassowary, plainly envisaged in the design of the rite, became the "subjective" source of what I subsequently wrote. I could not be—nor can an Umeda youth be—a Cassowary, but I could be the equivalent, the counterpart to a Cassowary in another Possible World. I was enchanted, so that when I began to write, words came to me effortlessly. Toiling graduate student! When I mention that 80 percent of *Metamorphosis of the Cassowaries* (and 100 percent of the chapter on the interpretation of Ida) is an unrevised *first draft* of my thesis, I do so not to provoke admiration and envy—and I should add that never have I again attained such fluency—but to lay bare the psychic sources of the mode of ritual interpretation I adopted in my book, which are now to some extent called into question. In my case, the cliché about fieldwork being an "initiatory" experience was more or less true. I was infused with a collective representation of selfhood dialectically negating the conditions prevailing throughout socialization up to that critical point, an antisocialization if you like. The Cassowary stands for the prospect, never fully realized, of desocialization for the developing Umeda male personality; for the anthropologist, likewise unformed, the cassowary provided a focal symbol for a kind of methodological disinhibition, obscurely linked to personality developments of a more far-reaching kind. Both the merits and demerits of my book stem directly from the somnambulistic manner in which it was composed. I recall an exchange that took place during a seminar at Manchester in which I presented some of my work:

> *Mancunian:* Dr. Gell, I'm sure we are all very impressed with your ingenuity, the way in which you manage to get everything to fit together so nicely but I'm sure that a large number of people here are rather skeptical, just because of this. I would like to ask you whether you ever suffer from doubts. I mean, don't you ever find yourself wondering if this isn't all just a bit *too* neat?
>
> *Gell:* Doubts? I have them now and then, but I *fight them down.*

This answer provoked a murmur of laughter among the audience, which was all that I was aiming for, but in truth, I was speaking misleadingly. At that time I had no doubts whatsoever about anything I had to say about Ida. It was never doubt that welled up from beneath the text my pen spun across the page, but always more of the same, more "ingenious" correspondences, arrived at, in fact, by the exercise of anything but "ingenuity." Under the spell of the Cassowary, I was infused with creative energy that cost me no effort of will whatsoever, so that the elements of the text—ethnographic notes and anthropological concepts—seemed to join up and form themselves into patterns with dreamlike facility. The end result, of course, is only an anthropological monograph no better than many others, and not half as good as some, of interest only to a small group of specialists. But that does not matter; the Cassowary, true to the essential role of such initiatory monsters, liberated psychic energy in unprecedented quantities, energy that (in an anthropologist) took the eventual form of a heightened intuitive grasp of pattern and order. In this exalted mood I wrote not only the least defective book I could have written, in the light of my limitations as an investigator and as an analyst, but, in fact, the only *possible* book, given the nature of the intellectual crisis in which it germinated.

These remarks may suggest that there are limits to the applicability of "scientific" canons of criticism to productions as irreducibly personal in nature as anthropological monographs often are. At the same time, the necessity of such criticism for the growth of knowledge cannot be denied. It is inevitable and proper that Juillerat's data and conclusions should be presented, not just as a self-sufficient contribution, but as furnishing a basis for a critical perspective on my work on Ida. Juillerat could have gone much further in this respect than he has. In any case, our primary, and shared, responsibility is to bring the remarkable intellectual creativity of the cultures of the Border Mountains area of Papua New Guinea to the attention of the educated public. On this point I know that I and Juillerat are in complete agreement, and stirring up a little controversy to this end will hardly come amiss.

LOCAL KNOWLEDGE AND THE OBSERVER'S MODEL

The kernel of my response to "The Mother's Brother is the Breast" is as follows: (1) I do not agree that there is an overall mythical exegesis of the pattern of the Ida ritual as a whole. I would maintain that to understand Ida as a complete performance, and as an institution, it is necessary to construct an "observer's model," guided by more or less the same "sociological" (that is, contextual) principles of interpretation that I did, in fact, adopt. (2) But this is not to say that mythical material, secret exegetical lore, and the like have no part to play in the construction of such an observer's model, still less that I have a monopoly on the relevant facts and observations that would lead one to make a suitable model or derive correct interpretations from it. (3) Juillerat's work with Yafar ritual experts (whom I could not identify in Umeda and who, if they existed, would not have imparted secrets to me because of my "bachelor-hunter" status) has enormously expanded our understanding of the concluding phase of Ida, but not in a way that contradicts my deductions about the significance of the *ipele,* or the general model of Ida that I present. (4) On the other hand, the Yafar experts do not seem to be able to provide a secret exegesis for the very figures that are, in the eyes of the general public at least, unquestionably the most important, namely, the Cassowaries (*eli*). That these are "Cassowaries" I cannot bring myself to doubt, since that was the first thing I was told about Ida, by informants whose eyes gleamed with excitement at this concept. In concluding this commentary, I will return to this crucial point, that is, the preeminence of the Cassowaries and their ideological significance. Let me begin by discussing those features of Juillerat's argument that are most attractive to me.

The most exciting aspect of Juillerat's research, from my point of view, is the new data and analysis he provides concerning the attributes, ritual actions, and mythological correlates of the *ipele-ifegê* bowmen. Even while I was in the field, it was apparent to me that the *ipele* were aiming their arrows at the setting sun. The visual impact of the image of "shooting the sun" was immediate and dramatic, but I did not have (or was not aware that I had) any supporting "sun" material on which to hang an interpretation. Now we have the myth of the "mother's miscarriage and death" (chapter 1) and all this is transformed. I consider it likely that the Yafar myth recounted by Juillerat is known (in some form) in Umeda and was missed by me through inadvertence, or because it is secret, or both. I did not look hard for exegetical material on the arrow-shooting, because in this instance I actually did have a genuine explanatory comment from informants, to the effect that the arrows, falling in the bush, would make it grow vigorously in the ensuing year. This was virtually the only "explanation" for a part of Ida that was volunteered, so I was inclined to give the statement due prominence and let the matter rest there. Clearly, I was wrong: the shooting of the *ipele* arrows is much more than an elaboration on the familiar theme of arrow———→fertilizing phallus.

With Juillerat's discoveries in mind, it turns out that there are at least two (fragmentary) lines of evidence in my own material, which are distinctly confirmatory of the position he takes. With all due modesty, I present them here. Juillerat says that for the Yafar, the sun is a female supernatural being. This possibility never occurred to me and I never asked about it. But I did not even need to ask, in a sense, because this is indicated quite plainly by the Umeda word for the sun, decomposed according to the system of "lexical motivation" that I employed extensively throughout my analysis, and that Juillerat also makes use of. The Umeda word for the sun is *akabea*——→AK + ABA + YA. *Akabea* begins with the segment *ak,* which, with the insertion of the semivowel, becomes *awk,* "nonkin/nonaffine outsider" (extreme limit of the social and physical universe). *Ak*,* not a word in isolation as far as I know, is the "syllabic inversion" (Gell 1978) of *ka,* the pronoun meaning "I" (cf. *ker,* "bone"). AK is anti-"I." To this is conjoined the segment *aba,* "sago flour" (——→*abwi,* "ripe," and so on) in isolation, but closely linked in terms of sound-symbolism to *ava,* "mother." I cannot interpret the segment *ya.* But *akabea,* "sun," invites comparison with a female supernatural being whom I was told about, whose name I recorded as *agwibagwa* (? AK + WIB + AGWA). This female spirit lives beneath the earth and controls plant growth (*wib,* "yam"; *wis,* "moon," and so on). The word for the sun seems strongly to suggest some kind of encompassing nurturant presence. I am surprised that I did not notice this before, but no doubt I was misled by a Eurocentric assumption that the sun must be masculine. At least, I can derive some comfort from the fact that the principles of symbolic inferences from lexical motivations that I placed so much reliance on in my discussion seem to accord well with Juillerat's fresh material.

The other line of evidence that I have at my disposal, which is consistent with the thrust of Juillerat's argument, concerns the ritual representation of the sun. The sun was represented in a particular kind of mask made in Umeda, though not in my time, and not, apparently, at Ida. A couple of months before the first performance of Ida that I witnessed (in 1970) at a time when I did not have any firsthand knowledge of that or any other Umeda ritual apart from curing rituals, I obtained information about a festival centering on the construction of "sun" masks, which I was told was no longer performed, but which had evidently been seen by my (quite youthful) informants. Sun masks were constructed on a rattan frame, with a conical fringe covering each dancer's head and shoulders (that is, like a cassowary/*aba*/*teh* mask in Ida). From the top of the cone a tall pole emerged, passing through the axis of a spherical form made of a number of limbum spathes, sewn together and stuffed with dried leaves. An outer framework supported the sphere, which was painted with spirit designs and decorated with feathers and leaves. Evidently a number of these masks were made for the festival, but I did not secure any details of the ritual connected with them. The enclosing spherical form stuffed with leaves is clearly a representation of a female parturitive entity, and my informants were at pains to stress how "heavy" (*kini*—the word also means "pregnant") the masks were. Were these masks shot at or dismembered?—what one would give to know! Unfortunately, once I had had the opportunity to observe a performance of Ida, these fragmentary data on an apparently obsolete rite, lost whatever salience they might have possessed in my plan of work, and I never followed up on them. Clearly, it is now urgent that more investigations be conducted. For all I know, the sun ritual may have been performed since my time in the field, for I was also told that Ida itself was obsolete, before it actually occurred.

I also prepared a note suggesting that at Sowanda, where Ida is performed but with many "dialectical" departures from Umeda practice, certain figures in the arena, wearing cassowary-type masks but dancing during the day, represent the sun. But once again, I failed to follow up on this.

SECRECY AND REGIONAL VARIATION

These hints in my own data, quite apart from my unqualified faith in Juillerat's prowess as an ethnographer, make it seem exceedingly likely to me that the mythic scenario suggested by Juillerat for the *ifegê* episode at Yangis is applicable to the *ipele* episode at Ida. Juillerat has thus achieved an important breakthrough in Ida interpretation. How extensively the relevant myth is known in Umeda is an open question. The Umeda certainly have secret myths and make a distinction between these myths and other myths that are known to all and sundry. These secret myths are called myths "of the path" because they are imparted in the deep bush between men of different communities, typically between *awnan* "bush" friends. Such myths have prestige because they are "foreign," and are extracted with difficulty from relative strangers, like kula valuables, or valuable "foreign" magical spells, plants, and the like. Given the existence of a chain of exchange relationships running between Yafar, Punda, Umeda, and thence north to Imonda and the Wasengla Valley, it is most likely that a secret story, of the kind described by Juillerat, is known to men in Umeda who participate in these exchange paths.

However, I consider it almost as likely, though only fresh research could confirm this, that a version, possibly less explicit, of the same myth is known to all adult Umeda men, and even youths, to whom it is not so much secret, as sacred, and hence discussable only in ritual contexts, as was much of the data I obtained on Ida.

I have the strong impression, reading Juillerat's account, that secrecy and the maintenance of exclusivity in ritual knowledge and offices is much more marked in Yafar than it is in Umeda. I paid a short visit to Yafar during my fieldwork, and I was immensely struck by the different atmosphere in Yafar, compared with Umeda. The Yafar were polite, but much more reserved in their manner than the Umeda. I noticed that whereas the Umeda had an irrepressible proclivity toward sexual raillery of the most explicit kind, which they did not hesitate to indulge in even in the earliest stages of an encounter, the Yafar never behaved to me in the same way, and indeed took pains to sit in a "modest" way, concealing their private parts. There was a brooding, constrained, secretive air about the place, which I put down at the time to the fact that Yafar appeared to live cheek-by-jowl with their in-laws.

It occurs to me now that the "constrained" atmosphere in Yafar, as opposed to Umeda, may have reflected a more general contrast in social organization. Yafar emerges as a more hierarchical village than Umeda, unless the contrast is purely one between ethnographers. I could not find any "big men" or widely acknowledged "ritual elders" or "priests" in Umeda, and it was not for want of looking, since I had originally intended to work on micropolitics. I was impressed to learn, when I visited Wamu village, to the south of Amanab, where the Hubers were then working, that there were hereditary heads of clans there. I was convinced that there was no comparable office, or even, I thought, the idea of an office in Umeda, where relations were exceptionally democratic, and neither birth nor age, nor even sex really, seemed to confer much distinction. Umeda descent units were so small and demographically unstable that I find it hard to understand how the mechanics of hereditary office might have worked there, if it did exist, now or in the past.

If I am correct in supposing that there is a sociological difference in the degree of formalization of social hierarchy between Umeda and its southern neighbors, then that might also explain the much greater emphasis placed on secret exegesis of Ida/Yangis and other ritual performances in the southern group of villages. If there is a priestly status group, whose social prestige in internal village affairs depends directly on the acknowledged and exclusive possession of religious knowledge, that is an obvious sociological explanation for the maintenance of a tradition of secret exegesis of the kind Juillerat has unearthed. And it might also explain the nonexistence of the same kind of tradition, or its relative deemphasis, in Umeda. Obviously, this is an urgent question for further research. It may prove in the end that Ida (that is, Yangis) in one sociological context is disarticulated from ordinary life and has to be understood as a form of symbolic capital belonging to an exclusive group of high-status men, whereas in another sociological context Ida is a public festival, designed essentially to regularize life-cycle phases, as I interpret it in my book. This possibility is suggested by the fact that in Yafar Yangis is (a) not a regular annual event and (b) not considered to be a Yafar ritual, but an exotic import from Umeda, whereas in Umeda Ida is a regular annual festival, and considered to be autochthonous.

Juillerat notes that Yangis apart, social and ritual life in Yafar has closer affinities with Amanab culture (that is, with southern villages, toward Green River and the Sepik bend, such as Wamu) than with Waina culture (that is, Umeda, Punda, Waina, Sowanda, Imonda, Wasengla, and points north). This could be significant. Perhaps there is a general "cline of increasing symbolic hierarchicalization" along a north-south axis, with Umeda/Wasengla at the "democratic" end, and the Amanab cultures tending to the hierarchical end. This "cline of increasing hierarchicalization" culminates, one might speculate, in the notoriously hierarchical Min (or mountain Ok) cultures on the other side of the Sepik bend, such as Telefomin and Bimin-Kuskusmin, where the office of ritual specialist is indeed highly developed (for a general bibliography, see Barth 1987).

Only more research, which it is by no means too late to contemplate, will enable us to grasp the Yafar/Umeda contrast in an appropriate regional and ethnohistorical perspective. That we can now begin to contemplate a whole series of exciting research problems along these lines is one of the beneficial effects of the ending of the period during which Umeda had to stand as typical of the cultures of this border region. No New Guinea culture can be understood in isolation, for there is no distinction between the comparative method and the writing of ethnography itself. Unless we are able to fill in the regional picture, there is a sense in which not one of the constituent cultures of the region can be said to be known.

I can indicate just how tantalizing and suggestive this emergent regional picture might be by turning attention away from the end of the ritual, which, as I have agreed wholeheartedly, is now much more intelligible as a result of the Yafar material, to its beginning, that is, the "Cassowary" episode. There is no doubt whatsoever in my mind, that the two dancers, painted black, who appear on the first night, (the *eli sabbra*) are publicly identified, in Umeda, as Cassowaries. But in Yangis, as Juillerat shows, this identification is not readily made, if at all. It would seem that the Yafar, importing Ida from their northern neighbors, have not imported the Cassowary image.

There is no need for me to discuss the symbolic interpretation of the Cassowary image at this stage, since I have already dealt with this topic at length elsewhere. But I would like to add something to my previous account that may go a little way toward explaining the readiness of Umeda to publicly identify the *eli sabbra* as Cassowaries, whereas their southern neighbors do not.

I did not work in the villages of the Wasengla Valley (such as Epmi, and Mindepoke) but I did visit them and I heard them described by the Umeda catechists who came from these large and powerful (and greatly feared) villages to the north of the Waina area. I asked about their Ida equivalent and obtained a little information that way, and I also read the report of a medical patrol to the area, which described a strange clustering of births suggestive of markedly reduced male fertility for a period after the performance of Cassowary dances in these villages. The report attributed this reduced fertility to the battering given to the testicles of the Wasengla Valley men by their exertions with the weighted gourd during these annual dances. What emerged from both these sources was that in the Wasengla Valley an annual ritual was (?) performed in which most, or even all, adult men adorned and masked themselves in a manner similar to the *eli sabbra* at Umeda and danced with the weighted gourd, not just for one night, but for some days, apparently. That is to say, to the north, the Cassowary role is not just the apex of a series of ritual roles, but was *the* ritual role. I am basing my remarks on hearsay, since no eyewitness accounts of Wasengla ritual are known to me, and this evidence needs to be checked, but it is surely suggestive in the present context. I saw a (lone) Cassowary dancer in Imonda (a small village, between Umeda and the main Wasengla Valley). This dancer was immediately identified to me as a cassowary, and the identification was made much more obvious by virtue of the fact that the large cassowary headdress was constructed entirely of cassowary plumes, not of sago leaves, as in Umeda.

Moreover, I obtained a fragmentary myth concerning the travels of an ancestral cassowary that emerged in the Wasengla Valley, and proceeded—through Sowanda, Umeda, and Punda—south toward Amanab, unraveling a string, described as a necklace behind it. I did not know what to make of this myth fragment, nor whether it had anything to do with the cassowary that figures in the Umeda myth of the origin of Punda, although in this myth, too, the cassowary proceeds from north to south (Gell 1975:226). But the northern origin of the cassowary (and also the Umeda idea that everything that comes from the north is powerful and threatening) is probably germane to this discussion. Perhaps, in order to discover a more complete mythic exegesis for the cassowary than neither I nor Juillerat can provide, the place to start looking would be in the Wasengla Valley. One might suggest that the Wasengla themselves could be approached, via the Institute of Papua New Guinea Studies, to set down their traditions, since even when I was in Papua New Guinea some years before independence, many of them were literate.

It is interesting to speculate on the possibility that the exegesis of the last phase of Ida may be indigenous to the villages to the south of Umeda, whereas the exegesis of the first phase may emanate from the north. If this were so, then one could both agree with the proposition that there is no part of Ida that is devoid of detailed exegesis, yet go on to deny that Ida, performed in any one place and time, by any one collectivity of actors, is understood primarily in the light of the *totality* of the extant exegetical material germane to its interpretation. This is the position I would be inclined—not particularly confidently, for lack of data—to take on the problem of indigenous interpretation. I hope that subsequent investigations will bring all this into much sharper focus.

RITUAL MEANING, INDIVIDUAL EXPERIENCE, AND SOCIETY

Meanwhile, I would stick to my guns on one major point on which Juillerat and I part company. Juillerat does not believe, no more do I, that the provision of indigenous exegesis in some form or other marks the termination of an anthropological account of ritual. Like me, he considers that the anthropologist has to do some explaining; explaining that the agents in the ritual cannot be expected to do themselves—from their point of view their behavior is habitual, meaningful, and in no need of explanation in a sense that would satisfy an anthropological investigator. Juillerat and I disagree primarily about the kinds of considerations that should motivate our explanations—Juillerat favoring intellectualist-cum-psychoanalyst considerations in this regard, whereas I favor what I have no alternative but to call sociological considerations.

This debate is as old as the hills. It has emerged recently in a new guise, which may help us to take a fresh look at it. In a remarkable article, Simon Harrison (1985) has pointed to the "disarticulation" of ritual practice and society in Avatip—a Sepik society somewhat akin to the Iatmul, although on a smaller scale. Harrison sharply reproves his colleagues for their unthinking adherence to a Durkheimian prejudice, to the effect that ritual mirrors society. On the Sepik, ritual life (dominated by esoteric totemic debates and ceremonies in the men's house, and the projection of an ethos of hypermasculinity) contrasts sharply with domestic practices and attitudes, which are noncompetitive, sexually egalitarian (emphasizing joint nurturant-productive activities), and based on villagewide consensus, not interclan rivalry. Male ritual activities are valued *just because* they have nothing whatsoever to do with life as it is lived—the men's house is a hermetically sealed Dramatic Society, in whose confines men can engage in self-aggrandizing histrionics without incurring the nemesis that would undoubtedly overtake them if they acted in this hubristic manner anywhere else.

It seems to me, leaving psychoanalysis out of it for the moment, that Juillerat could very well take up the anti-Durkheimian battle cry so forcefully uttered by Harrison, which is surely aimed at people like me, who maintain that ritual practices can be understood as a reflection of social processes taking place outside the ritual arena itself. However, I have two lines of defense. The first may be considered tautological, but I prefer to see it as a sociological necessary truth. Put simply, if it is the same men who do one thing in the men's house and behave quite differently outside it, that in itself is a social fact, which has to be explained sociologically.

Social life and ritual life in Avatip are not disarticulated—they are *opposed,* which is a very different matter. That is to say, they are dialectically opposed and thereby mutually implicated in a single nexus of sociological causation. The error is to assume that the relationship between the ritual frame and the encompassing sociological frame is one of simple replication, in symbolic terms, of the macrocosm in the microcosm. On the contrary, the ritual frame is demarcated, can only be demarcated, precisely by a series of denials of normative expectations as to practice and behavior locally accepted as rational and normal. How else would one recognize that a ritual is occurring at all, except by noticing that people were behaving oddly according to a normative understanding of means-ends instrumentalities and conventions of social intercourse? If Durkheimianism consisted of the proposition that ritual is normal behavior subjected to formalization, it would be doomed; but it does not. On the contrary, the relation between ritual practice and nonritual practice is arbitrary, and consequently informative, because it can be inflected at will, now transforming practice this way, now that, now overturning it altogether. Ritual practice is meaningful, not because it is modeled on or a model for nonritual social behavior, but because it departs from it, denies it, and hence makes it *explicit* in a way that, in the absence of this delineation of the *negative contours* of the parameters of social evidence, would otherwise be inaccessible to cognition. That is to say, the nonritual value orientations of Avatip are not disarticulated from the ones enunciated in the men's house, but are dialectically dependent on these very values, in that the moral character of nonritual behavior in Avatip is actually defined—quite explicitly according to local psychological theory—as a curbing of masculine spiritual power that is stored up in the men's house and its sacra. If Avatip male domesticity was not viewed against this background, it would not have the same meaning or virtue; indeed, it would not be virtuous but simply craven.

The second line of defense follows from the first. Avatip has been at peace for decades, but was in the past engaged in war and headhunting in the typical Sepik fashion. When one states that ritual values are disarticulated from social ones, one must be careful to specify what society, or what phase of society, because in pre-Pax Australiana times, the actual constitution of society, and its dominant values, would fluctuate rapidly and sharply according to the fortunes and phases of war. Male cults are without exception cults of violence, violence that in Papua New Guinea the imposition of the colonial peace robbed of its specific nonritual reference in the encompassing social world. Images of war and cannibalism have persisted much longer than these institutions themselves, for the good reason that without the images there would be little left for men to celebrate, and moreover, violence of a more pervasive kind continues even when its most institutionalized and dramatic manifestations have been curtailed.

Let me return from this digression on Harrison to the points at issue between me and Juillerat. Juillerat says that 'the most striking fact in Yangis, beyond its complex exegesis, is its very low level in practical sociological implications' (see chapter 1, "Sociology of Yangis"). Juillerat is no doubt correct in this assertion, as far as Yafar is concerned, in that Yangis is an extremely irregular affair rather than an absolutely normal one, as it is in Umeda (except in exceptional times). In Umeda, this generalization simply does not hold: performances of Ida are of concern to the full membership of the society for a great part of the year, and in normal times adult Umedas can expect to see four performances annually, if not more. Ida is not a rare, strange ritual, as it must be for the Yafar. Nor would it be comparable to an initiation ritual occurring once in 10 or 15 years, involving knowledge that would have to be kept alive by ritual experts during the lengthy intervening periods when no rituals were being performed. Ida is much more comparable to the Trobriand *milamila*. It is the climax of the year, sociologically important because it imposes synchronization on the whole range of gardening, hunting, lovemaking (and previously warfare) activities. Second, by mere familiarity and repetition, it seems to me inevitable that Ida activity becomes a major focal element in the pattern of life of Umeda men and women. Pick a teenager off the street here and his head is full of sex and pop music; pick an Umeda youth out of the forest and his head is full of sex and Ida.

Moreover, as I hope I showed in my book, there are innumerable cross-references between the global context of Umeda practical life and specific images and themes in the ritual. I may have misidentified many of them, but I am sure that there are many more that I just missed, because it would take a lifetime to track them all down. What I imagine is that when particular Umeda are participating in Ida, their minds are filled with a shining haze of half-glimpsed images drawn from real life and the imaginary life, flashing by half-noticed but never stable enough to be the subject of sustained meditations, as the press of fresh experience dislodges them from the focus of attention. I cannot produce an Umeda's stream of consciousness, so I cannot confirm this supposition; on the other hand, I cannot conceive why Ida should be, for them, so quintessentially worth doing, unless it acted to stimulate the imagination, the sense of abundant, almost overpowering alive-ness, in some such way. One informant said to me, describing the sensation achieved by putting on the fish mask and dancing, "You can really see everything," which I have always supposed indicated some state of expanded, synoptic, perception.

In a sense, this epiphany is the most inaccessibly intrapsychic experience imaginable, but at the same time, given the frequent performances of Ida provide an opportunity for Umeda males—and also females, who become extremely exuberant at times—to enter a condition of heightened awareness, a transfigured state of being, it is impossible to suppose that this does not have a marked impact on their sense of self and attitudes to others, moral dispositions, and the like outside the ritual itself. A man who is frequently drunk, is not the same, even when sober, as a man who is only ever sober. Every experience an Umeda has—production, reproduction, hunting, social interaction of all kinds, and relationships with, and understanding of, the natural world—is continually cycled through the images triggered by ritual representations that evoke and modulate these life experiences. What is important is what these images are and how they interact in different domains of experience, not what some ritual expert is prepared to assert is *the* explanation of whatever is being presented. If only he, or he and some other, can deploy this image from imagination, then that is an interesting fact about him, and possibly politically important, as I have already said. But it does not give one any insight into the much more important problem of how to understand the ritual process from the standpoint of the participants who do not belong to the "learned" category. Are they puppets? Dummies who will dress up and dance to order, without integrating the activity in which they are engaged to the totality of what they live and what they imagine?

Much more likely is that the learned explanation is the elaborated, canonical version of a collective representation that is accessible, in part or in whole, to the general ruck of performers, and moreover, even where the experts are concerned, it is the common image that thematizes the ritual experience, not the esoteric one. One way or another, people will attribute subjective significance to their behavior, in the ritual frame and beyond it, and will do so on the basis of their personal and cultural experience. The task of the anthropologist is to explain what there actually is out there, and that is what there is. Ritual experts are part of the problem, not the means to its solution.

Rituals occur in acephalous, antiauthoritarian societies such as Umeda because of a wholes series of convergent motivations in individual agents. The sociological problem of ritual is not what ritual "does for" society in a simple functionalist sense, but how ritual is an emergent property of social relations in these societies, so that the community cannot do otherwise than reproduce rituals, just as it reproduces people and relations. Juillerat advances a psychoanalytically based argument, to the effect that it is resolution and/or prolongation of oedipal desire for union with the mother that supplies the psychological ground conditions for the motivations that achieve coherent collective expression in the ritual drama, which culminates in the firing of the arrows at the sun. The mother is dismembered, and incest is avoided.

I am less prejudiced against psychoanalytical arguments than many of my colleagues, and I would not discount this argument, especially if, as I suspect, a version of the myth of the dismembered mother was actually common knowledge, in some form. But I am inclined to doubt very much that this is the whole story, or the most important part of it. First, the mythic schema relied on by Juillerat relates only to a phase of the ritual, a phase, moreover, that is not by any means the most salient for the majority of the participants. The *ipele* episode is the "ending" of the ritual, but not the ritual itself. In the same way, Don Juan being carried off to hell is the ending of Don Juan, but the Don Juan "myth" is about the seduction of all those women and the meal with the stone guest. For Umeda, Ida is unquestionably about the Cassowary dancers. We have a prejudice that makes us think that the end of a ritual (for example, communion) is the most significant part. I do not think this holds for Ida at all, since the Cassowary role is far and above the most prestigious one, and the night dance the high point of the proceedings, for all that it comes first.

And whatever the cassowaries stand for, it is certainly not the resolution of oedipal tensions or the avoidance of incest. In fact, the Cassowary is identified with most strongly, although the Cassowary is "bad." Is the Cassowary an image that can be seen as a projection of oedipal anxieties? Possibly, but I would suggest that in Umeda, where generations succeed one another with little overlap (there was not one man in Umeda with a son's son alive at the time of my visit), the Oedipus conflict of childhood is muted demographically by the widespread occurrence of bereavement early in life. What the Cassowary represents is not so much the threat of death (at the hands of a jealous father) as its consequences, that is, the solitude of survivors.

What the Cassowary evokes is an existential condition, which, in actual fact, is a reflex of the alarming demographic facts: "Cassowary-ness" is, to borrow Bourdieu's formulation, neccessity made into a virtue. Umeda men are alone in the world, like cassowaries. They are autonomous because they have to be; they belong to no social group large enough, or institutionalized enough, to secure the realization of their life-goals. The proceedings that follow the night dance of the casso-waries represent the unfolding (in a manner reminiscent of the neo-Platonic doctrine of the unfolding of Venus as the Graces, Cupid, or Hermes) of the constituents of the Cassowary as a global, encompassing image of the human condition.

I prefer the idea of the unfolding of the Cassowary to the idea of metamorphosis and regeneration on which I placed, I think, undue stress in my book. I do not find it at all plausible to think, at this stage, that the Ida ritual represents a "victory over death," since no Umeda ever gave me the slightest reason to think that they believed any such victory would be forthcoming or that they personally desired it. Umeda were not preoccupied with the fear of death, in the sense of their own personal extinction; what they dreaded was the consequences for them of the deaths of other people, on whom they depended. What the Casso-wary represented to the Umeda, it seems to me, is independence from social others, primarily parents; independence that would, in the end, be thrust on them willy-nilly, if it had not already transpired. It is in this sense, also, that I would interpret the scenario of the *ipele/ifegê* episode. The killing and dismemberment of the Sun-Mother—the source—is the unequivocal act of acceptance of the actual conditions governing exis-tence, in which mothers actually do die, consumed in the process of nurturing their offspring, who "eat" them (eat = shoot = copulate = cause to die).

I am skeptical of the idea that actual desire to commit incest with the mother is a genuine motive, even unconsciously, as far as Umeda males are concerned. The representation of the mother throughout Melanesia is monotonously geared to the provision of food, not so much milk as vegetable staples. Why import a complex of ideas about incest with the mother, historically associated with the development of our own system of family roles, childcare practices, sexual stereotypes, or ideas about purity into such an alien context, in which the mother role is both different in reality, and different in its images and representations? The mother who is killed and dismembered is the primordial source of nurture, of fulfillment, not the unattainable tabooed sexual object postulated by psychoanalytical theory.

The objections that seem to me to stand in the way of accepting a psychoanalytic theory of the motivations underlying ritual behavior are not so much that such motives are nonexistent (although sometimes they seem to be construed in a rather ethnocentric way) but that psychoanalysis is unduly narrow-minded about the spectrum of human interests and significant concerns. I think it is much more profitable to understand ritual as a kind of filter, which modulates the entire range of social and cultural experience of participants at the ritual scene, organizing and transforming this material under headings provided by a series of images. The heading of headings is the Cassowary image, which absorbs and annihilates all possible meanings and suggests a revaluation of all values.

How can one attempt to reconstruct the process through which ritual action transforms and organizes experience? As I have suggested, the process is one that takes place subjectively, subliminally, in psychological Real Time, and is hence un-get-at-able in any kind of question-and-answer session with informants. I would maintain that the only possible method is analysis by synthesis, that is, by the construction of a text whose formal construction is such that a mapping is established between a series of responses to images evoked in the reader's mind as the text flashes by, and a parallel series of images that may—one can never know—flash through the consciousness of a ritual actor. It is not what is explicitly said in the text that is important, but the resonances set up by the artful deployment of imagery. This image play, to be effective—and only if it is effective will it be at all realistic—cannot confine itself to the task of communicating the actual goings-on at a ritual or the statements made about that ritual by participants. It has to evoke the sedimented lived experience that is always in play during ritual and that in fact motivates it. This is what is really at issue between Juillerat and me. Juillerat thinks that one can get at the meaning of ritual by dealing exhaustively with the facts that are actually germane to the ritual, that is, description and native exegesis, plus putatively "universal" psychic motivations. I, on the other hand, believe that it is only by reconstructing, through literary artifice (and always inadequately) the totality and specificity of social and cultural experience, that one can assemble the materials for the image-play that actually communicates, across the boundaries of cuture, language, and history, the essence of ritual experiences.

This is the essence of my "sociological" creed, which turns out to be more of a literary method, perhaps, than a high-road to the making of empirical generalizations. It is not for me to say how successful I was in my efforts, but what really distinguishes my account of Ida, in comparison with Juillerat's of Yangis, is that it is much more ambitiously conceived as a complete text. I am sure that, as research work proceeds in the Border Mountains area, many ethnographic deficiencies in my account of Umeda and Ida will come to light, and I will be confronted by critics far less candid and sympathetic than Juillerat. But I hope that the superseding of *Metamorphosis of the Cassowaries* as *the* account of the area (which cannot come too soon, since there is much more to be discovered, more than I even suspected) will not deter others from attempting the difficult task of resynthesizing ritual experience in texts, constructing models of a grandiose kind, and, generally, behaving like anthropologists "under the sign of the Cassowary."

André Green

3 The Oedipus Complex as *Mutterkomplex*

In 1974–1975, a number of anthropologists and representatives of various disciplines (philosophy, mathematics, semiotics, psychoanalysis) gathered around Claude Lévi-Strauss to exchange views on the theme of identity. In my contribution to that seminar (Green 1977), I chose to compare Lévi-Strauss's view of the kinship atom with Freud's concept of the Oedipus complex (with its two sides, positive and negative), as it was formulated in a schematic way, but in a structural spirit, in *The Ego and the Id* (1923).

On that occasion, I observed that Lévi-Strauss's model, which introduces the maternal uncle as representative of the group, encoded all the relations between Ego (the child), the father, and the maternal uncle in formulations that set themselves up in symmetrical opposition, reproducing the two aspects (positive and negative) of the child's relationship with the father in the Freudian model. On the other hand, a relationship encoded by Freud remained outside Lévi-Strauss's view, namely, that of the child to the mother, who, as it happens, was attributed with no sign, either positive or negative. I also remarked that it seemed to me to be necessary, just as Freud had drawn a distinction between sexuality and genitality (by introducing the concept of infantile sexuality), to distinguish between sexuality and filiation from an anthropological perspective. If one were to take account of infantile sexuality, then the relationship between the child and the mother assumed a place that could no

longer be "neutralized" as Lévi-Strauss had done. Last, it seemed to me
that the introduction of the maternal uncle might be justified by the fact
that not less than two men are needed (one representing not only the
group, but the process of exchange) in order to "frame" the mother–
child relationship and to counterbalance the excesses (positive or negative) of the mother–child relationship. Bernard Juillerat has now asked
me to discuss the results of his investigation, which seems to confirm the
ideas that I have just summarized. His exceptionally rich raw material as
well as his remarkable analysis leads me to psychoanalytic reflections
that go well beyond the points that I raised in 1977.

PRIMITIVE AND PRIMORDIAL

Bernard Juillerat's invitation is to be explained by the fact that he himself has used psychoanalytical concepts to throw light on his interpretations. In fact, it is not so much that he directly applies these concepts to
his material, leaving the domain of sociology or anthropology, but that
he simply wishes to show that the concepts of those two disciplines do
come up against certain limitations. If our understanding is to go further,
it must avail itself—in his opinion—of concepts of a different order.
Thus, far from falling into the superficial individual-collective opposition that has traditionally attached psychoanalysis to the first and sociology to the second, he envisages, in contrast—and quite rightly—the
order of psychoanalytic concepts on the side of a timeless entity (see
chapter 1). Thus he alludes to the thesis of the timelessness of the
unconscious not only as far as the individual is concerned, but also in
relation to societies—no doubt because the meaning that Juillerat is
trying to elucidate operates in it on an infrasocial level. Although it
unquestionably springs from individual experience—that of the subject
in his relationship with parental images—its real implication lies in what
is most general in individual experience in the human condition. One
might speak of invariants in the sense of symbolic matrices common to
all men—which never appear directly, but only through sociological,
historical, and geographical interpretations that refer, in the final analysis, either beyond or short of the sociological. Is it not this that the
opposition of the sociological and the cultural is trying to define? In any
case, it calls for detailed examination.

To pose the incest prohibition as the demarcation line between nature and culture is not enough. Between that prohibition and social organization there seems to be a vast area of psychical representations on the boundary with the cultural concerning the body. Without doubt, by an imaginary return to a concern about the body that culture forces itself to think collectively—in other words to interpret—a demarcation is set up. It may be that the human condition throws men outside nature, while they continue to depend on it, and that this break, which may be the work of psychical activity, forces the human condition to conceive of the reintegration of man into a world from which he has been partly separated. Perhaps we have accepted without sufficient examination this syncretism that sets up communication between the human body, animals, plants, and stars as the sign of a primitive undifferentiation, whereas it ought to be interpreted in the sense of rediscovering a lost nature.

One can no longer speak of "primitive" societies, in the sense that they may be regarded as inferior to our own. That at least is the excuse given for that exclusion of any reference to primitivism from the vocabulary concerning them.

By trying to consider the societies that were once called primitive as societies comparable with our own, are we not trying to efface all the semantic resonances that the term "primitive" may possess, not in the sense of inferior, undeveloped, and crude, but in fact in the sense of others that are quite the opposite: the primary, in the sense of first, basic, fundamental, in short, *primordial?* In other words, perhaps what we were trying to do was to distance ourselves from the idea that those societies might offer us an opportunity of knowing the fundamental psychical parameters on the basis of which different historicities and social organizations are developed.[1]

What is remarkable in the study of this Melanesian society, as an example of primitive society, is that its system of collective psychical representations puts us in closer contact with what I have called the primordial, whereas this primordial is never the object of a direct analysis. Nothing allows us to claim to be reaching a state of transparency that would spare us the intervention of repression.

In chapter 1, Bernard Juillerat states: "Meaning determines structure and not the reverse" and "in Yangis meaning is linked principally to sexuality and reproduction." What we have here is a recognition that sexuality and reproduction are functions that produce and generate not only meaning*s,* but meaning. And that they possess a determining power of structuration, that is to say, an ability to organize their products.

My allusion to the primary, to the fundamental and to the invariant does not take me away from Juillerat, if one remembers that he writes "the sociological elements present in ritual or mythical analysis are, however, too close to psychology to be distinguished from the universal psychoanalytical material." But one does not get so close to the primary without a defense being established that tempers that proximity. It is called polysemy; that is why I propose to add a third to Juillerat's two preceding propositions: "Meaning is never univocal." The Yafar usually give more than one esoteric explanatory version and have no difficulty in agreeing that all do not converge in a single or unified view of creation, or in an entirely coherent view of the world. This is not a failure in logic, but on the contrary a profound intuition of the laws that govern the primary processes, in particular the fact that they ignore contradiction. But when these primary processes invest the field of consciousness they may serve the aim of disguise.

One may perhaps understand the different if not divergent versions that explain or account for a particular meaning, a particular ritual element, much less as a contradiction than as an index of the imaginary associativity that, implicitly, creates a relationship between two or several explanations, thus indicating the existence of inductive processes that link two aspects that seem opposed on the level of conscious logic, but that an unconscious logic brings together. It would no doubt be illusory to wish to go over all the representations adduced, or to hope that simply by bringing them together the key of the link between them would appear. We should rather consider that these explicit manifestations are the products of the transformation of an unconscious representation that is unknowable as such and that may be approached only through its offspring. This representation would seem to be a geometrical locus that urges the psyche to work in various directions, none of which would probably attain an enclosed coherence, for, if it did, that partial view would tend to be constituted as a totalizing system of meaning.

What we want, then, is neither transparency nor totalization. Two notions as closely related as sexuality and reproduction receive very different treatment in everyday life, and in ritual that suggests the difference that separates them.

SEXUALITY AND REPRODUCTION

Let us consider the Yafar through Yangis: their fundamental collective psychical representations establish in *primordial* categories the masculine and the feminine; their ritual activity, which is evidence of their fundamental preoccupations, is aimed at male control of fertility; their language abounds in real and imaginary anatomical figures of the sexual organs; discourse animates them metaphorically; and so on. Now, by contrast, sexuality in ordinary life is the object of strict prohibitions. It is made the object of a morality that suggests embarrassment and uneasiness when the topic is approached (Juillerat 1986:276). Outside the sacred context in which it is taken, sexuality would seem to be unapproachable. Generally speaking, it is better not to say too much about it.

As far as actions are concerned, there are a great many restrictions. The relations between "engaged" partners before marriage are subject to even more than the ordinary taboos. The young people must ignore one another, the boy seeming not to see the girl that is intended for him. He will even deny the future bond that must unite them. After the birth of a child, parents abstain from sexual relations until it is able to walk. Adultery is severely punished. Not so long ago, the sight— even involuntarily—of an act of coitus by a third party could be punished with death. One highly significant fact is that even so-called normal sexuality—and this seems to be somewhat stereotyped according to Juillerat's information—is regarded as an impossible act to socialize. It takes place outside the village, in the forest.

By shifting the stress to reproduction, the Yafar unburden their collective representations of intense aggressiveness. Although the complementarity of the sexes is recognized in ritual, sexuality gives rise to struggles in the myths. "Mistrust, lies, murder, abandonment between male and female characters or sometimes between old and young often characterize the mythical scenarios." The original myths speak of a climate of violence even before the appearance of man. The differentiation of a distinct human species separates the sexes: the women in the village, the men in the forest. Originally it was the women who celebrated Yangis, subdividing themselves into male and female moieties. Soon the men copulate with women whom they have surprised, then kill them in order to seize the masks and practice the ceremony that establishes social and ritual male domination. Nothing remains of that mythical past except the celebration of the ritual. As Juillerat (1986:279) remarks, it is the desire for the contrary—that of presenting a flawless unity—that dominates.

By linking all sexual representations to fertility—that is to say, by situating it on the side of life and death—this shift, which concentrates on it all the available semantic expression, says nothing about the link between sexuality and pleasure. On the other hand, fertility having become an object of thought, the ritual is offered as an attempt to respond to the mystery of gestation. Thus, the no less enigmatic mystery of pleasure is here occulted to the benefit of a collective overelaboration of phenomena bound up with deflowering, conception, pregnancy, and birth. What will be said by the collective psychical representations on these themes will tend to refer these various figures back to one another perpetually, stressing their analogical resonances in the imaginary. So much so that fantasies concerning sexuality—independently of reproduction—will reappear in this indirect, as it were, authorized way.

So we have some notion of how abusive it would be to believe that the recognition of the sexual derives here from a less mental constraint about it. The contrary is the case. Everything suggests that, in some occult way, sexuality might be a factor of major social disorder. Social prohibitions, rules of marriage, and kinship form a vast network of bonds that give sexuality certain recognized and strictly supervised modes of discharge.[2] What remains visible of the signification assumed by sexuality is, therefore, above all what reveals the implicit violence capable of being unleashed by a relaxation of the bonds that bind it. One may therefore consider reproduction as one of the modalities by which the creation of a new being makes it possible to contain, to transform, and to enclose sexuality in a body that will be subjected to the effect of the forces that inhabit it only to the benefit of a growth that places it in the service of the soma and of a social definition of the relations between the sexes.

The relegation of the sexual act protects from this potential violence not only the village, but also the witnesses most concerned in this activity: the children. The interruption of sexual relations until the time when the child reaches the age when he can walk certainly shows the extent to which growth takes place to the detriment of the sexuality of the two parents. The rare, but nevertheless existent practice of abortion demonstrates the unconscious communication between death and birth, since it is said on such an occasion that "the child must drop like a ripe fruit" (Juillerat 1986:269). That one of the most accepted causes of infanticide would be the one in which the father cannot be known certainly shows that society alone cannot take over the paternal role. It is possible to suppose that the sanctions bound up with transgressions of sexual prohibitions are replaced in the ritual by the implicit threats to reproduction or even the death of the product of the sexual act.

This, it seems, is never spoken of except in a preventive way in the spells that accompany all actions that one might call binding actions—that is to say, either of fixing various substances or elements, or more explicitly in the secret ceremony at the end of the hunting season: "To bind the 'possum' children, to bind the 'cassowary' children," and so on (see chapter 1, "Inauguration of the Hunting Period").

It seems to me to be scarcely conceivable that a ritual charged with such power concerning fertility is aimed only at fertility itself and does not, by implication, ward off the powers of death.[3] Those powers are never mentioned. On the other hand, it may be possible to interpret their presence in the form of a reinclusion of them within the powers of life, which brings us back to the Freudian concept of the fusion of instincts (of life and death). But who are those powers of death threatening? Since sexuality has been entirely turned toward its reproductive side, the danger can only concern the product of creation: the child. Yangis no doubt affirms that the boy is the most complete product of creation and that the course of sexuality consists, initially, in surviving possible destruction and acquiring that destructive power for itself, by socializing it.[4]

There is no direct link between the anxieties aroused by reality and the representations of Yangis. But it might be said that both meet at a silent crossroads. In reality, any conception presents the threat of a potential death that may occur at any moment and that therefore involves the idea of a mute and barely somnolent presence, ready to leap out of the shadows and strike its target. In the celebration of the ritual, the highly ostentatious evocation of the invisible forces presiding over fertility, far from being conceived as homage paid to the gods or even demanded by them, even runs the risk of unleashing the forces of death.

The occultation of the sexual in favor of the reproductive cannot prevent, on account of the analogies sustained at the imaginary level, suggesting through the threat of death the threat of castration, even in avoiding the question of the links between pleasure-transgression-punishment. Thus throughout the ritual allusion is made to it, always in a veiled way, sometimes on the occasion of a detail and even of a secret detail.

The explicitly evoked danger of letting the secret fall into the women's hands is to see the collapse of the phallic cult. It should never be forgotten that Yangis is a male ritual not only because it is carried out by men, but also because it is intended for men. And it is no doubt the same power that is creative (procreative) and destructive: the mother. An image of death stands in the background of this dramatization, that of the Great Mother. In fact, I am not sure that Yangis is concerned only with fertility. It could be that the implicit intention of the ritual is to reconstitute the course of the male human being from his conception to puberty. Not only is it a rite of passage, but also a recapitulation, the stress being placed perhaps not so much on membership of the society of men but on the difficulty of separating oneself from the mother. If male dominance were exercised more directly, it would be expressed mostly in the social hierarchicalization, which is discreet among the Yafar. And what if the absence of such social hierarchicalization were the sign of a failure to go beyond the primordial link with the mother?

THE SECRET

The highly dramatic and semantic concentration of the public phase of the ritual obviously catches the researcher's attention. It would be a pity if this were to divert attention from the secret phase of Yangis. This is especially so when, reading Juillerat's work, it is not easy to understand the reasons for the secrecy that must surround this phase, the length of which is important (it is approximately that of a pregnancy). An important difference may be of help here. For only the secret phase is accompanied by magic spells in the strict sense, the public phase being nonverbal. The reference to incantatory speech—usually prayer—helps us to get a better idea, through the request that is expressed in it, of the anxiety that underlies it.

The first moment of intense verbalization mentioned by Juillerat occurs during the rituals that take place around the coconut palm halfway through the secret phase preceding the hunting season by one or two months, which constitutes a "breach" of the restrictions imposed during this period. The words spoken on this occasion express openly the all-powerful character of the Great Mother to whom these prayers are addressed, the extreme dependence of men on her gifts, their enforced passivity as if they were reduced to the state of infant, and the fears of being abandoned by which they are besieged.

Similarly, at a later stage in this phase, we shall find signs of female predominance, in simulacra of warlike (and sexual) relations between male and female moieties. It seems that the image of sexual complementarity that the public phase strives to stress is less marked here. Only at one moment is priority given to the male principle. But this moment is decisive, for it marks the end of the restriction concerning fertility and the beginning of the cleansing of the village. The uprooting of a herb in the middle of the square by the elders, that is to say, the picking of the protective *roofuk,* runs the risk of allowing the *hoofuk* to spread and soften the earth. So it is the erect penis of the Master of the Sky that must strengthen the earth during a ritual copulation. The allusion to female castration is clear.

On the other hand, male castration involves no catastrophe. The *bêêbi* liana is associated—the invocations affirm this unambiguously—with a male principle and with erection. Now the cutting of this liana (for the making of masks) involves a certain liberation of the principle of growth. Cutting off the head of the cassowary—which is the equivalent of cutting the liana—or its penis or testicles, provides access to the *hoofuk* and allows reproduction to be carried out (see chapter 1, "Main Operations Carried on in the Enclosure").

For women, then, opening runs the risk of a seeping away of power; for men, it gives access to a sort of vitality. Only female castration, therefore, is to be feared. This figure, which after all is an isolated one, will be counterinvested by the many representations of an omnipotent Great Mother.

In retrospect, one may understand the first phase of the ritual as a desire to let the maternal female principle take its course without anything obstructing it. The phase of *hoofuk* predominance encourages passivity, the retention and abstention of intercurrent actions. It is also a phase of separation of the sexes, which may amount to the isolation of the female.

Everything seems to suggest an omnipresence of the Great Mother. Her corpse will serve as a space of ritual shelter. Of course the sticks that mark her extremities again suggest complementarity as a necessary condition for socialization and even for survival, but the periphery thus marked is nevertheless that of the dead body of the Great Mother. A little later it will be she again who will be evoked by the planting of crosses on each of the spaces of the moieties, but this time under a living, erect form. It is an action of binding (in order to hold together the vertical and horizontal branches) that is carried out in the body. The men then say that they are binding in blood, in the blood of the vagina, in the blood of the penis. The bond seems to me to represent both what makes it possible to hold the parts of the maternal body together and what presides over the conception of a new human being, well anchored in the uterus.

Last, on the eve of the opening of the public ritual, the men who have gone off into the forest to gather the vegetable material to make masks—this is called the gathering of persons—wash in coconut milk and eat the fruit before returning to the village. They then say their last prayers. Although these seem to solicit B . . . as much as W . . . (their blood, in fact), the incantatory requests are addressed more to the mother: "Let the children in the womb appear! Let the children in the amnios appear! Mother, mother!" This is a mere emphasis, for the penis is also called upon and the beauty of men celebrated, but it is predominantly maternal. These faint differences express an unquestionable dissymmetry.

These observations suggest to me the following hypothesis: the nonpublic phase of the ritual that excludes women and children must keep the secret concerning the recognition by men of female supremacy because of the power that motherhood confers on them. In fact, sexual difference or sexual complementarity accepts the equality of the sexes only outside motherhood. This creates a disequilibrium in favor of women that men must try to compensate for, in various ways. It may be that the conception of the ritual itself expresses this intention.

The existence in the midst of the secret phase of a hunting period lasting one to two months, the association of milk with game, the Great Mother's role as protectress of game, the game/children equation, the equivalents drawn up by Juillerat between the opening and closing of the flow of milk and the opening and closing of the hunting period, the magic spells that associate hunting and procreation, the figures associated with hunting that accompany mutual provocation in the similacrum of war between the two moieties already show during the secret phase that the hunt is the object of great polysemic condensation. As an exclusively male activity, it signifies one of the rare privileges that men give

themselves during the distribution of the game. One is tempted, therefore, to give it the role of a male rebalancing of sexual inequality in favor
of women as a result of motherhood. Its rich signification seems to me
above all to be centered on the link that it makes with the maternal
body, in the search for subsistence, at the same time as it provides a
symbolic equivalence to coitus, and therefore to incest, as the final
phase of the public ritual will show. But the fact that the opening of the
hunt must be preceded by ceremonies around the coconut palm—just as
the closing of the season brings the men back to it—and that prayers
must be addressed to the Great Mother makes me want to examine
more closely that privileged stage of the secret phase of the ritual.

This median stage, situated four months after the beginning of the
secret rituals at the midpoint of the duration of a pregnancy, begins with
the simultaneous cutting down of two totemic sago palms: a figure of
sexual complementarity, accompanied indeed by a crossed consumption
of the sago palm jelly, each moiety eating the opposite species. This
balance is broken by the ceremonies around the coconut palm, the
primary maternal symbol, the object of special solicitude, its rarity requiring that it be preserved. Here there is no allusion to a male element;
everything is maternal. The coconut palm being situated in the village
(the exclusive place of residence of the women), the women and children are sent out into the forest.

The words spoken—"Mother, give me!" "Break-open the children of
the possum! Break-open the children of the cassowary!"—when opening up the spathe, then "It is the mother's breast that is doing (this),"
while shaking the inflorescences and making the flowers fall, thus imagin-
ing that the children of the cassowary are falling together—suggest that
the products of the tree are gifts from the mother. The men who receive
these gifts in their open hands cupped together say they are "in the net
of the Mother" and those whose hands remain empty will say, "The
Mother has abandoned me." It should be remembered that it is the *ifegê*
who climb up the tree to carry out these operations. We can see signifying condensation at work again here: the fall of the inflorescences also
symbolizes birth (to break, to open), suckling (the flowers are assimilated to milk), conception (the hands symbolize the maternal uterus =
the net). To all these intricate figures is opposed a single content: the
abandonment by the mother, which therefore signifies sterility, maternal
unproductivity, famine.

The ritual marks in an impressive way maternal dominance unambiguously breaking the sexual symmetry. When these operations have been carried out, the *ifegê* come down from the coconut palm and are welcomed with words associated with milk and game.

The meal taken at the foot of the tree by the participants mixes the products of the coconut palm, magical rhizomes, and parts (heart and blood) of game: the incantation accompanying the eating of the food—"eat the blood of the mother's milk"—seems to me to be capable of being interpreted with a double meaning: (a) on the one hand, one might see in it an anticipation of inevitable weaning and of the need to seek elsewhere than in the mother's body for a form of subsistence that differs from it and that takes over from it; and (b) on the other hand, it might express a regressive fantasy that brings back the maternal food after birth, milk, to the earlier state in which the child was fed from inside the mother's body and not from her externalized product. The assimilation of game with the mother's body might find confirmation in that essential stage of the public ritual, the shooting of arrows toward the sun.

It might be thought that the ritual enacts the ultimate satisfaction of a cannibalistic fantasy, with regard to the mother, before the final break with her body makes it necessary to find food outside it. That the hunt should be bound up with the mother's body is shown by the return to the coconut palm to mark the stage that brings it to an end.

When the Yafar want to mark the end of the hunting period, they go back to the coconut palm and their invocations express a wish to bind or to hold in (that is, in the Mother) the possum or cassowary children. Earlier the game was a substitute signifier of the mother's body; it is now identified with the children. Whereas previously it assumed signification from a distancing from the mother's body, its capture now binds it once again to the coconut palm. Could the hunt not be regarded, therefore, as a form of fecundation, the incantatory "link" warding off the danger of abortion? That the mythical mother is a protectress of game is a notion that frequently crops up. Semantic links unite food and sexuality through the medium of the hunt.

Would it overestimate Yafar knowledge to note that the ritual preparatory to the opening of the hunt and the intense activity that surrounds it take place more or less in the middle of the secret period, which lasts about as long as a pregnancy, just as the period of fecundation is situated in the middle of a menstrual cycle? This would suggest a cleavage by which real human knowledge of fecundation and sacred imaginary knowledge coexist.

The ending of the hunting season might be regarded as an important limit of the secret period. For, henceforth, activity will be devoted to the strictly preparatory part of the ritual, that is to say, to achieving the material conditions necessary to its execution: the making of the necessary materials for decoration, the making of the jelly, the collection of firewood and leaves, and above all the preparation of the ritual area under the exclusive responsibility of the men.

At first sight, it might be thought that the symbolization, so intense in the earlier stages, gives way to a sacralizing activity devoid of specific content. I would prefer to believe, however, that all this intense mobilization might, in its nonfigurative signification, represent the internal processes of invisible eating. There would, therefore, be an unconscious identification between the growth of the fetus in utero and the various operations required to carry out the ritual.

The most remarkable impression that emerges from the preparation of the ritual, which nevertheless involves an ordered programming, is that, during the different phases, the symbolic contents relating to suckling, copulation, fecundation, and eating are called by interchangeable names, as if the manifest allusion to one of these acts evoked the others as its harmonics. Furthermore, it would seem that the temporal sequences take care to avoid reproduction of the natural sequence. It is as if each stage had to evoke others that would come after it or remember those that had preceded it.

SYMBOLIC AMBIGUITY

The public ritual is nonverbal, which means that its interpretation cannot be based on an analysis of actual words spoken, but must pass through information provided by informants. I have already stressed the remarkable Yafar tolerance to contradiction, both through the coexistence of various creation myths and through multiple interpretation of the same content. The nonverbal character of the public rituals seems to encourage polysemy. Should the unspoken nature of the public rituals be linked to the presence of women, who are thus deprived of understanding? In any case, this situation reinforces the symbolic ambiguity. By way of example, let us take the first stage of the ritual, that of the *êri*.

During the first stage of the ritual, the *êri sabaga*, the "two persons," or "humans," who in certain contexts have a male connotation, represent mothers on the point of transmitting their power to their daughters. However, the swinging of the sago palm leaves during their dance is supposed to recall coitus. But when the symbolic gender of the two sago palms is considered, the *êri sabaga*, the "two persons," must be identified as the vegetal metaphor of the divine anthropomorphic couple W . . . and B . . . . I am merely reproducing here what Juillerat says. We see how in some 20 lines there follow, in relation to this single representation, (a) a single-sexed male representation, (b) a single-sexed female representation (the mothers), and (c) a bisexed representation (the coitus of W . . . and B . . .).

To these polysemic condensations are added displacements in details. Thus with the initial phase, the dancers' bodies bear secret designs that allude to the death of the Great Mother (B . . .) in childbirth and to the fragmentation of her body, through which the unique breast becomes the sun. Therefore, condensation concerns not only elements belonging to synchrony (the difference between the sexes), but also to diachrony, since with the beginning of this stage, which is supposed to represent conception, a detail allows us to anticipate the amputation of the mother's breast, following her death in childbirth and the dismemberment of her body by the father. But why must this detail be kept secret? Would it not be because of the paternal violence that marks every stage in the development of sexuality and reproduction? A loud noise accompanies conception and already, during conception, anyone who can read the painted symbols may anticipate death in childbirth or maternal castration. Another secret: throughout the night, the dancers keep in their mouths a piece of cassowary meat given them by the priests. As they leave the arena, these pieces will be taken out of their mouths and placed in that of the *yis,* who follow the *êri*. But before the first hours of dawn the two priests will secretly give the *êri* dancers a cooked *abi* egg to eat. According to Juillerat, the *abi* egg represents the breast and milk. The first *abi* egg was born from the blood shed when the Great Mother's breast was cut off. We see that the secrets are intercommunicating. Here, too, one may well wonder about the reason for this secrecy. If one indulges in exegesis, it becomes clear that the mode of feeding the *êri* with *abi* eggs refers to the myth related by Juillerat. Now this myth involves incest, fratricide, an act of enforced cannibalism, and a birth assimilated to the defecation of the devoured body of the incestuous lover.

Examining only this phase of the ritual and the description of it given by Juillerat, one notes that the only two allusions made to secret knowledge concern mythical deeds involving great violence. Now the ritual evacuates or wards off this violence.

Let us return to the myth to which the *abi* egg refers. Note its duplicated and sexually marked structure, which leads to the incest between brother and sister-in-law and to the revenging fratricide, with cannibalism of the lover's body imposed on the adulterous woman, which leads to her paralysis, then to the bringing to birth of the lover's bones, which become the *ogomô* spirits. In feeding her sons, the mother makes them grow, as she becomes smaller.

The symbolization of the myth suggests the following:

1. the omission of the father and the mother

2. the replacement of the father/son relationship by the elder brother/younger brother relationship

3. the incestuous action of the *younger* brother, with the youngest sister, the elder brother's wife

4. the fratricide of the elder brother

5. the relation between cannibalism and conception

6. the symbolization between giving birth and defecation

7. the representation of spirits as the souls (children) of the dead

8. the feeding that empties the mother to the benefit of the children, which thus ensures their growth.

Thus, in the midst of a procreative ritual dominated by femininity and the complementarity of the sexes, a detail (the *abi* egg) alludes to a view of the birth of spirits as spirits of growth born from the consequences of an incestuous act in which the younger brother becomes the lover of the elder brother's wife. These spirits are born from the failure of an act of revenge: the elder brother forces his unfaithful wife to eat the corpse of the transgressor. Paralyzed, she is fed by two small birds invoked during the delivery (second symbolic fecundation by winged animals after the cannibalistic act). In turn, the mother seems to be consumed in feeding these child spirits. It then becomes clear that the duplication of the brothers and sisters, all of the same generation, leaving to survive only a difference in the elder/younger hierarchy, serves as a substitute to an oedipal situation. In the four-term myth, one individual plays no role (the elder brother's first wife, a silent element in the myth, but no doubt necessary to create the symmetry of the situations). The four roles are reduced to three, which brings us back to an oedipal triangulation, however well disguised.

Similarly, once the woman has been abandoned by her revenging husband, procreation gives birth to boys (and not one boy). Social survival being the lot of the elder, the younger brother is destined to become a rebel, punished and, in the final analysis, triumphant, since it falls to him to fecundate the elder brother's second wife. He pays for this with his life, but in a very Osirian way: his limbs give birth to children. The heroic character of the transgression is clearly indicated by the trumpets that announce from afar off their arrival at the Yangis.

Thus the ritual incorporates, absorbs, or feeds on a piece of myth, *pars pro toto,* and integrates it in its dramatization, but the allusive presence of the myth gives the ritual a latent meaning, reduced to its simple expression, linking fertility with a transgressive incestuous act, the cause of violence. At the level of the myth, the place of the conflictual relations (jealousy between the men or elsewhere between mother and daughter) is represented, the young triumphing over the old, even after death. At the ritual level, the conflictual relations are occulted, the creative, libidinal element attenuating the aggressive, destructive element in a complementary sexual harmony represented on several levels (vegetal, cosmic, social), operating a vast synthesis that never ceases to be polysemic, in which the male principle and the female principle may be seen to be given symbolic precedence, according to the stage in the ritual.

In any case, as Juillerat remarks, myth freely expresses fantasies without any consideration for moral or practical consequences, whereas ritual is supposed to be endowed with efficacy, which forces it to be more cautious. This confirms the presence of more organized defenses in the ritual. The symbolic ambiguity is part of this.

SEXUAL COMPLEMENTARITY AND HIERARCHY

There are two opposed visions in Yangis: that of sexual complementarity and that of the predominance of one sex over the other, as can be seen in the relations of the original parental couple W . . . and B . . . . On one hand, the conclusions of the analysis are not definite, but the stress seems to fall on the Great Mother, whose body is the object of rich projections. On the other hand, the *parental* male principle does not seem to be present in the representation or is represented only in already derived forms. The *fecundating* phallic principle seems to avoid too direct a representation. It would be tempting to see one of its expressions in the symbolic activity itself, in its "binding" aspect and perhaps in the transformations of colors or shapes. The system of correspondences between animal and vegetable species may also refer to its action. It would appear to be less embodied in species than existing *between* them, which makes it possible to establish the relationship that binds them together. Similarly, its actions may not be univocal: they may also consist in opening, breaking, and separating, as well as binding. To be more precise, it is in terms of binding that the other operations of separation should be considered. Generally speaking, the parental phallic principle seems to be more approachable through the result of its action, its products, one might say, than through its material expression. It could be said that it was more bound up with death if one remembered the extent to which the mother's body is devoted to it. And her death seems to be the result of sexual exhaustion. Indeed, the cassowary, after her death, shortens his penis, which is now considered too long. Should this not be seen as a manifestation of self-punishment? But perhaps the specificity of the male phallic principle is more directly bound up with the spirits that seem to be its specific form of creation. This seems to be true in the case of the *ogomô,* born from their father's corpse.

The divine maternal principle has its own specific embodiment, the coconut palm. It also has its original totemic locus, Umeda. The situation is very different in the case of the male principle. Although a locus, Sahya, is certainly assigned to it, the embodiment of the penis of the first god who emerged from the earth and was transformed into a sacred tree—which would, therefore, seem to be the equivalent of the coconut palm—concerns a species that has disappeared and therefore makes any ritual act around its vegetal materialization impossible, or better, only thinkable.

We are in the presence here of a mytheme referring to an absence—in any case to an impossibility of concrete manipulations, as in the case of the coconut palm, which suggests the figure of the dead father.

Of course, it is easy to imagine that each of the two moieties will give versions of myths of origin that privilege, depending on the case, the male or female moiety. But the direct allusions to W . . . in the ritual are less frequent than to B . . . . As Juillerat will have noted, sexuality is ambivalent. If the cooperation of the sexes is well recognized, symbolic power over reproduction can belong only to one sex at a time (Juillerat 1986:69).

Some will no doubt say that it is less necessary to place value on the phallic principle, since men have given themselves exclusive access to the ritual. But this does not explain the sense of discretion in the phallic presence, or rather its influence in a less visible mode, the mother's body being the theater of the gestative dramatization.

To posit the complementarity of the two powers, male and female, in the absence of any hierarchy between them, as the ritual behavior of the Master of the Sky and Master of the Earth seems to suggest, does this not share the Yafar desire for compromise to an excessive degree? After all, the sky in the end becomes the guardian of the inaccessible breast of the primoridal mother and certainly imposes by this fact the necessary distance from the mother's body. This acceptance of distance also gives value to the hunt, distance from the village, and the exploration of the forest space.

Castration—or at least what a psychoanalyst interprets as such—affects both sexes. Its imaginary dimension is clearly attested in the ritual phase known as *rawsu-inaag*. The two protagonists who occupy the arena are called "blood of the vagina" and "blood of the penis." And it is indeed the second organ that the imaginary takes as its target since it is said that during his first sexual intercourse, man loses a fragment of the skin of his penis.

There is an attempt, therefore, to attenuate sexual difference through a common reference to blood in both sexes, which may help to make up for castration anxieties. But really what we call castration—the imaginary wound inflicted on the penis—is interpreted rather as the occasion of an issue of the growth principle. Therefore castration is not equally distributed in both sexes, lessening the threat on the penis, and moreover is annulled in its dimension as an amputation. In any case, at the ritual level, it is never related to a context of punishment inflicted by a jealous father. Although one may suspect its existence, its cause is no less obscure.

Why speak of castration here? The question is worth asking. It does not find an answer at the ritual level—at least directly. Although the ritual strives to a certain coherence, to which Juillerat's description pays homage, it does so in performing a great signifying concentration, the reason for which is no doubt the necessary condition for it to be effective. This signifying concentration is produced by two different operations. One is positive and consists in tightening the significant elements of the ritual, binding them closely in such a way as to guarantee them great cohesion. The other is negative and consists in eliding the remnants or traces that cannot be eliminated from a subtext, represented in the ritual by features that can be explained only by reference to myths, present in the form of clues. Now it is at the level of these myths that there appear not only negative powers—these may be divined allusively elsewhere, but the linking of these powers with human affects (jealousy, envy, revenge, desire, and so on). The reference to castration would seem to be justified, therefore, insofar as it links certain significant elements with a violent connotation to an interpersonal, affective narrativity that necessitates a detour through myth. Although ritual strives to give a vision of the world that is self-sufficient—"Things are thus because they are thus"—reference to myth gives another version that might be called more "human" only approximately as far as the representations that convey it are concerned, but that, in the final analysis, is certainly the one to which it refers because it is the one that one finds in the depths of human motives that are commonly shared in mutual resonance, but not too loudly expressed. Yet what saves this level of psychologization is the fact that these various feelings are themselves related not to particular contexts, but to a general unconscious structure.

Even in this context there are no clues of a punitive paternal sanction. The jealous father forces the children to incest by imprisoning them in their mother's belly and at no moment shows castrating intentions. I see this as proof that the version of the Oedipus complex offered by Yangis is much less that of a *Vaterkomplex* than of a *Mutterkomplex,* in which the stress is put above all on the child's difficulty in separating himself from the mother's body (see also Green 1990a).

DISTANCE AND MASCULINITY

Consider now the place occupied by blood in Yangis and, more generally, among the Yafar. They call themselves *children of the blood.* The blood is always coded in the sense of a unifying factor. The imaginary stands here on the side of the fluid that symbolizes life circulating inside every body. But if this is the case, it is because when it is no longer contained in the body it becomes a sign of the danger of death, if not of death itself. In menstruation, it might also be the sign of sexual difference. For the Yafar, this differential value (between life and death and between male and female) is never taken into account in the imaginary. To the blood of the hymen will correspond blood from the penis (coming from an invisible penile-hymen); the blood will suggest neither a wound nor death. It is the original raw material from which all men spring. Implicitly, the first sexual relation is conceived as a shedding for both sexes in which the loss of a skin (internal or external) makes this act the equivalent of a new birth. Generally speaking, shed blood always gives birth to something.

Yet, I wonder, precisely in terms of the example of menstruation, whether blood is not the implicit signifier of the *hoofuk/roofuk* opposition, for the opposition between centrality and periphery that is directly implied may also be understood in relation to the blood "retained" by the mothers to feed the fetus (and therefore to the transformation of the blood into a living being) or, on the contrary, to blood "shed" outside—which, indeed, relates it to feces. In the second instance, this evacuation-shedding, this fall from the body would seem to express allusively what the unifying use conceals and designates negatively: castration.

Nothing in Yafar belief and practice suggests the practice of physical mutilation or painful trials, as is so often the case in rites of passage. But if it is not represented expressly or through explicit figuration is it not that it could not be identified as a localized and precise feature because it is erected into a more general principle that accounts for all that which falls, is separated at the periphery or at the surface?

That the end of Yangis—in the double sense of termination and purpose—should be the shooting of arrows toward the setting sun brings us back to the question again.

It is clear that the act required of the *ifegê* involves an insistence on recognition. Recognition of the separation from the breast no doubt, as also the invitation not to go back, either toward the earth (the intrauterine phase of life), or to infancy (the bowmen must point their arrows to the west and not to the east). This gesture may also be understood as a demand for the metaphorical recognition of *female castration* through the equivalence between baby, feces, penis. At this stage, it would no longer seem to be the breast as feeding organ that represents maternity, but the mother's body as a place to be penetrated, pierced, filled (indeed the sun must seize the arrows sent in its direction), maintaining in the background of this representation the idea that the object in question was part of that maternal body, separated from the rest and removed by the father far away in the sky.

However, this castration does not make the young man flee or drive him to deny it; on the contrary, the distance from the mother's breast may help him to confront it. For if Yangis opens with the act of conception, in the form of the "explosion" that accompanies the throwing down onto the ground of the sago bundles, it seems to me to end with the image that represents access to individuation as a state capable of reproducing the act that has engendered the future individual.

It is this act that is symbolized in the hunt. The hunt takes place, like all sexuality, outside the village.

In the hunt, the game is no longer immediately accessible to the hunter, as it formerly was in the mother's body. For not only is the separation imposed as necessary; it serves as an incitement to find once again the lost object, in another mode—that is to say, in my opinion, in an analogous mode that is supposed to be at the source or origin of what makes a man hunt. Namely, his conception was an act of hunting.

We are confronted with a splitting parallel to the separating of sexual pleasure and reproduction mentioned above: here it seems to unite and separate the pleasure of hunting and the need for food. Thus it may be conceivable that only women procreate and are capable of feeding their young. But it falls to men to enjoy sexual pleasure and the pleasure of the hunt insofar as each is identified with the other. Nevertheless, the anxieties seem to be mainly displaced on death either by abortion (inside) or starvation (outside).

Man is the master of distance. He places the separated breast in the sky, he goes on adventures in the forest, he reaches without direct contact thanks to his bow. In relation to a sexual imaginary, it may be said that whereas women's sexuality is pursued in their bodies through the pregnancy following coitus, men's sexuality is perpetuated when the penis has left the woman's body, not only because man finds substitutes for that body, but because he invents ways of acting that maintain his libidinal cathexes without that body being in direct contact with himself or having to experience its presence through his senses. But to embrace the extent of the field of projections and their quasi permanence is to testify to the vital importance that there is in making sure that the object is not lost.

Many myths use the powerful evocation of the death of the mother to signify the break of the link with the son. It would certainly seem that here the strictest incest prohibition is not enough to ensure for certain the mother-son separation and that it is necessary to imagine the mother's disappearance in order to avoid any risk of its occurring. But it is also meant to signify that, in any case, the primordial object that the mother represents is intended to be definitively, irremediably lost in its earthly existence. This fantasy seems necessary to the acceptance of the socialized existence implied by autonomy, the learning of techniques, however crude they may be, and insertion in the group network, however complex it may be.

THE OTHER AND THE INTERMEDIARY

The final phase of the ritual enacts, at the end of many stages, a clearly dramatized episode that is separate from the preceding phases by its frankly human characterization, although different from the vegetal and animal symbolizations that came before. This dramatization confronts the new beings produced by the succession of the preceding episodes, the *ifegê,* the sun, as maternal symbol, and finally a newcomer, the *anuwanam.* This character is not designated by any decorative symbol and owes his place in this ritual area to only two conditions: he had already taken part in a previous manifestation of the same type and therefore possesses a certain competence. Therefore competence is the sign of minimal sociality here, and the condition of having taken part in a previous ritual as a neophyte no doubt satisfies a de facto initiatory requirement, even though no particular sign nor privilege is directly accorded it.

These considerations throw light on the function of the maternal uncle. As guardian of the breast, he is certainly in a sense that masculine mother Lévi-Strauss speaks about. But it is just as important to stress that he is a nonmother, although the difference between him and the father is scarcely perceptible. He plays no repressive role. That is to say, here, social competence has nothing to do with social hierarchy or competition. The maternal uncle no doubt occupies an intermediary position in the process of achieving sexual otherness. Although the ritual first had to represent the *êri*—girls taking over their mothers' fecundating power—before acceding to the representation of the sons, one might see the figure of the maternal uncle here as a symmetrical, inverse process. In this case, sexual otherness is acquired and one is, in leaving the woman-mother, on the side of men. But the uterine double of the opposite sex represented by the maternal uncle in relation to the mother limits that otherness, which will be fully acquired only with the father. He is the separator from the breast, the guardian of the uterus, the initiator into games, the provider of instruments, and the giver of names. By presenting the consequences of separation from the mother in this way, one offers boys a consolation, but the myths cannot be fooled in this way and entrust the paternal figures with more selfish, more cruel, more ruthless intentions.

The treatment of the *ifegê*'s penis suggests it is being given a special value, not to say glorified. The penis is decorated, like the head that will wear the mask. It is wrapped round with vegetable elements (belonging of course to the sago), animal elements (feathers from birds of paradise), and even human menstrual blood. Last, the foreskin reveals the glans. Myth will provide an explanation of these practices by relating them to the tasks carried out by the father after the death of the Great Mother, making up for the interruption of a process of growth caused by the mother's death. But the ritual also gives the impression of a birth, although one that is identified here with sexual puberty (the emergence of the glans).

Of course, one may be surprised by the absence of the father. I see this as additional proof of the minimization, even the suppression, at the ritual level, of all forms of hostile relationships to which myth gives great freedom of expression. And even when, with Marilyn Strathern, one says of the *ifegê* that he *is* the father at the moment of shooting the arrow, one cannot but note the magical and nonviolent character of the substitution. In fact, the explicit omission of the father accords well with the repression of the complete oedipal representation, which is a way of showing, if only negatively, the relations between the paternal function, the enjoyment of the mother's body, and the prohibition signified to the child.

It is as if this stage signified, with the advent of the sexual as the culmination of the human, the field of the virtual, condensing birth and marriage.

Something else we learn from this phallic valorization is its metonymic deployment by bow and arrows. Thus the bodily sphere and the intervention of the male other go together. And if the male other possesses any knowledge, he shows by a demonstration of his own weapons that a renunciation had to accompany that acquisition: his arrow is headless. In fact, he has acquired intelligence only at the sacrifice of a sexual "omnipotence." His personification in the figure of the trickster no doubt condenses—through the combination of the play, imagination, and a certain physical weakness—the deviation of direct sexual pleasure toward an aim-inhibited pleasure, which might be referred to as the pleasant counterpoint of the tragic seriousness that is supposed to underpin the ritual.

DIFFERENCE, ANTAGONISM, PLURIVOCITY

The psychical process underlying what might be called Yafar thought may be subdivided into several levels.

The first—I mean the one that I shall mention first, for as far as the Yafar are concerned, one cannot know whether it comes first or last, that is to say, if it is situated by them as a primordial base, or, in contrast, as a limit beyond which one cannot advance in the interpretation—is that of sexual difference. It is what characterizes the divine couple W . . . and B . . . , clearly designated as male and female. It is also what defines the sago palm–coconut palm mixture, or male and female sago. And if the entire cosmos is sexualized, the principle of difference is observed.

The question is then posed as to how the no less fundamental *hoofuk/ roofuk* pair is to be situated. To some extent, it seems to overlap with the sexual difference, opposing the phallic centrality of *hoofuk* to the peripheral fallness of *roofuk*. But one may go on to think that, in this new context, the male/female opposition may not have a great deal to do with anatomy. What, according to the anatomo-physiological order, would seem to correspond to femaleness, such as gestation, would nevertheless be called phallic, if not explicitly, at least implicitly, because the principle of growth that governs its course is that of an internalized centrality. The fact that Juillerat indicates its dominant female connotation in no way prevents us from seeing it as a mark of the phallus, which here transcends its attachment to the male in order to signify contained power, active and no doubt hidden, just as the erection is a potentiality of the phallus inhabiting the nonerect penis. On the other hand, *roofuk* would seem to be attached not so much to the female as to castration. Its superficial peripheral location seems to mark above all the concept of "that which falls from the body, is separated off, is detached."

Thus it might be thought that the "real" categories of sexual difference, and even the representation of the divinities that ensure continuity, refer to a more abstract level, a phallic/castrated opposition. It would even seem that the notion of unity may be conceived only as the result of castration. It is the cutting off of that maternal breast, doomed to become the sun. Of course, the fragmentation of the female divinity B . . ., dead in childbirth, precedes her solar destiny. But it is specifically not a fragment like any other of that scattered body. It is distinguished from the others, separated from them first and placed in the sky as the organ that links the baby to the mother once it has acquired a separate existence outside the womb. Now we know that the Master of the Sky is on the side of the male powers.

With the *hoofuk/roofuk* opposition, sexual difference is duplicated by a dimension that can no longer be attached exclusively to synchrony. The idea of time appears with the transformations of growth that may swing beyond maturity to the decline that foreshadows rotting. Death and castration coexist, therefore, in the transition from sexual difference to that of *hoofuk/roofuk*.

The dual organization may seem to be the object of great permanence. Not only because it marks the fundamental signifiers to which one is tempted to relate everything in Yafar culture, but also through the insistence with which it is found in ritual, in the coupling of many of the elements of that ritual. It may not be enough to refer to sexual difference, since at the level of the *hoofuk/roofuk* opposition, even if that difference may be found, it seems to be covered over by another, which seems to place it rather on the side of the opposition of the life and destructive drives involving a reference to time. This more radically oppositional form is not an ultimate term, but serves more explicitly perhaps than the male/female opposition that it will cathect elsewhere, the idea of conflict. If the Yafar are scarcely oriented toward the conflictualization of sexual relations, one may on the other hand detect in Yangis, if only in the form of complementarity, the quasi permanence of antagonistic relations. And it is here that we find the second level that may be brought out after the conflict constituted by the dualistic organization. It is not that all oppositions are reduced to the primordial opposition, but it would seem to be as if, having posed the primordial opposition, conflictuality was to be found at many other levels, marked initially by the conflagration that inaugurates the throwing to the ground, ostentatiously and noisily, of the *hoofuk* by both male and female moieties. Divine copulation thus solemnly represented does not reveal a hierarchy, but the encounter of the two principles seems nevertheless to be carried out under the auspices of a collision produced by the meeting of two contrary forces. It would take too long to list all the forms in which complementarity seems to be duplicated by an antagonism. It would not take the reader long to locate them himself.

By adopting representation by pairs one realizes the minimal condition for representing similarity and difference. On the one hand, there is the extreme sexual difference illustrated by the primordial divine couple and its vegetable substitutes and, on the other, the representation of the mothers, soon to be supplanted by the daughters. It is a complex relationship in which similarity is present (by the absence of sexual difference), but in which difference is displaced to the side of the generations. Thus between sexual difference posed as an ultimate term (since it is not only human, but divine) and nondifferentiation, may appear an intermediary figure—from which the male is excluded—that accepts (sexual) similarity and (generational) difference. As Marilyn Strathern has clearly seen, a reading that brings out the homo- and heterosexual aspects is indispensable. The pair is the relevant figure to bring out within the couple the reference to the homo- or heterosexual criterion. It should be added, moreover, that the homosexual criterion seems more marked on the female side, not because female power, against which the shadow of parthenogenesis stands out, is regarded as stronger, but perhaps because a function of differentiation is attributed to the phallic signifier. This function does not necessarily operate directly, but also through castration. I am thinking here of the breast of the original mother B . . . and of the *rawsu-inaag,* more explicitly of the morpheme *raw,* which alludes to the fall of a part of the vagina, either during deflowering, or during childbirth.

When it is not expressed through castration, the phallic signifier will adopt as support the spirits of growth (*ogomô*), that is to say, the male principle that works the maternal kingdom—the spirit of growth, or more directly the primordial mother B . . .'s male children. Once again, one finds the constant principle of a grouping in pairs, with the exception of the seventh element, a cassowary, which is isolated. This odd element is called *the father* of the others.

These spirits are associated with fish, which, even more clearly, symbolize childhood (and not the spirit of growth or a divine child). They see their penis not hidden by a phallocrypt, but tied with a young foliole of the sago palm. It is remarkable that at this point in the ritual the mothers openly express a wish to take possession of their children once more. But that time is over; the internal play of the forces of maturity must lead to separation and the establishment of a distance from the maternal power. As long as this power remains in relation with the chthonic forces, its excessive vitality runs the risk of accelerating the process of maturity to the point of rottenness, that is to say, to death. This makes more understandable the obligation to place it in the sky, far from the surface of the earth. It would seem, then, that the central-peripheral problematic has been superseded here, the sun being both. Its separation is no longer a threat: it is a new order of things.

It would seem that the hidden transformations of the phallic signifier, from the time when it appears to emerge from the primordial blood mixture, make small animals (fish or termites) coincide in symbolism with the representation of the child as a whole, which may be condensed into that of his penis. Later, both elements seem to be dissociated when the child is regarded as such, while the phallic signifier is detached in the form of the bow and arrows—arrows whose male sexualization (the three tips) has to be all the more marked in that it is related to membership of the female moiety. There may be accession here to a new status in which the separation of the phallic signifier of the child's body no longer has the signification of a castration, but, on the contrary, that of an extension of his power through the effect of action at a distance. But such an action requires an apprenticeship, advice, a guide—in other words, an *orientation* of the libido. It is then that the other intervenes as practiced human being, whose competence in whatever domain confirms the fact that the rupture of his symbiosis with the chthonian world has well and truly been consummated.

This omnipresence of antagonism begins with the third level of operation, which tempers the preceding one, the avoidance of univocity. Duality here takes not only the form of functioning by pairing off, but also that in which a single interpretation is not enough to exhaust the content of a figure. There then opens up the vast system of correspondences that enables us to relate a feature of the ritual to multiple explanations. What is remarkable about this, however, is that plurivocity in no way produces incoherence; on the contrary, it brings out the network of resemblances that relate the different figures of procreation, gestation, childbirth, and deflowering.

Each of these stages, though well individualized, insofar as it may be given a different interpretation, cannot claim to absolute singularity. Could one not more easily grasp what it is that gives the foundation to the correspondences? A set of relations seems to emerge in most cases. The correspondences regularly involve the following factors:

- The passage from the outside to the inside, or the reverse, which is materialized either by the penetration of the penis in the female body or by the emergence of the child from the mother's body.

- The allusion to a mixture produced in an atmosphere of more or less concealed violence.

- The quasi permanence of the representation of figures in twos, which is resolved in a unitary figure that plays the role of third party at the end of a series of pairs and whose function seems to be conclusive.

The exceptional richness of Juillerat's work has given me a great deal to think about. I wanted to carry further the psychoanalytic hypotheses that he himself advanced. These do not seem to me to be questionable and are faithful to the mode of psychoanalytic thought. My reading has tried to show that in the general framework of the Oedipus complex, conceived as anthropological symbolic matrix, Yangis presented a version of it that stressed the mother-child separation more than the castration complex as an expression of the *Vaterkomplex*. There may, as I have suggested, be a relationship between this way of experiencing and viewing the Oedipus complex and the absence of social hierarchy. This would then justify describing the Oedipus complex also as *Mutterkomplex*.[5] From this point of view, since the mother is the only member of the oedipal trio to have a physical relationship with the other two, the father and the child, fantasies of mother–child separation will no doubt be predominant. Paternal intervention will be not so much a sanction as the establishment of the distance necessary for the performance of the symbolization.

NOTES

1. On the illusion of the notion of "archaic," see Green (1986, 1990b).

2. "It would seem . . . that marriage or the approaches that lead to it are antithetical to sexuality as order is antithetical to disorder" (Juillerat 1986:276).

3. Among the Yafar, the infantile mortality rate up to the age of five is 55 percent (Juillerat 1986:271).

4. It is remarkable that male domination in social life is not too noticeable among the Yafar, except as far as the distribution of game is concerned (Juillerat 1986:517).

5. We have found in the myth of Theseus as described by Plutarch another example of a similar configuration.

François Manenti

4 Yangis: Enacting the Unconscious

Applied psychoanalysis is a dangerous game. Anthropology functions as a lure for that very special hunter, the psychoanalyst. To reinstate the individual within the body social and to deduce the all-purpose individual from a broad cultural field are high-risk ventures that often misfire.

Yet who can blame the psychoanalyst if he recognizes, in the anthropologist's "savage" cultures, themes to be found in his own clinical practice? It is tempting indeed to read myth as the rebus of a dream and ritual as an enactment of the unconscious.

The Oedipus complex is the cornerstone of psychoanalyst theory. Although some analysts have reduced this complex to a family triangle reflecting modes of desire, Lacan argued that it forms the basis of the logic of the unconscious, which Freud articulated through the Oedipus myth. In this chapter I explore the significance of the Yangis ritual from the psychoanalytical point of view, in which terms such as "father," "mother," and "incest" far transcend individuals and their acts; they are, so to speak, arrangements of psychic molecules that have their own specific rules of composition.

In approaching an anthropological text—text being the form in which the information dealt with here comes to us—we make certain assumptions,[1] for instance that "savages" are no different from us as far as the aforementioned "psychic molecules" are concerned. In my reading of the Yangis ritual, and of the myths associated with it, I thus attempt to isolate and exemplify what seems to me to be an elementary particle of man's cultural being.

SEXUAL TOTEMISM

In chapter 1, Juillerat has shown that the totemic pair is to be regarded as the parental couple, a concept that overlaps with that of the so-called primal scene (in which the parental couple copulates). This fundamental fantasy of obsessional neurosis may be understood as far more than a "sexual affect," in that it concerns the essential notion of *Jouissance*,[2] which for Lacan (1966) is fragmented into phallic *jouissance* on the male side, and the *jouissance* of the other on the female side. Since woman is defined as being "not all" in phallic *jouissance*, all supplementary *jouissance* is to be added to the female side. This phallic *jouissance*, a corollary of the phallic phase, is co-present when language is acquired. In Lacanian terms, this means that language is bound up with the signification of the phallus, which appears in two distinct forms, the symbolic and the imaginary phallus. This distinction leads us to regard the primal scene as something other than the mere satisfaction of a "sexual need"; in fact, it enables neurotics to imagine themselves caught up in a whole, in a totally fulfilled *jouissance*, which is assumed to have existed in that mythical age preceding man's entry into culture, language, and the problematics of sexuation. The primal scene evokes both the male and female aspects of *jouissance*, thus fantasizing a specific link between the two.

During Yangis, it is the men who assume both sexual roles as represented by the *Araneri* and *Angwaneri* moieties.[3] The fact that the social group is divided into two sexual moieties and that the world of the Yafar is classified according to these moieties, shows that sexuation is more than a question of biology, and that it needs to be inscribed as such if man's universe—his culture—is to allow him to exist as an individual. This helps us to understand the etymology of Yangis—"man-woman-sago jelly," terms indicating the fusion of the two sexual principles in conception.

Juillerat (1986:67) shows that the copulation of the divine pair is followed by a period inhabited by primordial beings who, while possessing a dominant sex, contain elements of both male and female. This period reminds us of pre-Oedipal, "pre-symbolic" nondifferentiation, when a word refers not to one, but to all significations. In Lacanian algebra, this is the "space" of the uncrossed A, the space that, in the imaginary, is correlated with the mother, indicating the "stage" at which the self-image is undifferentiated from that of the maternal whole, and also the time of undifferentiated *jouissance*.[4]

HOOFUK

In the Yangis ritual, the term *hoofuk* refers to the fertility principle and appears to represent a central concept. Although this fertility principle is to be found in both sexes, it carries a female connotation. As a sexual force, it reminds us of the Freudian concept of libido. Freud, however, underscores the "male" character of the libido. Is there a contradiction here?

The fact that the power of fertility carries a female connotation may be understood in several ways. The fertility associated with motherhood is not, of course, difficult to grasp; but the association with maleness is rather more complex. In the mythical history of Yafar origins, the divine couple and the naturally androgynous species were replaced by two distinct sexual communities; at this point, women gained control over knowledge and ritual (Yangis). Male domination resumed during the ensuing period with the murder of the women. If, for Freud, the sexual drive (the libido common to both sexes) is male, this is due to its active character, in opposition to female passivity. The murder of the women corresponds to the establishment of society.[5] This is akin to what Freud called "activity." Juillerat shows that the first night of Yangis, which, ritually speaking, forms the basis of bisexual fusion, brings into play specific "strong" and "weak" forces (see chapter 1). These can be viewed in terms of activity/passivity, notions associated with the sexual drive, which must not be interpreted too mechanistically. The terms refer to the journey out and back undertaken by the drive. One may also associate these terms with the problematic of the two types of repression distinguished by Freud and Lacan, which also raise the question of origin. For the speaking being, origin can only be deduced after the event and thus is retroactive. It is this apparent contradiction that is at stake here.

Between active and passive, male and female, it is difficult to decide which comes first. "Activity" requires a "passive" support that, in a sense, is anterior to it; yet passivity requires an act of choice. This is how I read the mythical female anteriority and female connotation of *hoofuk*.

MYTHICAL ELEMENTS

It is easy enough to identify the divine couple W . . . and B . . . as the parental couple, as it is to see that the existence of these divinities prompts society to question its origins. Here, too, onto- and phylo-genetic problematics are mixed. However, this mixity is not proposed as scientific truth, but rather as fantasy—an other truth. The weight of interpretation suggests that myth is there to be decoded—it is quasi-oneiric. In my view, myths of origin do not speak of the origins of society as a whole, but of the individual as a social subject.

A dual problematics is inscribed not only at the level of the primor-dial couple. The birth of the *ogomô* takes the form of a series of twins, just as the two *ifegê* are born of two streams issuing from the maternal blood produced at B . . .'s "miscarriage," which leads to her death.

In the psychoanalytic field, duality is interpreted in relation to various logical levels in the structure of the subject. Freud familiarized us with the notion of narcissism, the relation of the "self" to one's own image; Lacan introduced the notion of the mirror stage in order to show that the self can only be identified through the other. It is the mother who at first occupies the place of this other. She is the locus of "everything"— nothing is counted, nothing is named. The Oedipus complex then intro-duces the subject to signification, as for instance the hypothetical mean-ing of self. In the Freudian paradigm, this stage is marked by the murder of the father, which is linked to his incorporation. The importance of sago jelly in the Yangis ritual reminds us of the theme of constantly reiterated incorporation.

After B . . .'s death and the birth of *ifegê*, B . . .'s body is morsellated by W . . . . This act marks what might be called phallic *jouissance*, that is, entry into the symbolic sphere. Unlike the above-mentioned significa-tions, the fact of the father's presence introduces the notion of absence, meaning an absence of signification. Naming a thing excludes it from any other possible meaning. To give meaning to an object, which in turn gives it its being, determines its place in the world and limits the locus of the possible.[6] Father W . . . names the *ifegê* and, in dismembering B . . .'s body, creates the animal and vegetable species. It is particularly striking that the first part of B . . .'s body to be cut off is her single, central breast, *uneg tot*. This part supports the Lacanian notion of the imaginary phallus, to which Freud also refers.

The imaginary phallus is the mother's phallus as hallucinated by the child; it is the child's strategy of reparation for the paternal act of naming.[7] It must be understood from both the mother's and the child's point of view. The logical assemblage underlying the term "mother" makes it clear that the term can only be understood in relation to an other; the mother is only "mother" in the child's eyes. The imaginary phallus has its origin in the discontinuity between mother and child. It is the father who, through his presence, organizes this discontinuity. The naming of the *ifegê* and the creation of the species occurs at this point, and it is also at this point that the phallus is stowed away.

In "The Dissolution of the Oedipus Complex," Freud shows how, in a young girl, the phallic phase entails an eroticization of the clitoris, which thus becomes a phallic equivalent. An illustration of this theme is to be found in the Yafar myth concerning the dance-step *ogohyaag* (see chapter 1 and Juillerat 1986:258), which consists of swinging the ritual phallocrypt, *suh-wagmô*, legs apart, so that it bangs against the bone-belt to mark the rhythm of the dance. According to the myth, only the woman (*garbôangô*) wore this penile cover, which was attached to an outsized clitoris. This represents the imaginary phallus. Juillerat (1986:339) tells of a myth in which the amputated penis Wefroog is metamorphosed into a lizard, which makes love to a woman by sucking her clitoris (an initial reference to the breast–penis relation). The myth continues: while the woman goes looking for wood, her daughter Afwey discovers the lizard, which she and her father kill and eat (another allusion to the breast–penis relation). After the mother's return, another lizard appears and bites off her clitoris. It should be noted that the myth culminates in the daughter's pregnancy.

The clitoris–penis–breast relation, which appears at several levels in these mythical accounts, reveals the complexity of sexuation. The terms designating these organs are eponyms of elementary logical functions in the structure of the subject. W . . .'s act of cutting off B . . .'s central breast represents, therefore, the paternal position in the dissolution of the Oedipus complex.[8] Mother and child are now situated in the paradigm of sexual, totemic difference, which is also that of self and other.

Why should the breast have been chosen as a phallic substitute? This correspondence is in fact commonly encountered in clinical practice.

Moreover, it permits us to distinguish between the phallus and the male sexual organ. In *Totem and Taboo,* a work much decried by anthropologists, Freud emphasizes the murder of the father of the primal horde and the cannibalistic ritual that follows.[9] Of the three types of identification involved here, Freud calls the first, "identification with the father by incorporation." This relates to cannibalism, whether actual or symbolized (as in the ritual of the Christian Eucharist). Much has been written about this first type of identification in an attempt to understand its chronological role in the formation of the subject. There is, however, a contradiction between this and the fact that the mother is the other with whom the child first identifies. Taking father and mother strictly as persons, there can be no convergence; but with the notion of the imaginary phallus hallucinated as part of the mother, it becomes possible to resolve this apparent contradiction. What Lacan calls the symbolic phallus indicates the co-production both of the lack and naming. The dismemberment of B . . .'s body refers back to this lack, indicating both pure existence *and* what it fails to be.

The murder and incorporation of the father are marks of the problematic of naming. They should not be interpreted solely as affects attached to the Oedipus complex. In fact, the dead father's incorporation is the very substance of lack. The Oedipus complex is here reduced to a question of language: without lack there can be no existence, no possible signifying chain.

The breast is the part of the mother's body that corresponds to the infant's first need. Food is therefore associated in an archaic way with the notion of lack. It now becomes clear why the breast should in turn be associated with the phallus. The coalescence of the two notions is what gives rise to the imaginary phallus. That B . . .'s amputated breast should be placed in the sky and become the sun—a Yafar correlation between milk and light (see chapter 1)—recalls the link between symbolic incorporation and vision, which is possible only through the image of one's own body (unlike real images, one's body is always elusive, and cannot be seen). The relative homophony noted by Juillerat between *noofuk* ("sight, looking, eye") and *hoofuk* shares this logic of lack.

RITUAL ROLES

Let us return to the Yangis rite and the order of appearance of the characters, noting what is of psychoanalytic interest.

Eri

The two *êri* represent the primal couple, itself related to the two sago palms. The two sexual moieties are therefore present from the outset. The exchange of *hoofuk* through the ritual *hoofuk fatik* ("dropping of *hoofuk*") clearly indicates the notion of copulation, which psychoanalysts call the "primal scene." Note, on the one hand, the piece of cassowary meat placed in the mouths of the two moieties by the "priests"—the food is not incorporated but handed over to the two *yis*. On the other hand, the egg of the gallinaceous *abi* causes day to dawn. During Yangis, the village square is called *abi kebik,* in reference to the process of gestation (through the intermediary of the nest).

Cassowary, however, refers to the maternal ancestor. Juillerat indicates the nutritional value of this "character" as "Cassowary-coconut palm" (1986:413). In the myth, the itinerant Cassowary cannot feed all the inhabitants and is killed. Juillerat observes that he is stoned—not killed with an arrow, which would signify incest. Curiously, this killing marks a rejection of incest, and also the fact that there is choice.

Rawsu-inaag

The literal translation of *rawsu-inaag* is given by Juillerat as "in the blood of the hymen." The term *raw,* we are informed, designates the side part of the vagina that "falls" during first sexual intercourse (or childbirth). The part that falls refers in my view to a correlative loss in sexual relations. This requires some explanation. Lacan states that the "sexual relation" does not exist, suggesting by this provocative notion that there is no attainment of a common goal—on the contrary, that there can be no locus of unity in our perceptions of sexuality, even if orgasm and its cry occur together. Sexual relations bind the subject to death and to its avatar, lack. Loss and bleeding are not, for the Yafar, associated with the female alone, as is shown by the existence of the terms *emwêêg taf* ("blood of the vagina") and *hwig taf* ("blood of the penis") indicating the blood lost by the *êri* in the course of copulation. The loss operates in the same way for both sexes.

With the appearance of the *rawsu-inaag,* the *êri* begin dancing in the center wearing the ritual phallocrypt, *suh-wagmô;* the *rawsu-inaag* themselves wear the "everyday" phallocrypt. This difference indicates that the latter are excluded from the process of copulation. This exclusion from sexual relations may be interpreted as yet another clue to the role of the *rawsu-inaag* as embodying loss.

Juillerat interprets the presence of the *rawsu-inaag* as weak, in opposition to the strong action embodied by the appearance of the *êri*. This can be seen as an instance of what Freud pinpointed in terms of activity/passivity (male/female). However, I am tempted to interpret *rawsu-inaag* as pure loss and not as passivity, which as such is caught up in the active/passive dialectic.

Yis

The term *yis* clearly refers to sago jelly. The fact that the two characters may be called *afwêêg hoofuk* and *fenaw hoofuk* indicates a relationship with the two totemic species. Juillerat reminds us that sago is the vegetable metaphor for sperm. The dance of the *yis* accompanies the making of the two moieties of the ritual jelly by the priests. Juillerat's interpretation of this—namely, that the important thing is to mix something red (representing the female part) into the jelly so that it "solidifies," and that this solidification represents the formation of the embryo—seems to me to be incontrovertible. Yet here again, it is not impossible that the addition of red ochre evokes the cutting off of B . . .'s breast.

The importance of the sago jelly leads one to ask what determined its choice. Cooking may be seen to represent the change from "nature" to "culture." From the psychoanalytical point of view, the fact that the choice centers on something to be eaten is no accident, but rather a precise indication of the problematic of admission into the body social as an admission into *being* in its paradoxical relation to the notion of *object*. The food to be taken is pure essence, an "outside self" quite distinct from the ego. Food must be objectified if it is to be ingested into the ego, thus losing its object-ive nature. We shall later return to the links between the concept of phallus and incorporation; but I would here again insist on the association between this concept and the notion of lack, of which the red ochre additive furnishes a clear indication.

The *yis* are associated with Oogango—the "wild melon woman" whose name is derived from similarities between her body paint and the *öög* melon. This mythical figure has her "negative counterpart" in Ahgoango—the "toad woman" who is all black, and who dies trying to paint her own body. Oogango is also said to be a child of W . . . and

B . . . , and seems to have been named by W . . . and painted with the menstrual blood of B . . . .

One informant has remarked that the body paint of the *yis* and of the Fish is the visual expression of *hoofuk* and the mother's blood. We find associated with *yis*—with sago jelly—a whole series of ideas relating to the generic notion of image and body image. That the body of Oogango was painted with the blood of B . . . reminds us of the narcissistic "wound" inflicted by the fact that the imaginary perception of our bodies occurs only with an image returning from the locus of the other; and that Ahgoango died in the course of her attempt to paint her own body illustrates the lethal factor vehicled by the imaginary of the body, mourning its eternally lost real image. The convergence between the scopic dimension and food and the fusion of the male and female principles show the relationship between body image and the recognition of sexual difference (if there is fusion between the two totemic male and female principles, this is because they are *not* confused). Here, the paradigm of lack takes us from the murder of the father (and its frequent correlative, his incorporation) through to the incest prohibition. It should be remembered that Oedipus recognizes his father in the dead rival, and, having himself become an incestuous father, blinds himself and begins his wanderings.

Ware-inaag

Juillerat's preferred interpretation links the *ware-inaag* to the place where many mythical characters go after death—a place at the edge of the world, from which one does not return. The term by which these characters are often designated—*yis na mingik* ("leftovers of sago jelly")—again connotes the loss personified by *ware-inaag* and *rawsu-inaag;* in fact, it designates what is lost of sexual fluids during conception (the making of the ritual *yis*). The role of *rawsu-inaag* seems to me to overlap with that of *ware-inaag:* it refers to the loss correlative to the recognition of sexuation, which, in turn, is eminently correlated with the admission to language.

Eri and *rawsu-inaag* on the one hand, and *yis* and *ware-inaag* on the other, do not, however, constitute two equivalent pairs. The first seems rather to represent "proto-oedipal" enactment, whereas with *yis*—in particular the notion of cooking—we pass from a divine primordial couple to a social expression of its essence. It may be said that the first pair is an aftereffect of the second—it is first assumed to be primary, then marked as such by the ineluctable evidence of the second.

Sawôg, Ogomô, *and* Kwoy

The *ogomô* appear during Yangis in the form of three masked sexed pairs, each representing the *Araneri* and *Angwaneri* moieties; pairs to which is added a solitary *ogomô*—the Kwoy, or Cassowary, who is a sexed *Araneri*. The *ogomô* spirits are assumed to come to Yangis from distant lands formerly occupied by certain Yafar clans. Their presence in the masque poses a threat to the dancers. Juillerat relates them to the maternal domain, and more specifically to the male principle at work in the growth of the fetus. The male principle is apparent in the Kwoy; his particular relation to the other *ogomô* has therefore a specific meaning. This brings to mind the myth linking the *ogomô* and the *abi* egg.

From the incorporation of the young murdered brother—guilty of breaking his elder brother's sexual monopoly—are born his bones, which immediately become the *ogomô* spirits. Although the *ogomô* have rejoined Yangis, their mother finds them again and feeds them a cooked *abi* egg. Juillerat reminds us that the first *abi* egg was born of the blood lost during the excision of B . . .'s breast (an amputation that marks the "overture" to B . . .'s dismemberment).

The number of *ogomô* (more than two), the process of their birth, their relation to the *abi* egg, and the fact that they bear the names of the seven principle clans, link them specifically to the cutting off of B . . .'s breast as the moment of accession to language—the so-called phallic signification. This notion is confirmed by what Juillerat considers to be their association with the male principle at work in the growth of the fetus. Indeed, if the phallic phase is so called, this is because it is *initialized* by what relates to the male, as represented W . . .'s action. The only *ogomô* who does not appear as part of a pair is the young Cassowary, Kwoy; he is sexed as belonging to the male moiety.[10] Whereas all the *ogomô* have a male connotation and have black bodies, Kwoy is unique in that his body is red. The Cassowary is in fact totemic in origin (the *êri* have in their mouths a piece of cassowary meat that they do not incorporate).[11] It should be remembered that although the figure of the Cassowary can be understood in a polysemic way, it may be read as the father of Freud's primal horde—one endowed with total, undivided *jouissance*.

In my view, the *ogomô* may represent what there is of pure loss consecutive to the fact of naming (entry into the phallic phase). The red body paint of Kwoy, who is regarded by one informant as the father of the other *ogomô*, refers to his anointment with menstrual blood, and in fact embodies imaginary castration (in this case, it is the whole body that is seized) prior to possible situation in the problematic of paternity-filiation.

Although the *sawôg* wear the same masks as the *ogomô*, their body paint is different. It is noteworthy that there is no seventh *sawôg* corresponding to the Kwoy. It appears that, one or two generations previously, they wore neither these masks nor the phallocrypt, *suh-wagmô*, but had their heads draped in a net and their penises uncovered, suggesting a position close to that of the child.[12] If the *suh-wagmô* associated with the steps of the *ogohyaag* dance is viewed as the work of conception, this would explain why these characters—as conceived but not conceiving—do not have to wear it. Furthermore, their lateral position relative to the *ogomô* places them on the feminine side; the net formerly worn in place of the mask expresses the female sex.[13] The mother's words, "My child, my fish," clearly express this same analogy. The fact that she attempts to catch the *sawôg* indicates an anticipated risk of a forced return to her. They are children, yet not wholly so; they are on the side of the mothers, the women. The femininity in question here is not that of the biological sex—girl or boy, each has to be situated relative to perceived sexual identity, or sexuation.

Note that this marginal position corresponding to femininity (as spatially expressed in Yangis) is also the position of what seems to be associated with loss in *ware-inaag* and *rawsu-inaag*. When Lacan claims that "woman does not exist," he means that "woman" designates what is not entirely involved in phallic *jouissance*—it is introduced for the subject by the invention of a father who names and thus dismembers the maternal whole, the undifferentiated whole (A) of significations.[14] Whether in the Lacanian or, as here, the totemic sense, "woman" designates a particular locus of lack, an incompleteness. This is where phallic signification no longer resonates.

We have related *ogomô* and *sawôg* to the notion of loss; this raises the question of whether the same loss is involved in both roles. In the first case, the loss is bound up with naming (the clan masks, the equivalence between bones, and the dismemberment of B . . .); in the second, it is above all a question of body's separation from the mother (this is evident from the mother's cry, "My children, my fish," and her attempts at capture with the nets).

In the observed ritual, *ogomô* and *sawôg* are both said to represent the work of *hoofuk* (*hoofuk na gafungo*). The two dance steps— *ogohyaag* (central) and *ira* (lateral)—are present. Juillerat reads *ira* as "the female growth principle that provides the child with flesh." *Hoofuk* would thus appear to be responsible for the losses required for the "birth" of the *ifegê*. The *ogomô* represent symbolic and loss *sawôg,* the loss of body image. Once one's own body is separated from the mother, it can only be perceived through naming and the loss of an ideal body-to-body perception that would somehow "bypass" the other that naming implacably establishes.

Freud invented the concepts of word representation and thing representation (*Wortvorstellung, Sachvorstellung*) to indicate the logical loci of these two losses. On a paradigmatic axis, they may also be viewed as reflecting the problematic of the two *jouissances*—those specific to sexuation and to the double.

Koor

Most strikingly, informant B views this character as representing *suweegik,* the dangerous vapor that emanates from women—originally from B . . . during pregnancy or menstruation. What is the nature of this threat? What causes its perception in fear? We know from psychoanalytic practice that the bond between mother and child is not a simple or univocal one. For the mother, the child may embody her lack of phallus, in which case she may become omnipotent in the child's eyes. The mother who thus places the child in the position of the imaginary phallus in this sense reifies him. Menstrual periods are clearly linked to sexuality, reproduction, and sexual desire. That Yafar society should have been able to see in this a mark of imaginary castration seems also to be borne out: the *koor* precedes the *amof* and is regarded by Juillerat as that which must be set aside as soon as possible if one is to terminate one's pregnancy successfully. This renunciation permits a disengagement of the maternal, narcissistic image, which corresponded to the satisfaction of the subject's desire for the father of the primal horde (given that there are several levels of paternity, which cannot be reduced to the simple fact of "being daddy"). In this sense, the *koor* indicates what has been defined as the ideal ego.

Amof

Like the *koor,* the *amof* mark the end of pregnancy. Juillerat's suggestion that these characters be viewed as referring to the rupture of the
amnios (see chapter 1) is plausible. The fact that the treatment of swell-
ings includes an incantation related to the elimination of termites and
the *hoofuk/roofuk* polarity observed by Juillerat seem to support this
hypothesis. By their very presence, the *amof* represent something other
than the *koor* who precede them; in no sense can they be said to be a
repetition of them. No notion of danger is associated with them; they are
not linked to *suweegik.* Yet the myth places them on the periphery of the
dance area—on the side of the women. The *boof-amof* equivalence that
emerges in the myth is reminiscent of the duality inherent in every being
from birth. The fact that the Yafar give each individual member, male
and female, a left and right name (see chapter 1, note 36, and Juillerat,
1986:383) seems to me to be fundamental in this respect. The correlation
between these names, and the peripheral location of the *koor,* suggests
imaginary structuring, in the sense of body image. *Boof-amof,* which
initiate the paradigm of duality, again evoke for me the double *jouissance* bound up with the imaginary division of the subject, which is also
introduced by naming.

Sawôg, Eri, *and* Yis

As Juillerat shows, the reappearance of these characters does not appear
to indicate anything other than the need to reiterate the "powers" required for the coming of the *ifegê.*

Ifegê *and* Anuwanam

The characters of the *ifegê* constitute the climax of the Yangis ritual;
they embody the totemic and sexual moieties, and the birth of the children. The fact that a specific treatment of the penis is necessary for each
ifegê, and that the penis itself is a duplication of the body as a whole, is
not only particularly significant, but also problematic. The relationship
of the penis *as organ* to the whole body is to be understood in terms of
the theory of lack and the mirror stage. Freud stresses women's *Pe-
nisneid* (penis envy): the mother is fixated on this organ as a result of the
inaugural lack resulting from entry into the symbolic, the social sphere.

The organ, then, corresponds to a demand for completeness. Thus the clitoris may be fantasized, hallucinated as a phallus (which, for this reason, is not to be confused with the penis). Furthermore, so-called phallic *jouissance* is associated with the clitoris. Entry into the symbolic sphere involves a grasp of the body, which must no longer be fragmented, discontinuous, dismembered.[15]

When placed in such a way that it responds to the mother's demand for completeness—a logical instance whereby every demand must, for the child, find a response until the demand itself ceases—the body assumes the position of the imaginary phallus. The term "imaginary" refers to the "grasping" of the image, but, as everyone knows, the image of the ego can only come to us through the other—however "savage."

That the body of the *ifegê* should be the replica of their penises shows that the imaginary phallus bears down on the whole body in its specular grasp, and that the *ifegê* are still in this position.[16] In order to transcend it, they need the presence of the *anuwanam* (initiated guides). The term *ifegê*—literally "original men"—refers to the three-pointed arrows. Exegesis indicates a penis–arrow relationship. Note that each *ifegê* uses a special arrow point, depending on his membership within one or other of the sexual moieties.

The two *ifegê* embody both *jouissances,* as paradigms of duality. But they need the presence of *anuwanam,* who is initiated[17] and who appears in the ritual unpainted, wearing the everyday phallocrypt; he is said to represent their maternal uncle. The essential role of the *anuwanam* is to divert the *ifegê* from their mothers, represented as the earth (on which are to be found the small lizards that can be caught with the help of those special arrows, which are also termed *ifegê*).[18] However, the *anuwanam* shows the *ifegê* the sun—the only relation to the mother that is allowed them. This sun, the cut-off breast of B . . ., may be partly understood as the imaginary phallus. Does this contradict the fact that the *anuwanam* designates it as possible, and even necessary? In a way, it designates a hallucination of maternal completeness that, in the final analysis, is dangerous. B . . .'s excised breast embodies imaginary castration, which is the castration of the mother, but also the possibility of one's own castration; in this sense, it suggests castration anxiety. This anxiety has two aspects. The one most usually referred to relates to anxiety as such, but the other suggests a liberating factor associated with it. In fact, castration anxiety is what may enable the child to avoid being made equivalent to the assumed total *jouissance* of a mother as the receptacle of the undifferentiated totality of significations; this is sug-

gested in Yangis by B . . .'s body before its dismemberment—a signifying body that is supposedly self-sufficient, and that also symbolizes the
chthonic world, the body of the earth-mother at which, in the initial
stage of their appearance, the *ifegê* aim their arrows.[19]

The liberating aspect of castration anxiety appears in the ritual in
relation to the character of the *anuwanam*. As we have already noted,
this character represents the *ifegê*'s maternal uncle. The question of his
role is not new to anthropology. But how is it to be understood from a
psychoanalytic point of view? Intuition leads us to view this uncle as
embodying the paternal question. The importance given to this relationship is understandable, given that the uncle could represent a father of
whom one can be sure. The interesting aspect of this position is that it
indicates doubt as to paternity. This doubt overlaps with the question of
jouissance, of sexual difference, and thus, in the present case, with that
of sexual totemism. Doubting a father amounts in fact to doubting that
he can completely satisfy the mother's desire. This allows the child to
situate himself in relation to the inherent lack of signification in
language—a lack of which the symbolic phallus is the signifier.[20] This
doubt again designates the place of the empty whole that enables one to
speak, to be a "social being." The character of the *anuwanam* must
therefore refer to the Lacanian notion of the name-of-the-father—a
notion that is plural, and that is eponymous with the loss that the *ware-
inaag* and the *rawsu-inaag* designate at different points. The *anuwanam*
protects from incest by designating the castration of the mother. That
the maternal breast—the sun—should be placed in a male sky indicates
the phallic, linguistic connotation of castration. The shooting of the
arrows by the *ifegê*, which the *anuwanam* permit, marks submission to
the social law of which language forms the armature.[21] That the sun
should be the source of light certainly demonstrates the convergence of
the imaginary and the symbolic. The self-image can only be grasped by
accepting specular and symbolic losses—involving a renunciation of the
signification of one's own being that requires one to think of oneself
endlessly.

CONCLUSION

My reading of the Yangis ritual leads me to consider it an enactment of
what forms the theory of the subject. At this level, I view ritual as a
"formation of the unconscious" in the same way as a dream or a slip of

the tongue. Some will be surprised to discover among our Papuan con-
temporaries the myth of Oedipus as elaborated by Freud at the turn of
the century in Vienna. Can this be seen as proof of the existence of a
collective unconscious in the Jungian sense—a reservoir of archetypes? I
do not think so. Rather, I believe that since the dawn of speech, that is,
since the Upper Paleolithic period at the very latest, man has been
subjected to the same psychic constraints.[22] Obviously, differences in
culture and technology reveal a wide variety of answers to these constraints, but the relationship between the individual and his or her culture, however theoretical, remains essentially unchanged and produces
the same effects in human "nature."[23] There is no collective unconscious, no generally agreed *Weltanschauung,* but there is equality as far
as the roots of being are concerned.

The existence of myth and ritual raises the question of why they
should be so necessary. Each group, society, or culture forms a consensus around these formations. The mere fact that such a consensus can
exist enables us to posit the existence of culture. Culture has its own
styles, its own specific way of dealing with technology. As we have seen,
a culture that loses consensus dies, and with it the men and women who
make it up.[24] If, as I have suggested, myth and ritual (like dreams and
slips of the tongue) may be read as formations of the unconscious, then
they, too, need to be interpreted. Dreams have been interpreted since
time immemorial, as have slips of the tongue (although these have invari-
ably aroused laughter, which in itself suggests meaning emerging from
nonsense).[25] This brings us to the question of exegesis. In my view, its
nonexistence is practically inconceivable, although whether it is close to
that of anthropology is quite another matter. Myth and ritual are both
mediators of conflictual drives as mirror image, metaphor, and meton-
ymy of the structure of the subject. They also represent a strategy and
give the individual his or her necessary anchorage. To recreate the structure of the subject through myth and ritual is also to submit them to a
voluntary servitude on which the human being's reception into the social
sphere depends. Myth and ritual have different functions as part of this
strategy: the first corresponds to the pure symbolic order, whereas the
second requires enactment of the body. There can be no myth without
ritual, however unspectacular. Yangis shows this clearly: through it, the
individual—the socialized body—must deal with the question of the ego
as an instance of misprision (*méconnaissance*), as noted by Freud in his
second topic.[26] Myth and ritual *must* be read, as must the two repres-

sions corresponding to the symbolic order (speech) and the imaginary order (one's own body). This is how the universality of the Oedipus complex may be understood.

NOTES

1. This is not the place to demonstrate my initial assumptions, which the reader can find in the literature.

2. There is no adequate English translation of this word. "Enjoyment" can be applied to rights, property, and the like but has lost the sexual connotation that the French still retains (*jouir* is slang for "to come"). "Pleasure," on the other hand, is preempted by "plaisir," and Lacan uses the two terms quite differently. "Pleasure" obeys the laws of homeostasis whereby, through discharge, the psyche seeks the lowest possible level of tension. *Jouissance* transgresses this law, and thus is *beyond* the pleasure principle.

3. *Ara na êri* ("people of man") and *angô na êri* ("people of woman"); *ara na ruwar* ("children of man") and *angô na ruwar* ("children of woman"). This etymology permits the existence of individual men and women within each "moiety."

4. In terms of Lacanian mathemes, this refers to S_1, S_2, signifying "unary" and "binary." From this point of view, there is no transition from S_1 to S_2, but an eternal return to S_1.

5. Although sexuation existed before, there were no relations between the sexes.

6. "The world" is here understood in the sense of Wittgenstein's definition in the *Tractatus Logico-Philosophicus:* "The world is all that is the case."

7. Which, as we have seen, is perceived by the child as murder.

8. Juillerat notes that, although it ought to be W . . . who cuts B . . .'s breast, according to one informant it is the original Cassowary who does so—thus referring to an original couple of Cassowaries (see chapter 1).

9. Although this work may be challenged on anthropological grounds, it nonetheless represents an attempt to relate Freudian theory to primitive reality; in my view, it remains an exemplary piece of research from this point of view.

10. At least, according to one informant.

11. Is this a prohibition, a taboo of the kind that says "one does not eat one's totem"?

12. Here considered principally as the child of the mother.

13. It may be wondered whether this corresponds to a reality, or whether it exists only as a result of fantasy.

14. Which Lacan writes as "Ła Femme."

15. If B . . .'s dismemberment refers to entry into language as an identification with units having relations among themselves, it is because species are born from disjointed limbs that the myth does not refer to a prelanguage, fragmented body.

16. The terms "children of blood" and "bloody sago shoots" clearly indicate that their existence is correlated with the cutting off of the imaginary phallus, which, from another point of view, is what they are.

17. "In production, sex, hunting, killing, ritual" (see chapter 1).

18. "The *ifegê*'s arrow was like their penis: looking downward for the mother; but this was bad" (see chapter 1).

19. And, as a result, was not caught up in the metaphorical-metonymic chain of language.

20. This refers to the notion of the "incompleteness of the symbolic."

21. "Lalangue," as Lacan writes it.

22. I regard representative art and burial places as proof of the "presence of absence" that inaugurates language.

23. An analogy may be found in Mendeleev's table, which, with a finite number of fixed elements caught up in a precise knot of interrelations, is enough to furnish the elements of a multitude of occurrences in nature.

24. See also the work carried out in a different region: J. Empéraire, *Los nomades del mar* (Santiago: Univ. del Chile, 1963).

25. See Freud 1905.

26. Especially after "The Ego and the Id" (1923).

Marilyn Strathern

5 The Mother's Brother's Child

Like Alfred Gell before him, Bernard Juillerat invites the reader to a superb performance. The temptation is to continue the performances and play with the relationships between the acts, the actors, their actions, and so on. Certainly I shall make-believe that I am at liberty to interpret their interpretations as though I "knew" these West Sepik peoples. However, I want to suggest that, among their many aspects, the Umeda and Yafar performances display a sequence of gender transformations common to societies across Melanesia, and putting the initial analysis into this framework will constrain one's scope for play.

Indeed, I doubt if the power of the Ida-Yangis production depends entirely on its theatrical setting, or that the performance stops at the end of the rite. Gell sees the Umeda ritual as culminating in the emergence of the young bowman, while Juillerat dwells on the unadorned Yafar "mother's brother" who acts as the bowman's preceptor. Both figures can be regarded as points of departure for further metamorphosis— which one surmises will be continued in the context of conjugal relations, affinal exchanges, claims for brides, and so on. If I respond to Juillerat's invitation to question the universality of meaning provided by the Ida-Yangis, then I do so in relation to certain Melanesian universals in the presentation of such relationships.[1] I also respond to his suggestion that the incestuous imagery explicit in his exegesis could be considered a "mediative language or . . . a symbol to say something else about reproduction." I would like to see how far one might get if one threw out once and for all[2] any notion that the Umeda and Yafar are struggling with the symbolism of Western metaphysics and its conceptualizations of "nature" or "culture."

FIND THE FATHER

One of Juillerat's contributions lies in the prominence he gives to sexual differentiation. Central to his intriguing interpretation is the discovery that when the bowman[3] aims at the sun he is aiming at a single maternal breast. Both authors see the last act with the bowman and his preceptor as a restoration of "humanity," Gell in terms of the bowman's role as a human hunter, Juillerat in reference to the undecorated, "already socialized" mother's brother (MB). Gell stresses the cultural repression of the bowman with his bound penis and bound arrow-shaft (1975:289ff.), and of his companion, an "old man" whose life has run its course. In fact, Gell argues with stunning force that the whole Ida sequence is composed not of many figures, but basically the one figure in process of metamorphosis (the cassowary-bowman) (1975:296). "Beginning by incorporating nature . . . into itself, the society finishes by assuming responsibility for nature, by 'culturalizing' the very process of natural regeneration" (1975:295). "Order" emerges as the bowman emerges. Juillerat expands the initiatory overtones to this analysis. The bowman is the initiand, his companion an old man who is also his mother's brother, known by a term that means he has already been through initiation (Yangis) festivals, and thus reached full humanity. Juillerat suggests he prompts the bowman to shoot at the appropriate breast rather than return to his mother's womb; so that this founding intervention creates "social order over nature," "the establishment of society," "culture against and out of nature." Parricide is averted, for the son is lured away by the guardian of the breast (the mother's brother) from seeking confrontation with the guardian of the womb (the father, F). Hence the father himself is not present.

I could not agree more with Juillerat's comment that "males can only be produced by females." But this, to my mind, suggests an analogy with male initiation sequences elsewhere, not the reverse. If Juillerat is right, then we have to consider that at the end there are two figures on the stage: the bowman and his preceptor. And if the performance produces anything, then we have to understand it as producing the *relationship* between the two of them. In Gell's terms, the end of the rite recapitulates the relation between junior/senior generations, in reversed time. In Juillerat's terms, the relevant relation is that between nephew and mother's brother, the novice and the man who represents "society." Throughout, both authors comment on the interplay between reproductive powers and their absence. But the terms *nature* and *culture* are quite intrusive.

Suppose, rather, that the encounter of the two characters summarizes the connecting of two other ideas: the potential for reproduction and the reproduced thing, which is not itself reproductive. The old man/MB is a "completed" figure and, in relation to his junior sister's son, having produced is no longer reproductive (in this he is a version of the fetuses; on being produced, they likewise are not themselves reproductive).[4] Juillerat suggests that the mother's brother is another face of the male personage who mediates between mother and son, and that because the MB is present then the F must be absent. Based on a different reading of the gender symbolism, I make a different suggestion. Of course the father is there: *he is the bowman.* The young man is (filiatively) his own father. We know this both through the displacement of generations and because the bowman is endowed with the chief attribute of fatherhood— it is he who is reproductive.

Whether it is bound with limbum material or decorated with red sago shoot and women's skirt,[5] the penis is already a child: the bowman is already fertile. What the rituals have produced is the potent "father."[6] For it is only thus as a male with a detachable part to bestow that the man can confront/shoot a "mother," which he does in her unambiguous feminine form as in turn a detachable part of the mother's brother (the breast). These rites fall into a large class of performances in Papua New Guinea (initiation rituals, bride-wealth negotiations, ceremonial exchange) that are concerned with transforming a completed (reproduced) person into a reproductive (reproducing) person. To reproduce, men and women have to become momentarily differentiated from each other as entirely "male" or "female," the differentiation being created through the possibility of detaching, or being detached as, an opposite sex part (Gillison 1980). We might say that the sign of reproductive power is a person's ability to so detach parts of him or herself. The resultant single-sex identity creates the condition for embarking on a new cross-sex relation.

GENDER RELATIONS

One problem with a reinterpretation of this kind is its play with the connotations of male and female. We require in its stead a theory of gender forms. This I would derive from the general conditions of gift exchange, as is found across all Melanesia, whose economic form is that of consumptive production (Gregory 1982). The diagnostic predominance of personification, the conversion of things into persons, creates a temporal ambiguity between the things people produce and the relations that produce people. Relations (between persons) are the source of things; things are signs of these relations. But each already implies the prior existence of the other.

The items that circulate in a gift economy are to be understood as objects having value in the regard of persons. Transactions thus both imply and anticipate the production of objects; and without the objects there would in turn be no relations. The Melanesian impetus in production, then, is how to bring about those changes in relations that will indeed create (coerce) regard in others. For insofar as they are the completed product of an interaction between differentiated social others (partners, parents, or whatever), products *cannot in themselves reproduce* (wealth cannot produce wealth, babies cannot produce babies).[7] Consequently, persons alternate between a state of being active reproducers, and being the outcome of the acts of others. The move from active to passive state is indicated in their gender form.

The crucial distinction on which we need to focus is not that between male and female but between same-sex and cross-sex relations. The relations may appear oppositional, between equivalents, or that of an asymmetrical pair as encompasser/encompassed; and may be between the parts of a person or between two or more persons. A same-sex encompassing relation yields the all-male and all-female figure, an identity between the whole and the parts (as in images of parthenogenesis). A same-sex oppositional relation defines two partners as equivalent, in which case the relation between them may well be mediated by an opposite-sex object: "males" exchange "female" wealth (as in ceremonial exchange). A cross-sex encompassing relation allows a contained entity to emerge differentiated from its source (childbirth). A cross-sex oppositional relation results in feeding or penetration: one person's effect on the other in an unmediated mode (an example being relations between spouses). In their transactions with one another, active persons thus take on the attributes of a single sex, or as a result of the transactions of others can be conceptualized as androgynously—and passively—male *and* female. The separation of gift from giver, the thing transacted from the person of the transactor, allows the object (including persons) so created to mediate between discrete partners and thus itself create/ indicate the relation between them.

Gell emphasized that the two characters at the end of the Ida—senior and junior—offer a synchronic representation of a diachronic process. Taking the Yafar pair, we may note that the "male" bowman—from one point of view, all penis—stands with arrow tip, which from another point of view is an androgynous confection of male and female that recapitulates the male and female construction of the fetuses.[8] The "male" figure thus has at his disposal something that both does and does not replicate his identity. Detachable from him, it is a "female"-produced fetus or androgynous "thing." The mother's brother, on the other hand, is constructed as an inherently androgynous figure, at once male and female. In disposing of a part of himself, his breast, he extracts a feminine attribute. This is a male act (see Gillison 1980; Weiner 1987). In detaching the woman from himself (his sister in marriage), he thus becomes all male, thereby separating his own identity into male and female aspects (see Damon 1983), an essential step for his own reproduction. But detachment (reproduction) can only be done with violence. From the viewpoint of the vital sister's son, reproduced from the mother, the MB may equally well be regarded as now lifeless, like a discarded placenta.

My remarks do not do justice to the recursive sequencing and repositioning of these images. I merely wish to substantiate the point that we require a theory of gender forms. Otherwise our analyses fall foul of Western notions of sexual attributes that take a single-sex identity for granted, as when we suppose that a "mother" must represent a "female principle." It is clear that the gender of a mother, to continue the example, may be constructed in more than one way—in a potentially reproductive state as a detachable "male" part; or as a "female" detached from a male clan or a male mother's brother; or as an androgynous envelope for a growing fetus that at the point of birth will be conceptualized as a male extraction from her female body (see Lewis 1980:chap. 6). The mother is thus an all-female figure only at a specific moment in the extractive process, and the same applies to other gender identities. Those center-periphery relations, of which Gell and Juillerat make so much, suggest that the margins constitute an androgynous envelope for a single-sex identity; only the moment of creativity requires that the relation between them be polarized into male and female.[9]

As both Gell and Juillerat indicate, such equations require an appreciation of their dynamism—for since, as they say, the whole Ida-Yangis sequence has to do with fertility, it deals with the production of new identities out of old ones. No equation can be stable, because each anticipates its transformation. The combining of male and female elements in conception (whether oppositionally or in an encompassing relation) will produce the fetus, but for the fetus to reproduce it must be internally split in turn, so that its male and female parts become detachable from one another. Werbner (1984:268, 281) observes the alternation between the logic of pairing and nonpairing, between boundary crossing and encompassment. I add that the prime oscillation is imagined in gender terms not between male and female, but between a single sex (either male or female) and a composite sex (androgynous) state. To give some substance to my remarks, I shall briefly suggest how the sequence of Yangis dancers can be seen to engage in such an oscillation.

Here we shall find some reason for the redundancy of Umeda and Yafar symbolism. Sequences are repeated over and again because there is no temporal stopping place. Each position anticipates the next, the process being embodied in the figures. We can understand the mythical Yafar cassowary as simultaneously/sequentially all male, all female, androgynous, and a male-female pair. One state elicits another, the "cause" of different effects receding with each transformation. This means that the overall rites themselves are necessarily incomplete—the figures in their ultimate "human" aspects indicate that these relations have consequences for the further conduct of human affairs. Implicitly, since it is not possible to give the evidence here, I wish to draw on analyses of male and female initiation rituals from elsewhere in Melanesia, including, one way or another, the ethnography and ideas of most of the other contributors to this exercise. In the end, however, it is irrelevant whether we define these performances as initiation: the gender transformations, as I have hinted, are not confined to any one type of ritual sequencing, nor indeed to what we call ritual.

MONOCHROME AND POLYCHROME

Juillerat tabulates the attributes of the black *ogomô* dancers and the polychrome "fish" dancers that succeed them. He suggests one represents maleness-centrality, the other femaleness-marginality. Why do I wish to suggest a different gloss? Because of their sequencing. The polychrome figures are associated with fetuses, netbags, young sago shoots: they are children, and as products conceptualized as androgynous. These androgynous beings figure twice in the sequences: after the *ogomô* and *kwoy* who comprise six black dancers and one red, and after the earlier *êri* and *rawsu-inaag* in which the red and black figures are paired in sets of two. The polychrome dancers themselves prefigure the termites (*amof*), which are the emergent fetuses. These androgynous polychrome figures, I suggest, incorporate within themselves a cross-sex relation: they are the outcome of an interaction between the sexes that has already taken place, a sign of a cross-sex oppositional transaction. During the course of the rite, this oppositional cross-sex relation becomes an encompassing one, which means that the fetuses can be extruded, and subsequently made partible. They thus become subject to a dual transformation—into the mother's brother on the one hand and the red bowman on the other.

A cross-sex transaction depends on each party or partner achieving his or her own single-sex state. And single-sex (all-male or all-female) figures have indeed appeared at the beginning of the sequence: first the *êri* (black) and *rawsu-inaag* dancers (red), then the *ogomô* (black) and *kwoy* (red). Again it would be a mistake to see the colors as simply denoting "male" and "female." Rather, I would imagine that the single color denotes a same-sex *relation* between the parts of the person, whether all red *or* all black. This is indicated by Yafar in terms that Juillerat found ambiguous: the sense in which the first set of dancers (*êri* and *rawsu-inaag*) are all female (mothers), and the second set (*ogomô, kwoy*) are all male (fathers).

But a single-sex state anticipates a relation with its opposite; thus the figures also appear in pairs. Juillerat notes that on the one hand the *êri* are represented as mothers of the sago palms, but at the same time portray a sexualized pair. The *êri* duo is then repeated in a male version, also incorporating a sexualized pair. As he brilliantly concludes, the "apparent contradiction in sexual identities is in fact the result of two superimposed representations: one synchronic, about reproductive sexuality, the other, diachronic, about filiation" (chapter 1, "Sexual Identity . . ."). These are two types of generative relation—the latter same-sex, the former cross-sex. The one is transformed into the other in "reproduction." Consequently, we have *both* mother-daughter, father-son sequences *and* the mothers as both male and female, the fathers as both male and female. Such cross-sex polarizing of a single-sex entity is a common Melanesian theme: one is reminded, for instance, of the double flutes played during Sambia initiation, male and female, like the mother's two breasts (see chapter 1, note 56; Herdt 1981). We have to take seriously the representation of the one (male) as indeed a "version" (both flutes, both breasts) of the other (female).[10]

From this perspective, the colors black and red must be seen as alternatives of one another, as in the alternation of senior and junior generations (for example, Gell 1975:323; "all seniors" or "all juniors"). As Gell says, "The colour-code of body-paint in Ida is . . . the codification of a set of relationships internal to Ida itself" (1975:323). The generations then are analogues of the sexes. As long as their members are the "same," like the same-sex relation of exchange partners, the one gender cannot turn into the other. This is true whether they are paired symmetrically in an oppositional relation or asymmetrically presented in an encompassing one (Gell stresses the smallness of the Umeda counterparts to the *rawsu-inaag,* armed as they are, by contrast with the huge *êri;* Juillerat a center-periphery relation). The one is, I would argue, *already a version of the other.*[11] Only as separate entities can the mothers/fathers subsequently enter into a relation that will jointly reproduce something that is neither of them alone (the polychrome androgynes). What is required is proof of their ability to enter into such a relation with another and thus of their difference.

Mothers and fathers emerge as alternatives of one another, appearing on different occasions. They represent single-sex states with a potential for reproduction. This is made apparent in the sago symbolism of the identities involved, as it is in the mask names. Sure enough, then, the mothers (sago palm and blood of the hymen) are followed by *yis* (transformed sago jelly) and *ware-inaag* (remains of sago jelly), while the fathers (original sago jelly and menstrual blood) are followed by the *sawôg* (or *yis abuk,* the transformed red sago jelly) and *koor* (rotten or discarded blood). In each case, the parent (mother/father) is symbolized as a duo, an unmixed pairing (*êri* and *rawsu-inaag; ogomô* and *kwoy*). The fire and water transformation produces two elements: an androgynous composite fetus (*yis* and *sawôg*) and discarded remnants (*ware-inaag* and *koor*). The latter, I suggest, prefigure the final mother's brother appearance as a corpse. The message is that a transformation is necessary from a single-sex state before there can be a (composite) product. What is true of mothers is also true of fathers. So there is a *repeated set* of transformations: first the mothers, then the fathers. The first is an all-female representation only because it is the "same" as the second, all-male. The Yafar shout in their spells: *yis* of the penis, *yis* of the vagina![12] The one is the other; if *yis* are born of maternal blood, they are born of paternal blood also.

I would thus reread the classification of elements that Juillerat (chapter 1, table 1.2) opposes as male and female principles: the left-hand column (polychrome) is of cross-sex relations in their completed, combined form (androgyny); the right-hand column of same-sex relations, in the instance of a single-sex configuration (here all male).

We are dealing, to borrow Roy Wagner's idea (1977), with analogic gender. Male and female are versions of one another; they are essentially alike, and human ingenuity is required to differentiate them. Human ingenuity is required because it is in the act of differentiation (not in the state of being different) that production or procreation is possible, that fresh identities are extracted. Differentiation often requires violence, certainly energy. The recipient is forced to accept the item—that part of the other—that will establish the identity of the donor. Similarly, procreation is forced on the potential mother by the father—his part will grow within her. She must then yield the increment back; childbirth thus becomes an extractive process, as is claiming a bride from a body of men.

This is relevant for our understanding of sexual dualism. The differentiation to which analogic gender relations lead is achieved by polarizing male from female, female from male. Versions of one another, they become opposed as equivalents in a cross-sex relation. This polarization may appear as a transient effect. Indeed, the creation of moieties seem to have this character. They belong to performance, synchronic representations of a diachronic process. For the moieties "freeze" (see Harrison 1984) polarity between the sexes; they are oppositionally paired, and at the same time the one encompasses the other in being oriented toward what each will extract from themselves to give, a perpetual debt of origin.

Male and female are analogic equivalents. The forms cannot turn into each other. By contrast, transformation does occur between (active) single-sex and (passive) cross-sex forms, for this is the relation between cause and effect.

It is too simple to talk of diachrony and synchrony: we also need a recursive metaphor, one that will indicate how time runs both backward and forward. Gell's general remarks about time and the representation of the oscillating generations are pertinent. Ida "symbolic" time reverses "process" time (1975:335). Up to now I have referred to sequence and event as though they unfolded in process time: that is, as though the polychrome androgynes are the temporal product of paired single-sex creatures. It is clear, however, that the "product" may already be present before the event. The outcome is prefigured, a consequence I have also suggested of moiety relations, for they separately produce for one another only because they have each been so produced by the other themselves. What looks like oscillation in time is thus an effect of the oscillation between same-sex and cross-sex relations: each form does indeed turn into the other. One set of relations can only be made evident because it is a product as well as the cause of another set. And one becomes another ("reproduces") through the mechanics of gender differentiation.

DIFFERENTIATION AND DETACHMENT

Ultimately, polarization between male and female is accomplished through the separation or detachment of the "parts" that make up the androgynous person. A relation is possible because detached parts can be given and received. Conversely, the ability to detach a part defines a single-sex state. Thus the potent monochrome *êri* (Gell's cassowaries) whom Juillerat interprets as "mothers" and Gell as "belonging to mother" (1975:182) are also represented as composite figures, phalluses encased in skirts. But the point is that they have the wherewithal to enter into an oppositional relation. They may be internally polarized, a male (female) with a detachable female (male) part to give; or else they may be conceptualized as the recipient of a gift or the object of unmediated influence from another (where possession of an orifice is analogous to possession of a detachable part). Juillerat's *êri* are all-female (black or red) mothers because they are able to come into a relation with opposite-sexed others, both through their detachable breasts (the white markings), and through being fed eggs. Gell's black *eli*, identified with mother's brothers at one point (1975:324), whose penises grow long during the night's dancing (1975:184), "emphatically male" (1975:226) under their huge encompassing masks, are the game for which hunters will seek (1975:244), the wives who come from outside, objects of another's quest. (The cassowary MB is a male source of females.) In this Melanesian context, to be reproductive is to have the ability to initiate a relationship through a part of oneself, to create an object that will draw the interest of another.

The detachment of the mother's (brother's) breast is necessarily effected by a male (see Weiner 1987), in an image that prompts analogies with the Massim myths of serpent cutting and wealth creation (see Young 1987). Indeed, the mythical excision of the white breast from below the neck—a favorite place for wearing shell valuables—is reminiscent of the decoration worn by the Bedamini initiator at the head of the new group of initiated (Sørum 1984:323).[13] The mother's brother has given part of himself (his sister in marriage): but if this happened at the moment that the bowman appears (the MB shows the breast), it has also happened before he appeared, for the red bowman himself was extracted from the mother. The bowman returns the mother's brother's child not in the form of wealth or food[14] but in the form of a miniature child itself (the bound and skirted penis/arrow). In incestuous imagery, the mother's brother has indeed lost the head to his arrow (chapter 1; Gell 1975:206)—not because he cannot shoot the sun (Juillerat suggests this is a prohibition on access to his sister's breast), but because *it is the sun/breast that is his "head,"* and that the bowman encounters.[15] Yet again, the action is prefigured: the head is on the bowman's arrow before he even begins to shoot (in the form of the miniature child). Bowman, arrow, and penis are already "bloody sago shoots" (the mother's/MB's "sons," cf. Gell, 1975:144).

As far as the succession of generations is concerned, the son was already a parricide at the moment of birth. In being separated as a "male" from a "female" body, he filiatively displaces his father. It is only by the father's active engagement with the mother (a cross-sex relation of opposition) that the father reproduces an entity that simultaneously does *not* displace him: the son as an androgyne and a sign of the interaction between a differentiated parental pair. The father *thus reproduces for his wife's brother:* he produces the sister's son (ZS). Only by producing a sister's son, an entity different from himself, can he (father = son) survive the whole process of birth.[16] Perhaps the hesitation of the Yafar bowmen echoes the expressed vulnerability found in other Melanesian performances—of dancers to the gaze of others, of donors at the hands of the recipients of their gifts. For it is essential to the father's survival that the mother's brother accept the gift of the child (Gillison 1987), and allow the arrow to penetrate the breast. This is no longer the displacement of one partner by another but the mediation of a relationship through the "exchange" of (making equivalent) the parts that each differentiated partner has at his disposal.

Yet there is an asymmetry between the two figures. One may see MB and ZS as equally eliciting the masculinity of the other (see Wagner 1986b). Or we may see the MB as the senior androgyne who has the particular potential of eliciting maleness or femaleness from his own sister's child: he separates breast from body.[17] By putting the ZS into interaction with the severed breast, he thus creates him as a father. Whereas the androgynous fetus has the potential to be masculinized or feminized (that is, to be made reproductive), the finally completed person (the androgynous MB) in losing his head becomes like a corpse—perhaps foreshadowed by the ghost-clown.

As Juillerat observes, the Ida-Yangis sequence is about both procreation and filiation. Its own play with the dark/light sequencing of sunset and sunrise has to do, I would infer (see Biersack 1982), with the making visible of processes normally effective because they are kept hidden. This is serious play indeed. Yet, in a sense, the activity has no outcome: the figure of the senior man/mother's brother is undecorated, because for the rite to be effective its meanings must be transferred to the as yet unaccomplished production of sago and children, the development of relations between affines, sister-exchanges, and the rest.

To return to my starting point about the nature of gift economies: the breast is created as an "object" (chapter 1, note 50) on the mother's brother's part. But the object can only appear in the presence of the bowman, in the same way as the mother's breasts are, as it were, only feminized in the presence of the child they nurture. Objectification (the breast) is here an outcome of the relation between mother's brother and sister's son (mother and son); it is the product of a transaction between them. At the same time, it is also the cause of the transaction, and the very item that is transacted. This recursive sequencing—an object at once the outcome and cause of a relation—defines the "gift." Whether one is dealing with detachable brides, children, or wealth, we may say that parts of persons thereby become objectified in the course of transactions. But this is not the terminology of those who live by these operations. Their imaginative concern would seem to be to separate cause from effect—to make intervention apparent. In one sense the gift (the child to be created) cannot exist prior to the relation between the mother's brother/mother and sister's son/father; in another sense, the premise of exchange requires the gift to be the cause of that relation (the child already exists and must be extracted).

Not all Melanesian societies act out these processes in the same way. But they do seem caught up in the idealization (after *idéel,* Godelier 1986) of gift relations. The problem, so to speak, comes long before the substitution of wealth for persons: it is inherent in the personification process whereby persons stand for other persons (M. Strathern 1985), and relations are created through consumptive production. A "person" is an object of relations between others, nurtured at the hands of others; to be an active partner to a relation, to become a transactor him or herself, requires a transformation of identity. In Ida and Yangis this is imagined through the successive metamorphoses of androgynous and single-sex figures.[18]

NOTES

1. The references to Juillerat throughout this chapter pertain to chapter 1.

2. This chapter was first written in 1986. I have, of course, "continued" to do this in various contexts, including M. Strathern (1988).

3. I use the singular to refer to the figure (rather than the number of actors).

4. True not so much because he is situated "outside the reproductive family cell" (chapter 1, note 90) but true *at this instance* in the ritual, when he bestows reproductive potential on the bowman. Insofar as he (the mother's brother) *has aleady produced* (the red bowman), with nothing more to detach, he reverts to an androgynous nonreproductive state.

5. Phallocrypt, mask, and netbags are all containers. I suggest the bowman's exposed/bound penis reveals (yields) the normally hidden fetus.

6. In the following discussion, I call the *ogomô* dancers "fathers." Yafar refer to them as "male children." Male children in a reproductive state *are* "fathers."

7. Contra the symbolism of a "commodity economy," where productive consumption predominates (Gregory 1982). "Objects" include categories

of persons—those objectified in the transactions of others. The position I adopt here on Melanesian gender symbolism is argued at length in M. Strathern (1988).

8. The mythical father ties his sons' penises up with a bandage, thus binding the blood, as in conception. Not the emancipation of man from "nature," but the procreation of a fetus from both mother and father.

9. On the first day when *ogomô* and *sawôg* (see below) are both on stage, the androgynous fetuses (*sawôg*) dance on the periphery; on the second day of the *amof* performance, the ritual has moved to the point at which the fetuses are to be detached through the bowman's violent act— and *sawôg* as contained fetuses dance in the center, *amof* as emergent ones on the periphery.

10. Thus the two moieties are *both* replicas of one another *and* paired as male and female, the sago palm like penises full of semen, the coconut like breasts full of milk. The analogy is underlined by the fact that their "children" are not children of the semen, or children of the milk, but equated as children of the sago palm blood and children of the coconut blood. On pairs, see Schwimmer (1984) and A. Strathern (1979).

11. Mothers/daughters are in a relation not of "regeneration" but displacement. Thus, simultaneously each is already the other. By "reproduction" I refer to the connotations of increment (growth) found in cross-sex mediation.

12. At the moment of transformation (leaping over the fire) the *yis* dancers say "*Hoofuk* [grease] of the penis sago jelly, *hoofuk* of the vagina sago jelly. . . ."

13. The Bedamini dancer has a representation of a vulva painted on his chest, a pearl shell fragment in his beard.

14. Gell (1975:109) mentions the meat that the hunter owes to his true wife's mother's brother (and see chapter 1).

15. I am drawing directly here on suggestions made by Gillison (1987) apropos the Gimi mother's brother, and the son's encounter with his father. It is in shooting at the sun/breast that the son does, of course, displace his father, a real parricide. Thus the father is both there (in the person of the bowman) *and* not there (displaced by the bowman). His shooting place, so to speak, has been taken. The breast itself is both a female counterpart of the male MB *and* an androgynous precursor of an active relation between female and another male for whom it will be an object. The new father (son, sister's son) is simultaneously the product of

earlier relations *and* in this potent male state (about to detach part of himself) able to embark on a new relation.

16. On the reproductive functions of brother and sister for one another in an agnatic context (Bimin-Kuskusmin), see Weiner (1982).

17. The severed breast is the female counterpart (M as "female") of the now masculinized body (MB as "male"); alternatively, maleness may be held to reside in the act of differentiation itself, and the MB having excised the object of value from himself becomes a useless placenta or corpse (the dead, rotting mother, a bloody remnant).

18. It does not matter how the sequence starts. The actual performance bursts open with single-sex figures, but this is already a creation of the performance out of the androgynous actors, the enclosed space, and the like.

Roy Wagner

6 The Imagery Keeps Its Scale: An Obviation Model of the Yafar Yangis

The analysis of the Yafar Yangis offered here is based on Juillerat's source material. However, the ethnographic context framing this discussion was initiated by Alfred Gell's analysis of the Umeda Ida, and therefore it seems appropriate to open with a comment on that analysis.

A positive feature of Gell's analysis is its tendency to digress in an effort to do justice to the condensation of images. Gell is aware that each image provides at once a range of sensory effects and potential analogic relations that exhaust the capabilities of linear description and the explanatory expectations based upon these capabilities. Gell's use of Roland Barthes's syntagmatic and paradigmatic functions, and of Turnerian insights, provides a "thick" ethnographic description of the ritual action in the sense that it exhausts a series of cultural oppositions and categories. We are left to marvel at a scenario and a performance that can effectively coordinate so much complexity. But, of course, the complexity is artificial—it is a product of the analyst's dissociation of condensed images into linear oppositions and categories. The difficulty with Gell's analysis is that it goes to work on an artificially complex product and so misses the scale of the images themselves in sequence and transformation. It is a characteristic difficulty of the semantic or semiotic, structuralist, and social-anthropological approaches that Gell has pressed into service. The central problem is perhaps the Saussurian notion (and the Western tendency that that notion rigidifies) of the sign, which uses image solely as the enabler of abstraction and so disallows the meaningful transformation of images in their own right.

The alternative approach, which accords with much received anthropological wisdom, but little current practice, is to assume that it is images, in their transformational sequence, that are held consensually in the culture, rather than signs, or sign-based glosses of the images.

The range of potential analogies or glosses (interpretations, what it might mean) evoked by a verbal image or trope, or by a tactile, kinetic, or visual one is indefinite, possibly infinite. The only certainty and the only concreteness lie in dealing with the images themselves. A sequence of such images in transformation thus operates by enabling and canceling whole ranges of analytic possibilities. This movement—a calculus, as it were, for possibilities of relationship—forms the indigenous experience of the ritual as a concrete, imagistic power.

What is the "order," or structure, of such a sequence? As with other cultural phenomena, models and other heuristic devices are useful in gaining an analytic entree. But if the properties of image are retained throughout the transformation (e.g., if the sequence keeps to what the mathematics of fractals calls its own self-scaling), then a linear gloss or heuristic will be rendered arbitrary and self-contradictory by the paradoxes engendered in the transformational process. Thus the only viable heuristic is one that models self-cancelation or obviation within its own articulation (that expands the self-contradictory properties of metaphor, for instance, into articulative principles). From the standpoint of indigenous experience, the argument of a gloss or "order" is subsumed by the power of successive image transformations, and the only certainty, and the only concreteness, is to deal with the images themselves. The most honest statement of this experience to an outsider is frequently misunderstood as a kind of nescience, an indication of the nonanalytic nature of the "pragmatic" native. In fact, it betokens a more comprehensive insight than anthropology has yet owned up to.

Because it is schooled by image transformation, indigenous commentary on the significance of ritual and its phases is indispensable to an understanding of ritual on its own scale. This is particularly true for "secret" or withheld knowledge, which frequently affords privileged access to the cohesive integration or unity of the whole, the single encompassing image, so to speak, that is serially accomplished by the transformations.

This is evident in the secret (male) proceedings that occur some time prior to the beginning of the Yangis—the felling of the two totemic sago palms and the inauguration of the hunting period. These rites, and especially the hunting inauguration, which involves all the major performers in the Yangis, serve to establish a ritual symbolization of *hoofuk* via an inversion of the normal spatial significance of coconut and sago. Sago, which is village-peripheral, is treated in terms of the duality of human gender and reproduction—the two palms are felled simultaneously, through a concerted action of human mediation and communication, and their products are exchanged between the moieties. Coconut, which is village-central, is treated, through the ritual identification of its *hoofuk* with that of bush creatures, as village-peripheral. The coconut *hoofuk* is plural rather than dual, and its flowers fall randomly (like hunting luck) on the men below. This inversion, which is actualized in the hunting inauguration, sets up a powerful reciprocal trope, by which human reproduction and that of the primary human staple, sago, can each be effected through the mediation of the other, and under the ministrations of men.

Thus the inauguration of hunting is properly the act that sets the Yangis in motion, implementing the mode of female, earth-related *hoofuk* as peripheral to the central, dual, and gendered mode of sago, in which the *fenaw* sago, male but ritually gendered as female, takes the place of coconut. The small rite of rebinding the coconut spathe, which closes the hunting period, can thus be understood as diverting the coconut *hoofuk* to the two other transformations it undergoes in the Yangis: blood of intercourse, and *hoofuk* of pregnancy. The initial identification of maternal *hoofuk* in the rite of hunting inauguration stands as the first term in a triple mediation of peripheral *hoofuk* images (figure 6.1): *hoofuk* of killing (blood of the game), *hoofuk* (blood) of intercourse— medial between killing and nurturance—and hoofuk of pregnancy, that of nurturing the fetus.

But the ritual identification of the coconut, and hence maternal *hoofuk,* as plural and peripheral, is only conceivable or viable as a function of the inversion by which sago, the other term of the opposition, becomes central and gendered. The mediation of types of maternal *hoofuk* in figure 6.1 is therefore itself mediated by a congruent sequence of types of paternal sago *hoofuk* treated as culturally central and gendered images. These amount to the three critical acts of human procreation: intercourse, conception, and parturition (movement of *hoofuk* into, within, and out of, the uterus). Otherwise contexted within the

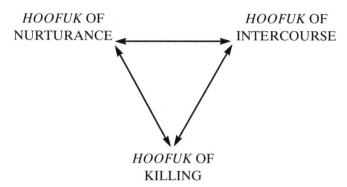

Figure 6.1. Plural, peripheral *hoofuk*.

female body, they are performed, under the terms of the ritual inversion, by men, who enact the roles of the respective genders via the identities of the *fenaw* and *afwêêg* sago varieties. Hence the two *êri,* the paired earth and sky priests, and the two *ifegê.*

It is not simply a mediation of oppositions that constitutes the ritual, but rather a reciprocal mediative movement among concrete images, each of which condenses a range of oppositional potentials (central/ peripheral, male/female, nurturative/killing, ingressive/egressive, etc.). Processually, the reciprocal mediation of the female *hoofuk*/male *hoofuk* series can be understood as a sequence of dialectical closures (thesis-antithesis-synthesis), the concluding term of each (synthesis) forming the initial term (thesis) of the next. Hence the gendered act of intercourse (B, in figure 6.2) mediates the transformation of *hoofuk* of killing (A) into *hoofuk* of intercourse (C), in that intercourse is a human inward act of penetration. *Hoofuk* of intercourse (C) synthesizes the opposition of A and B in its enactment of human gendered and engendered blood, the "wound," as it were, of procreation. The act of conception (D) mediates the transformation of genital bleeding into the nurturant *hoofuk* of pregnancy (E), which in turn synthesizes the opposition of C and D in its expression of a contained, generative fluid. The act of parturition (F), a wounding of the mother from within, so to speak, mediates, via the expression of this injury through the *ifegê* shooting arrows at an external matri-image, the final, external resolution of the ritual.

The final synthesis, at G, might be explicated in several ways. Following Juillerat's evidence, the firing of the *ifegê*'s arrows at F might be

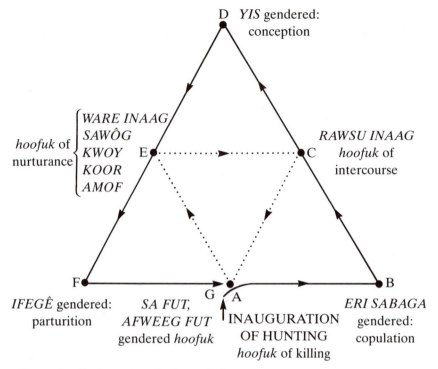

Figure 6.2. Reciprocal mediation and closure.

understood as a seeking of, or attack on, the maternal breast, identified
with the sun. It might also, I suggest, be seen as the penetration of the
birth orifice from within by the neonates. It would seem, however, that
the nonspecificity of the image to either of these alternatives accommo-
dates both of them (and others besides). In either case, and in any case,
the image of the white breast milk or white sunlight falling down recapitulates the cascading of white coconut inflorescences at A, very much
as the notion of the sun replanting the arrows as shoots of coconut and
sago reverses the symbolic inversion established at A.

   Movement of the Yangis itself can be followed from A to G, counter-
clockwise along the other periphery of the diagram in figure 6.2. But this
movement also obeys the retroactive implications of the synthesizing
closures, GEC, which form, in fact, an image of the maternal (plural,
peripheral *hoofuk*) mediation in reciprocal (clockwise) motion. The ef-

fect of this "symmetry," a property of (synchronic) image retained through its temporal expansion, is to render initial images understandable through the action of subsequent closures. Thus the coconut inflorescences in the hunting inauguration (A) may be spoken of as "blood" through the synthesizing action of C (C-A implication); the genital blood at C acquires reproductive capabilities through the synthesizing action of E (E-C implication), and the pregnancy *hoofuk* at E obtains nurturant properties from G (whether G is understood as a fall of breast milk or sunlight).

The cumulative development of the Yangis as a totality can be understood through the successive cancellation, or obviation, of mediational series. Thus, in figure 6.2, the initial synthesis, at C, is followed by an antithesis at D. But this fourth term, D, can itself be treated as the synthesis of a new series, BCD, thereby preempting the mediation and canceling the significance of the initial term at A. Beginning at the *yis* (D), then, the Yangis can be conceived as a succession of mediative replacements (figure 6.3, indicated by arrows), each substituting an internal action for an earlier external counterpart. Hence the *yis,* at D, replaces A's external fall of bush *hoofuk* with an internal union of (gendered) human *hoofuk;* E supplants the ingressive repletion of the uterus via intercourse (B) with the internal repletion of pregnancy *hoofuk;* F substitutes the penetration of the uterus from *within* via the sago "shoots" of the *ifegê* and their arrows, for the penetration from without imaged by genital blood at C. Each of these substitutions is itself imaged by a color: white for the *yis*-coconut hoofuk (D-A), black for the *suh-wagmô* of the *êri* and the central "black" *ogomô* at E (E-B), and red for the blood of the *rawsu-inaag* and the "red" sago-shoots (*ifegê*) at E (E-C).

The effect of the respective white, black, and red substitutions is to replace externally active with internally active agencies, with *hoofuk* proper. The center and turning point of this transformation is the *yis* (D, figure 6.2), significantly the substitution of internal, gendered sago *hoofuk* for external, peripheral coconut *hoofuk*. The "spine" of the ritual, so to speak, is formed of the sago-coconut contrast that constitutes its enabling condition. The sun is in fact the resolution of the spatial analogy (bush-peripheral/village-central) whose inversion frames the significance of the Yangis itself. When the emergent sago "shoots," transformed into arrows, are directed at the sun, the sun reestablishes the original disposition of the totemic trees, thus concluding the ritual by

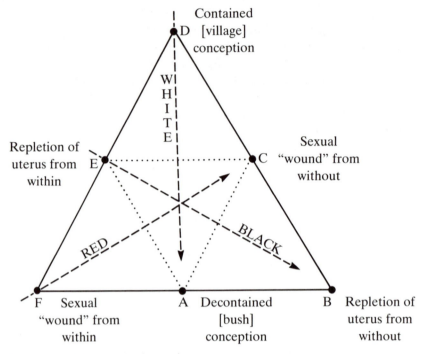

Figure 6.3. Egression for ingression.

dissolving its enabling trope. The sun itself is white at the central mystery of the ritual, the *yis;* it is red in its setting, as the *ifegê* fire their arrows; then the red gives way to the black night of *êri,* and the cycle begins again.

Remember, however, that the foregoing analytical observations are only partial realizations of a ritual effect that is conceived and enacted wholly in concrete terms, through a succession of images. The various sets of dialectical relations that I have adumbrated operate simultaneously, as implications of a single condensed movement, or enactment. The ritual itself, as modeled, cannot be said to possess, or to represent, a "structure," for it is as much an action of canceling and negating structural features or orders as it is of positing them. For this reason, I have used the term "obviation" to name the model. By the same token the ritual, as analyzed, will only be grossly misunderstood by applying to it such notions as "communication" or the encoding of a "message" or of "information." The Yangis is ruled by the unsaid: it is far more effective at keeping its meanings—encapsulating and subsuming them as secrets within secrets—than at letting them go. As for the more common social science tendency to "find" cosmological or sociological abstractions (for example, fertility, nurturance, social "forces" or "interests") within the imagery, any number of such generalities might be identified, and all are obviated in its working out. If the Yangis is a "game" (to use another facile heuristic ploy), and if its "rules" amount to the inversion of the central/peripheral order of the totemic trees, then the game ends in checkmate, and what is checkmated are the rules.

How, then, are we to understand a ritual like the Yangis? Its power, epitomized in the obviating "inward" turn that commences with the *yis,* is that of the embodied self-realization of *hoofuk,* which is so forceful that it overcomes even men's efforts to enact it and the rules and orders by which this enactment is essayed.

Richard P. Werbner

7 On Dialectical Versions: The Cosmic Rebirth of West Sepik Regionalism

> Every word engenders a word which contradicts it, every word is
> a relation between negation and affirmation. Relation is to tie
> together othernesses, it is not the resolution of contradictions.
> Therefore, language is the realm of dialectic which ceaselessly
> destroys itself and is reborn only to die. (Paz 1978 [1967]:140)

Upon ending his study of Yangis as ritual among Amanab speakers in
the West Sepik village of Yafar, Bernard Juillerat had the courage to
make a new beginning. He asked his colleagues for their comments. This
reopened the debate surrounding Alfred Gell's splendid account (1975)
of the Umeda festival of Ida. The people of Umeda, who are Waina
speakers, live near but not next to Yafar. The village of Punda mediates
between them. It turns out that we are commenting on an already dou-
bled and even redoubled commentary; that we are participating, not
unlike the people of the Sepik themselves, in a kind of agonistic discourse. The versions of practice and interpretation are contested. Being
agonistic, the discourse proceeds from version to counterversion largely
by negation, and not only by affirmation; and being beyond final resolution, it invites revision. An authoritative conclusion escapes us.

My own contribution follows three general theoretical interests,
which I want to introduce briefly before the main body of my text.[1] The
first is the approach to regionalism (see also Werbner 1977, 1979, 1985,

1989); the second, the nature of the egocentric perspective and fantastic logic in the festivals; and the third, the dialectics of discourse (see also Werbner n.d.).

A regional perspective is required for the interpretation and analysis of the regional relations imaged in Umeda and Yafar origin myths and actualized in their festival practice. The evidence now emerging from these and other virtual hunter-gatherers of the West Sepik (Gell 1975; Huber 1975; chapters 1 and 2 of this volume) calls to mind Aboriginal regionalism. The Aboriginal sacred geography, with its elaborate sacred sites and tracks of the dream-time, seems more highly developed (Maddock 1983). But the existence in the West Sepik of widely interlinked festival circuits and routes around sacred central places is only now beginning to be recognized, as are the links between the Australian hunter-gatherers and the virtual hunter-gatherers of Papua New Guinea.

Here my interest is not in a culture area approach. The cutting edge of this approach is mere spread, and its empirical hypotheses are dominated by the distribution of types, by variation from one extreme of the area to another in, say, the importance or increasing elaboration of the priesthood, the flutes in initiation, the representations of the Cassowary. One of its methodological objectives is to explain typical variation according to simple principles (for an African example, see Kuper 1982). The culture area approach is useful for overcoming naive holism, the tendency, once dominant in Melanesian research, to study a small group, little community, or tribe as an isolate, a whole unto itself. But for our purposes, the culture area approach is inadequate. At best, it is one of those methods of comparison that discloses distinctive specificity (Holy 1987). The concentration on correlations within the culture area directs attention away from coordination. This approach obscures the wider organization of a region and stultifies our appreciation of regionalism itself as a culturally known and culturally constructed reality. In this approach, cultural reality stops with the little community or *the* culture.

The regional approach enables us to appreciate certain flows between central places and across communities or cultures. But what are these flows? How are they constituted or controlled? And what is their importance for the reproduction of communities or cultures in relation to each other? I raise these questions not so much to answer them all at once, even in a preliminary approximation, but to open the field of problems.

In Umeda, and I infer in other nearby parts of the Lowlands, the paucity of cross-societal trade or barter in *material* things, like the restricted circulation of women as wives, is striking. It is all the more so by comparison with much of the Highlands. But if the flows of things and persons are contained within very short-range exchange networks, the same cannot be said for *immaterial* goods, for powerful knowledge (see Harrison 1990). Powerful knowledge is bartered extensively. As secrets, such knowledge is bartered within partnerships that are institutionalized for trade between partners from unlike cultures and hostile societies.[2] The barter would seem to be a factor in the differentiation between the secretly knowledgeable old men and the ignorant young men. The villagers participating in this cross-societal and cross-cultural flow of knowledge develop complementary yet opposed perspectives regarding the indigenous and the exotic. Their festivals are distinct cultural reworkings of their exchanged knowledge. But the process of reworking is a mutual one. Or, to put it another way, the different perspectives are constitutive of each other. Festival regionalism is a dialectical relation. The conversion of a whole version is systematic, from village to village. It is not my contention, however, that the outcome is a "culture system" (with all due respect to Juillerat's Epilogue in this volume) across different parts of the West Sepik. On the contrary, regional relations are "partial connections," to use Marilyn Strathern's phrase (1987, 1991), which need not, and indeed do not, add up to the totality of a single whole system.

Juillerat carefully records a significant number of differences between the festivals of Ida and Yangis. Ambiguities are also apparent from Cassowary myth and masquerade. But virtually all the rites reported (not by Gell but by Juillerat) and the greatest differences between Ida and Yangis occur in nonpublic moments. Juillerat's new evidence comes primarily from the sanctuary or *intra*village events, not *inter*village events. With that courage that characterizes his whole project, Juillerat frankly admits that he is puzzled by the differences and the ambiguities. I suggest, however, that he is puzzled in a way that the Yafar and their neighbors are not.

Juillerat recognizes no systematic conversion of the Cassowary cult from neighbor to neighbor. Or, if he records a variation, he leaves us with the impression that he was more fortunate than the youthful Gell in being able to learn more, with better access to nonpublic rites and esoterica. One good field worker coming on the heels of another undoubtedly has the edge, at times. This is so particularly in a region of this kind when the second is a more mature man. In this region, the youth is a hunter who is not expected to know all there is to know. After all, secret, inaccessible knowledge is proof of and, perhaps, the very means to the power of elders over youth. Maturity, experience, innermost knowledge, these are virtually synonymous in this region. But there is more to it than that, and we must not let our own disposition for seeing things temporally get in the way of our appreciation of differentiation in social space.

The people themselves understand the relativity of performance. Moreover, they insist upon it. Each village has its own esoteric and highly private, indeed secret, rites. These are known in depth only to insiders. For that very reason, the rites are disparate and yet capable of being coordinated within a wider region across villages and across cultures. The disparity is either unseen, or if it is recognized, it is taken to be of local concern only. Hence people from different villages and different cultures can say that their performances are similar, that Yangis is roughly like Ida. This "similarity" is an aspect of affirmation in their regional relation in tension with the negation by the "disparity" between them. Across villages and cultures, the people need not fully share or publicly broadcast their fine understanding of performance. On the contrary, they have the privacy, at least for themselves and without effective contradiction, to assert a version of their own to be *the* significant version. Secrecy is protective of vital self-knowledge.

To give a key example, about which more must be said later, in Yangis but *not* in Ida the hunt is inaugurated with an intravillage rite at a central coconut palm. The performance takes place some four months *before* the masquerade. This intravillage rite first enacts breast-feeding then weaning. The gift of flowers, from the coconut addressed as "mother," prefigures the gift of game. There is an anticipation also of other events, including the very last, in the subsequent masquerade. The game, like every mother and the coconut itself, comes to Yangis's center from an external source (coconuts like mothers being gifts from mothers' brothers for sisters' sons). It is a gift elicited by a scantly decorated and unmasked man. The same man, subsequently, is to reemerge newborn in the apparent finale of the masquerade. As the Original Man, he is the village ancestor and thus ultimate hero, the Arrowhead. This rite is for Yafar villagers. Umeda villagers, like Gell himself, may well be ignorant of it, although Punda villagers say, according to Juillerat, that they and Umeda villagers do perform it also.

But why should Yafar, and not Umeda, anticipate the masquerade with breast-feeding then weaning? And why, in Yangis not Ida, should all this be the "mother's" gift of game elicited by a man about to be a newborn hero in the masquerade? In other words, why does one village, and not the other, perform *this* flashback, so to speak, with the outcome as preliminary (breast-feeding and weaning) *before* the cause or antecedent (cosmic rebirth) (see Weiner 1980 on reproduction and the anticipation of an outcome)? The answer is in the dialectically related perspectives on origins, on selfhood, community, and the cosmos. I show this more fully in due course.

To return to the conversion of secret knowledge into unacknowledged differences, what the villagers publicly broadcast the most is the blowing of their own phallic trumpets. Outsiders take the blowing to be a signal of intent, not the bird song of insiders, in all its fine nuances. It is, as signal, simply a moment of division or bracketing. No longer is there to be the obliteration of the divide between inner wind and outer wind that prevails during the festival masquerade with its trumpeting. Outside and inside are now opposed, not to be fused. Accordingly, free passage and easy social intercourse across territories are stopped. Hostilities may break out between villages within shouting distance. Some have no direct marital or cult exchange with each other. There is, to use Bohannon's phrase, a "working misunderstanding" across villages and cultures. They do not have to understand each other's version, from the other's perspective. They all have to understand how their own performance fits from their own vantage ground at their own center. And for the cult to operate, each center must be central in its significance for its own villagers.

The point I am leading up to is this. Umeda and Yafar belong to a single regional cult. This has certain center-periphery relations of a cross-cultural kind that I have found to be typical of similar regional cults in Africa and elsewhere (Werbner 1977, 1979, 1989). The Umeda hold the cult festival annually, the Yafar at the end of the period it takes to build up a herd of semidomesticated pigs, perhaps a dozen, for a major kill, a period of roughly a decade. I am not suggesting, of course, that the festival with its feasting on game, on the products of men's hunt, is occasioned by pig kills, which are tied to women's rearing. It may be, however, that the game festival and the pig kill are gender-specific alternatives, as are hunting and pig rearing. And it would seem that the Yafar slaughter their pig herd some years *after* Yangis, 1971 and 1978 for recent pig kills, 1976 for the festival (the decision for a pig kill is reached by the whole village).[3] The frequency of performance befits the people at one heartland and one hinterland of a regional cult.

My suggestion does not imply that the region must be stable in membership or that the content of regionalism must be constant, fixed like the slope of the land. On the contrary, where the community itself is precarious (see Werbner 1989) it is not surprising that the region too is precarious; that regionalism is ephemeral. Villages may introduce an exotic festival and later abandon it. Opting for an alternative, they may redirect their center-periphery relations. Or, they may participate in more than one region at a time, performing in different regional cults. The precariousness and ephemerality is all the greater because certain peripheral villages perform a festival, and thus actualize their regional membership, erratically. In each village the people themselves understand the relativity of performance according to *current* placement within the regional cult. The alternatives in myth and masquerade depend upon whether you are at an original center of the regional cult or any of its derived centers at a periphery.

Between a center of centers and a peripheral center, there is a perpetual relationship, to use the term Audrey Richards made so familiar to Africanists. This perpetual relationship is aptly imaged to be between "mother" and "daughter." It is not a matter of their being women, of course. The terms of the perpetual relationship extend it over time (the distinct generations) and across social divisions (the circulation of women between clans, among the Umeda and Yafar, and between hamlets, among the Umeda).

Indirect exchange is involved. A third and mediating partner is implicit. This triad is the minimum for the perpetual relationship of mother-daughter: (a) mother's natal unit, (b) her marital unit, (c) her daughter's marital unit. With the expectation of sister exchange, the inclusive relation is thus: a $\longleftrightarrow$ b $\longleftrightarrow$ c, without a direct gift from (c) to (a); their relation is indirect, and mediated by (b).

I must stress the importance of the expectation of sister exchange for the paradigm of the relation. On recently having second thoughts about gift exchange, Gell has cast doubt on the cultural significance of sister exchange (1987). But here sister exchange is not an artifact of Gell's early espousal of "alliance theory." Moral value is attached to restricted exchange. This is evident in the representation of sister exchange. It is insulting to address someone as "father's sister," at least among the

Umeda. This person ought to be called "mother's brother," according to her husband's role, in recognition of the fulfillment of the return marriage in sister exchange. "Father's sister" implies a canker, the corrosion of an exchange relation by the default on return.

In this regional cult, the Umeda village is the "mother" center, the Yafar village a center of the "daughters." But this must be seen in terms of the triad. The Umeda-Yafar relationship is mediated by a third village, Punda. Via Punda, the Yafar are able to import knowledge of Ida from Umeda.

Punda is the small linking village between somewhat larger ones in a chain of villages. It cannot be the only partner for either of the others or form an actually closed connubium with either, given, among other things, its inadequate population of women and game. Punda is a *direct* partner of *Umeda's*. Among other things, Punda and Umeda coordinate their bush-village movement in Ida, speak the same language, practice sister exchange, and have hamlets in territorial partnership or bush association. At the same time, *Yafar* is also Punda's *direct* partner in sister exchange. Punda has borrowed from Yafar the countersorcery cult on which, in turn, Umeda depends (I say more about this later). Punda's placement in the relation between Umeda and Yafar makes it in a sense, I infer, "mother's brother" to both. In character with being a mother's brother, Punda is a partner that, in reciprocal exchange, mediates between nonpartners (on the importance of this for redoubled dual organization, see Werbner 1989).

Major difficulties confront us in appreciating this perpetual relationship as the triad it actually is. First, Punda has not been studied in depth; little is reported about it. Second, the difficulty seems to stem from a cultural achievement that characterizes the festival representations themselves. In each case, a third partner is implicit yet the representation appears to be dual, not triadic. Thus, each relation is reduced to direct and simple reciprocity, which is of course more evidently certain and controllable. Given these difficulties, and allowing for some distortion my method introduces, I mainly speak here of Yafar and Umeda, *as if* they were the only partners in their regional relation. (We might say that the obviation of the triad and its conversion into the appearance of a dyad is one way that the men master the actual relations between their villages and others.)

In Umeda, Ida is held to be indigenous. Yangis is exotic for Yafar. Yangis is borrowed in a way that the people themselves regard as changed, if not fundamentally, at least as befits the relationship between "mother" and "daughter."

For obvious reasons of space, I cannot say much here about the borrowing. I must keep to certain essentials about how the indigenous and the exotic versions are made to fit the image of "mother" and "daughter." These essentials are first, the appearance of the Cassowary; second, the alternation in performance; third, the importance of clowns; and fourth, the anticipated outcome of the performance.

EGOCENTRIC PERSPECTIVE AND FANTASTIC LOGIC

In creating a cosmos around themselves, villagers make their village a regional focus in relation to others. I will say more about this shortly. First, I want to say something about the egocentric perspective and the fantastic logic in their festivals. The men's masquerade in Ida and in Yangis is time for the ambiguous trickster to come out, the as-if and the might-be or the might-have-been. The masquerade is not a time for certainty, but for hope and the suspension of disbelief—in brief, for fantasy. The irresolvable contradiction is, however, that for each man the prospects depend upon women in their relations to himself and other men of different generations, different communities, to the insiders and outsiders of his mask, which, we shall see, is a *male womb*.

I find that Gillison's remarks about Gimi fantasy and phallic imagery brilliantly illuminate West Sepik rites and, indeed, some of the differences between masquerade in Ida and in Yangis to be discussed later:

> In Gimi thought, the power to create is derived from the union of sexual opposites *in a male form* [italics in the original]; the hollow penis is also a womb; menstrual blood is also semen when it emerges from a real or symbolic penis. . . . Once these opposite forces coalesce (in ritual or in the mythic past), they become an indissoluble object, which can be possessed at any moment only by one sex (i.e. by forces which are in daily life distinct). But this formulation is a precarious fantasy (Gillison 1980:170).

In West Sepik masquerade, this is recurrent: the representation in a *male* form of relations with and between females as well as males. Be it vagina, womb or breast, it is all a bit of penis in the masquerade of Yangis and Ida. And the same is true of their emissions and fluids; each belongs as semen does to the penis, semen being the food *par excellence* of the fetus in gestation as in insemination. In the endless transformations of the West Sepik trickster, the cosmos is masculinized totally. It is an "incorporation within an aggrandized male realm" (Gillison 1980: 170). Both the trickster and his cosmos seem engrossed in, to use Bronstein's illuminating phrase, "the narcissistic self-embrace."

Here the penis part is the whole, and the penis whole is the part. Hence the womb is a penis-womb, the breast a penis-breast, and so forth—all bit parts cast in a male form in all-encompassing synecdoche. Synecdoche is in my view a pervasive trope in the masquerade. It is the trope for the male gift (the penis as whole and part). As befits the masquerade of the male gift, this pervasive trope encompasses the part-to-whole relation (in imagery, head-to-penis, for example) along with the outcome-to-origin relation (in imagery, leaf-to-stalk).

There is more to the relation between the gift and the trope than that, of course. The dynamic appearance of metaphor in the masquerade is myriad.

THE DIALECTICS OF DISCOURSE: THE STORY IN RETROSPECT

This leads me to the third topic of general interest here, the dialectics of discourse, including our own. Some might think that Juillerat's project is simply another instance of a current vogue in the West: "writing about writing," Lyotard (1984 [1979]), an influential French critic of postmodernism, has captured in a neologism the somewhat narcissistic nature of the trend. It is "adlinguistics". The appearance in Juillerat's project of trendy adlinguistics is misleading, however. In my view, Juillerat's project, like Gell's report, is proof of the powerful impact of experience in New Guinea on anthropological thought. I speak, of course, as one who has never been to New Guinea.

By experience in New Guinea, I mean primarily the experience of the people of New Guinea, and only secondarily the experience the ethnographers bring to New Guinea. Recent ethnographers have come away with a sense of the importance of metamorphosis. There is an infinite regress in which experience is understood to be transforming (on recursion in ritual and the circular nature of the gift, see especially Gillison

1980, 1987; Strathern 1986a). Juillerat, like Gell before him, empathizes sensitively with the people of West Sepik, indeed, so much so that his study now turns back upon itself and, of course, back upon Gell's study from which it originated. It is as if the unfolding discourse is in the power of the trickster, that creature of endless and continual transformation who figures so largely in the masquerade of Ida and Yangis and who, for the people of West Sepik themselves, is so absorbing.

Trickster as the unconscious and primordial self plays for us all, as Paul Radin taught us in his classic on the Winnebago trickster (Radin 1948, 1956). What is archetypal is this: the Winnebago trickster, like the West Sepik one, "is basically the male principal, a kind of Priapus," able to transform himself and, like a woman, bear a child (Radin 1953:339). That the Winnebago trickster "resolved nothing" is the nub of Radin's conclusion (1953:338), as it is mine about the West Sepik trickster. Irresolvability is at once the outcome and the origin of dialectical thought, and it is dialectical thought that is constitutive of the trickster, and I hope of much of my interpretation that follows.

Before I add my own commentary, however, I want to go back over the story of our discourse. In the beginning, *perhaps,* Alfred Gell found that the Umeda had little to say about their festival of Ida. Gell tried to overcome this paucity of comment through the considerable force of his own commentary in *Metamorphosis of the Cassowaries,* his study of Ida (1975; see also 1978, 1979). In turn, Gell brought forth Juillerat and a host of exegetes, including me, with their commentaries in *Man* on order and disorder in Melanesian religion (Brunton 1980a, 1980b; Gell 1981; Johnson 1981; Jorgensen 1981b; Juillerat 1980; Werbner 1984; for an overview see Wagner 1984; see also Jedrej 1980). Most, and I exclude myself here, were Melanesianists. They could not accept that Gell had broken a Melanesian code.

Was the code Gell's own invention? Or perhaps, even more skeptically, was the very notion of a code a twist in the Western imagination? If so, the code would now be dated, the intellectual currency of the 1970s being out of fashion in the metaphor- and image-minded 1980s and 1990s. In any case, discourse was too disorderly, too uncertain and tentative, some said "inarticulate," to allow code breaking in Melanesia. "Too many imponderables," as Andrew Strathern ponders skeptically, elsewhere in this volume, on my own disclosure here of the structuring of regional discourse in West Sepik. If the "big man" was a fit, *public* subject for commentary, secrets were for keeping. To disclose them would throw everyone off balance. Perhaps this was why no one could or would give Gell any exegesis about what mattered most to them: the unspoken, perhaps unspeakable, reality.

But what was the unspoken among the Umeda seemed to be spoken, or we may well say *quoted,* among the Yafar. Juillerat told the Yafar about the Cassowary discourse in Gell's version. The Yafar countered with their own version, itself already something of a "quotation" of Ida. With the quotation came, as we might expect, interpretive comment or exegesis. The quoted had to be put in its new context. One means of converting the quoted into the contextualized and thus the appropriated was exegesis. Along with the exegesis came men expected by the people themselves to know how to transmit exegesis. Myth was told in fragments: no man would or perhaps could tell the whole story. The very idea that all fragments had to fit together into one story or one view, without contradiction and opposition, was unacceptable.

Juillerat's project is thus all the more appropriate. In our disparate commentaries, the method of dialectic prevails, as it does in comment and in myth. The projected outcome is interpretation, not absolute but relative significance.

The perspective from which a fragment was told was not revealed, at least in the account we now have. Nevertheless, Juillerat considered, in his *Man* correspondence (1980), that there was some perspective from which it could all be put together. The effort to put the whole in writing made him change his mind later. Perhaps one basis for his effort was the impression a pair of men in each hamlet was expected to give. This was that they had total possession of quotation and exegesis. It was their divine right to direct the version of events in Yangis. With the cultural competence to have their say about the unspeakable, they were themselves divine. In the three hamlets each pair incarnated the first divine couple from whom the Yafar moieties descend. No one could speak more authoritatively than these divines, or priests in Juillerat's terms. Their Yangis version of Ida was produced and directed, according to appropriate parts, by the one divine of the above and sky (the male moiety) and the other divine of the below and earth (the female moiety). The whole was beyond the capacity of any one alone to recount or to direct and produce. The original Ida, prior to its conversion by exegesis with more elaborately directed rites, lacked such divines or priests. Authorities achieve greater scope as the process of quotation develops.

A brief aside on the disputed priesthood: Gell found none in Ida, but

Juillerat claims that Ida, like Yangis, had priests; that Gell simply missed them. But Gell relies on first-hand knowledge, Juillerat on hearsay, on the opinion of outsiders in the next village, Punda. Their opinion may be an extrapolation from practice in their own village. Be that as it may, if priests had an importance in Ida anything like that in Yangis, they would be too hard to miss. Gell is the more convincing about the practice of Ida. The absence of priests in Ida seems to fit, as Gell suggests, an areal variation increasing along a north-south axis from no priesthood to highly developed ritual office.

The pair of divines in each Yafar hamlet were, like their moieties, customarily opposed. They and their followers were recurrently provoking each other in the agonistic intercourse of moieties. It may be that the three pairs competed or simply took turns to have the festival in their own hamlets. Juillerat did not manage to get any two divines or his main pair of confidants to give him exegesis in each other's presence. Inner secrets had to be told by one man from a moiety at a time, privately, even though he was aware of and even alluded to the other's confidences.

Yangis, called ritual by some other exegetes, was "labor" under the divine priests' direction. During Yangis, other men also divinized themselves, as deliberate, conscious artists, in their art of painting with its significance for the body's relief, in their music with its release of the inner earthbound self, and in their aesthetic play with all the senses.

Of course, the women, too, had labor, unmistakably creative in their bodies. But the art of the men's labor was to make the women's labor out to be mere craft, or the low art. The women's labor, from the men's perspective, was an outer envelope the high art discards. The men fancied themselves, in their aesthetically high labor, to be earthbound birds, such as cassowaries, whose birdsongs from phallic trumpets, like their phallic arrows and their actual penises, could still rise to the greatest heights. It was an escapist fantasy, but one that was *momentarily* realized in the actuality of performance. In actualizing their fantasy, the men put themselves at the very center of their universe, with the best of it around them for consumption, including the best of the women, of course. But, and in no way does this detract from the reality of the fantasy, the men also knew that the movement could not, would not last. It was with the women that the men always had to return to low labor, to being earthbound, to being themselves secluded from free intercourse. Agonistic as each kind of labor was, so, too, was the relation between the kinds of labor agonistic, *inescapably* agonistic.

In the correspondence of *Man,* Juillerat reflected on the way the agonistic labor had been brought together, despite doubt about its original narrative and its practical outcome: "The correspondence between ritual and myth was clearly established, just at the point when I had begun to doubt it" (1980:732). His doubts returned, however, perhaps because of the very communicative effort in commentary on the expression of the inexpressible, or perhaps because of the incompleteness of the correspondence.

Nevertheless, Juillerat remained convinced that there *was* correspondence and that it was between Ida and Yangis, allowing for supposedly superficial differences. Hence the study of Yangis *seemed* to enable him "scrupulously," in his words, "to list the errors in interpretation found in Gell's work," although it was not and never has been his intent to do so (1980:733). Yet it was as if his version, too, had to be one among others, each relative, none final. Irresolvability, like recursion and reflexivity, was and is inherent in the doubling and redoubling of quotation and commentary. Here Juillerat challenged us to become a part of it all once again; and I am personally most grateful to him for that.

REVIEWING MY OWN CONTRIBUTION

In a recent book (1989), I have revised the interpretation of Ida that I originally gave in *Man* (1984). The revision is accompanied by a further chapter on festival regionalism focused on central places. It traces the perpetual relationships across communities, the coordination of point-to-point relations, and the ranked spheres of exchange over access to masks, women, and land.

Reading Juillerat's manuscript and other contributions to his project has opened my eyes to what I believe I saw rather dimly, or not at all, before. It is not so much that I now consider what I wrote before wrong, given the evidence then available to me. Even then I was uneasy about the part of my analysis that dealt with certain actual sequences in masquerade. At that stage, with the available evidence, some of the analysis had to be "tentative and something of an approximation," I suggested (1984:286). Of course, the difficulty was not merely the evidence, but the limitations of both the evidence and the analytic framework. At that point, moreover, I was ignorant of the discourse across cultures between the West Sepik villagers themselves. It seemed to me that Gell was the translator and I was, in my turn, a reinterpreter.

How could I have known that the Waina and Amanab speak to and past each other, as undoubtedly do Gell and his exegetes, myself included? How could I have known that the West Sepik discourse is at least two-sided, each side contesting with the other, indeed *negating* the other's version? Why did I assume that agonistic discourse was for the likes of Gell and me, not for the Melanesians? Perhaps I ought to have seen more of ourselves in them, and not been so captivated, in my arrogance, by the difference between us.

Upon reflection, I find the strength of my earlier interpretation of masquerade to be not in the actualities of performance, but in the figurative sources for performance. A set of such figurative sources I would now call a *metaphoric series*. The conversion of the figurative sources during performance, the actual play upon primary metaphors, creates a *metaphoric sequence*. Such conversion of series into sequence is important (see also Todorov 1982 [1977]:222f.). In this chapter, I do not have the space to say much about that, but I discuss it more fully elsewhere (n.d.). For the present, I want to say that with my strength in metaphoric series and my weakness in metaphoric sequence I saw linear aspects of the masquerade perhaps too clearly. It was at the expense of dimness about a type of recursive transformation (see also Strathern 1986a, 1986b)—that is, transformation that turns back upon itself.

I did not take the view some attribute to structuralism, namely that it implies what Gillison calls "a big bang theory" (1987:171). A patent absurdity, it is structuralism without dialectics. It is, according to Gillison, the absurd "theory in which everything categorized with the 'here-now' or the self (e.g., culture and the male) is valued above everything categorized with the 'there-before' or the discarded other (e.g. nature and the female)" (1987:171). Here the inertness of *nonrelation,* which is implied, is a total denial of transformation, on which even the most mechanical structuralism must depend.

The view of *relation* that I still share—it provides the epigraph for this chapter—is the one Paz puts in dialectical terms in his brilliant essay on Lévi-Strauss and structuralism (1988 [1970]). Hence my view of the festival as a whole, including the masquerade, was not simply linear. I suggested that the festival as a whole regeneration embodies a hazardous oscillation between life and death. There is a dialectic of repeated destruction and repeated creation, man being born only to die again.

WHAT IS A CASSOWARY?

Much of our discussion turns upon an answer to the question of the Cassowary. Hence I must put my view briefly here, although it is something of an aside. Cassowaries are imaged in alternative figures, in different villages, according to a perpetual relationship of "mother" and "daughter" between the villages. If I am right, then Cassowary is an idea first, an associated image second. The image figuring the Cassowary is the variable, the idea the constant. The association in performance of idea and image creates that richness in felt experience, beyond words, which empowers masquerade. Nevertheless, at the risk of some oversimplification, I am tempted to say, in *my* words, what reference and what sense it has, as idea. Cassowary refers to the earthbound bird. Cassowary has the sense of descent, of having come down from a coconut palm (the maternal Tree of Life) and of being the origin of all who come down (offspring). This is imaged in the mythic representation of the primordial figure of the Cassowary with his legs and lower body parts emerging from a coconut above.

Following Gardner (1984), I would go further and suggest that this idea of descent is closed; it turns back upon itself. It is an idea that includes self-sufficiency in production and reproduction. The Cassowary as a bird, like the Australian Emu, "is endowed with certain essential characteristics of both men [an erectile penis, a rarity among birds] and women [a cloaca through which it defecates *and* reproduces] [and] displays the same capacity for self-sufficient and self-closing productive cycles" (Gardner 1984:141). Calling a complex representation a Cassowary associates it with powers of, to use O'Flaherty's phrase, "unilateral creation" (1980:28).

THE END OF MYTH AND RITUAL

I proceed from the hypothesis that actual experience is imaged in myth (Lienhardt 1961), as are cues or premises of actual practice (on the myth of the flutes as the Gimi organizational premise, see Gillison 1980:169). I do not agree with the view that divorces myth and ritual, as Gell does when he argues that ritual, unlike myth, "on the whole ends on a note of harmony, resolving the situation with a resounding cadence and a unanimous 'amen' " (1975:342). Neither in Ida nor in Yangis does ritual displace myth; such displacement is a *nonrelation,* contrary to the actual play of dialectics. Nor, as Gell suggests also, is it only "myths which seem to elaborate certain themes indefinitely, never reaching a full close" (1975:343). It is precisely because such transformation is continuous through origin myth and masquerade throughout Ida and Yangis that the divorce of ritual from myth is untenable. Ida without the myth is like Aida with music and no libretto, no cue for the sotto voce.

It is important that we appreciate an underlying premise about time and subjective transformation. Origin myths and origins themselves are inescapable in Yangis, for what the masquerading men seem to be reassuring themselves about is a relation between the past and a present without a future, only a past once again. In reality, despite any appearance to the contrary among women and others, the world is still the same as it ever was. Their events are the events of a perpetual relationship.

Origin myth is the cosmic scene on which the performance is enacted. Or, since origin and outcome are recursively transformational, we may also say that the performance is the proof of the cosmos as it was originally, the original cosmos being the unending outcome of the performance. The most coherent interpretation, and in my view thus the best, is the one that recognizes as many cues as possible from origin myth.

I would go further and argue that Gell's own interpretation of Ida loses more of the force of his insight into metamorphosis the less it follows the transformations in myth and the less it recognizes in both myth and ritual the same dialectic. Juillerat is right to see a limitation in Gell's account of myth, and I readily admit that it is a fault that extends to my own initial approach to Ida. But the fault is not simply a matter of exegesis; rather it is a failure to pursue far enough and systematically a fruitful direction of analysis.

That said about myth, what can we say about Ida as ritual? To be blunt, Ida is not ritual; and any of us who follow Gell in translating it as ritual risk being misleading. The same holds true for Yangis. The people of West Sepik have no ritual, at least judging by Ida and Yangis.

As Gell records, with his characteristic eye for the telling evidence, Ida is a whole of antitheses. Ida is said to be the alternatives that people undergo at opposite seasons, one at the center, the other at the periphery (on the importance of an oscillation between center and periphery among more conventionally recognized hunter-gatherers, see Lee 1976). In part, Ida is all that people undergo while they are ingathered at central hamlets, during the masquerade festival with its brief high season of indulgence in the luxuries and good things of life (see Werbner 1984, and 1989). In another sense, Ida is the alternative to which people are subjected while living in long houses or even family shelters, when they are dispersed in exile from the center. Much of the labor isolates them, primarily husbands with wives and children, at the periphery of the bush in the low season. This occurs before the festival during the many months of monotony, with the lack of sexual relief of a casual kind (the liaisons of the festival) and with only the relief of the occasional success in the hunt. In this low season, there is no villagewide visiting. Pursuit of game across territories not in partnership is banned. Also banned is any resounding across territories, except briefly after game is killed, when trumpeted ejaculations invite affines to come and share the kill. Otherwise, at this time, noise and shouting are used for carrying on hostilities between villages. In brief, Ida's low season exaggerates seclusion for men, whereas Ida's high season is for inclusion, par excellence.

In Ida we may see the notion of labor itself. The totality embraces alternatives that men and women "pass through," as it were, from 'labor' to "labor," both of which are labor. We may understand what one kind of labor is in relation to the other by knowing the prime social place of each. Inside the garden house in the periphery of the bush takes place the women's 'labor' of present birth, attended by the husband as a bystander. The husband and other men are silenced about this labor. This is their season for seclusion. Not the men, but the women are then giving up an inner part of themselves. The men's "labor" of primordial birth in the village is the rebirth from the past of immortal potency. Inside, at the center, the silenced bystanders are the women. It is at the center that men include other men, such as their mother's brothers, by sharing masks that are male wombs. At the center also is where the men are the ones giving up an inner part of themselves, their own substance in union, of course, with the substance of their sexual opposite. The manifestations of the men's gift are many. Yet the men's gift is one and the same, from the past to the present. It is the inner part and thus divine gift of themselves: semen.

To say that, of course, is to speak in the poetics of imagery. This is the imagery of the men through which they "labor" not only to masculinize the cosmos but also to divinize their masculinity: to put Priapus at the center of the universe with "Man is the penis" as their "root metaphor" (on "root metaphor," see my discussion in n.d.; and Pepper 1942:38–39, cited in Turner 1974:26).

AFFIRMATION AND NEGATION: *HOOFUK* AND *ROOFUK*

In Yangis or Ida, *as a whole,* the alternation between female 'labor' and male "labor" is a *relation,* not a nonrelation. Female 'labor' engenders affirmation, which the people themselves call *hoofuk* (*hofoy* in Ida). So, too, does male "labor" give rise to discarded negation, *roofuk* (*tofoy* in Ida), *and* the *converse.* At the Yafar village center, men during masquerade are said to be the *hoofuk.* Immediately afterward, still within the center, a second performance indigenous to Yafar and not imported from Ida makes them revert to *roofuk.* Labor for men is a play of antitheses, just as it is for women. The difference is perhaps in the striving of men to take priority over women, who are in copulation, Yafar men state, the first to lie down on the earth.

Albeit "crude," to use Juillerat's term, this statement of present priority is, for the Yafar, nevertheless fundamental, axiomatic, and certain. Hence the men's counterassertion about their own primordiality, which they fantasize and realize in performance; they "labor" to give "birth." Their masquerade proceeds through phases of copulation, insemination, gestation, and parturition. But instead of mortality, the outcome of the women's "labor" of "birth," the masculinized version is a realization of the return to origins, to beginnings and immortality. Primordialism is arrogated to themselves by men through the reversal of time in masquerade. And it is this negation of women's time par excellence, their time of *undeniable* affirmation, which I think motivates the men's masquerade as fantasy. It is as if with rising then descending flights of birdsong from phallic trumpets, with the arching flight of a penis as an arrow, that they themselves momentarily escape once more from bondage to the earth and women below, only to have to descend again. The men, who climax in the end of masquerade by releasing the potency of their penis-arrows, run for their lives, away from women. This climax is a play with life and death in which men put their life substances and, indeed, their very lives in jeopardy, for the sake of cosmic renewal.

The appearance on the surface, called *roofuk* and imaged as "skin, bark, envelope, *sterile* (my italics) debris covering the soil in cultivation" has to be "peeled off," as Yafar men put it. This transformation is essential to reveal, and thus free, the vital and hopeful inner reality, the *hoofuk.* Objectified, *hoofuk* is the "heart of all tree trunks," coconut water as white substance in the uterus (that is, penis), semen, and menstrual blood as semen.

It is during the masquerade of Yangis that, for men, the appearance (*roofuk*) is overtaken by revelation, (*hoofuk*). That is because it is then that inner reality, always a union of sexual opposites, is exposed in a male and phallic form. For example, the climax of Yangis has masquerade figures of masculine androgyny. Their urethra are smeared with menstrual blood, their penises are plumed decoratively to appear as if clothed in a woman's skirts. The *hoofuk* as revelation, while androgynous, is a coalescence of forces possessed by one sex, and it is thus masculine. A dangerous alternative, the *hoofuk* of females (or outsiders) is obviated when the masqueraders, said "to be" the *hoofuk* are revealing male insiders (on obviation in myth and ritual, see Wagner in chapter 6 and 1986a). In other words, the masquerade is the time for women and *other* outsiders not to be the *hoofuk,* which they otherwise threaten to be. The relationship between insider and outsider is agonistic; it is dangerous for each. Here the underlying image is that of the exchange relation. It is an image of the gift that has a vital, salvageable part of oneself (*hoofuk*) and a sterile, discardable part (*roofuk*).

When some become the subjects of *hoofuk* and hope, the rest become the objects of *roofuk* and despair. This is to put it transformationally, in accord with an oscillation in the year, in the life cycle, and indeed in the communal cycle of villages (such as the triadic chain of the Umeda, Yafar, Punda [on triadic chains and regional organization, see Werbner 1989]). It is a subjection of insiders to the centralizing experience of inner revelation and seductive revitalization in all its sensuousness—in sight (opening eyes in the mask), in sound (trumpets), in smell (perfume and smoke), in touch (the soothing feel of turmeric all over the body), and in taste (flesh of coconut and flesh of smoked meat, an identity of flesh—oneself). But this centralizing subjection depends on outsiders being the object of concealment and containment, being "silent, invisible, inaccessible" (Gillison 1980:170). Such outsiders are desirous but relatively deprived in all their senses, in a word: peripheralized. Total self-absorption is the exclusion of the other. Or, rather, it is to know the other only as oneself, not as other. That is, in Bronstein's phrase, "the narcissistic self-embrace."

But who is the seducer, and who the seduced? Who includes whom? Who really *is* in containment, the one in the mask or the one in the skin? We have to ask because the people themselves ask and have to ask. The best answer is the very question itself. It is the recognition of ambiguity and the significance of ambiguity. There is, as Gillison suggests for Gimi, something precarious about the fantasy being enacted. It is as if the men have to reassure themselves with hope against the fear that the very *hoofuk* of the women and other outsiders *is* the men's *roofuk*. The opposed forces seem to be locked in a ceaseless struggle with one threatening to overwhelm the other. Each gives and takes from the other, but the giving and taking between insiders and outsiders, between center and periphery is precarious. The precariousness of cross-unit sociality is in the nature of the gift.

This precariousness is remarkably evident in the center-periphery relations between hamlets in a community or region (see Werbner, 1989). The plenty of insiders preconditions the hunger of outsiders. In part, that is because it is impossible to *give* to all at once. Giving elicits the desire to be given, which is a hunger for the gift. In part also, it is because giver and receiver or taker can never truly be one and the same, if it is to be a social and not an autistic relationship. This problematic relation of the gift in center-periphery relations is expressed in the origin myth about Cassowary giving food to some villages or hamlets, then leaving them starving by going on to others. It is evident, though I cannot discuss it fully, that these virtual hunter-gatherers have an uneasiness about what guarantees the redistribution between generations, both within and between their hamlets, of their preserved and stored luxuries, smoked game and coconut. This uneasiness tied to the division of labor between the generations would seem to be connected also to a problematic relation between foraging and cropping, as well as between storage and sharing.

THE OUTCOME OF A WHOLE COSMOLOGY

In Yangis origin myth, the cosmos *is* an organic whole. Dismemberment of the whole produced its parts. The cosmos came out of the dismembered parts of that primal unity, a coconut, which became the first couple, *afwêêg* and *fenaw* sago palms. The fundamental conception is that to cut open the primal being's penis, which is its head, along with the testicles, "is to have access to the *hoofuk* and allow reproductive process to occur" (Juillerat, chapter 1). The result was an archetypal gift, with a salvageable and a discardable part, the one being fertile, alive, potent (*hoofuk*), the other being sterile, dead or ready to rot, no longer potent (*roofuk*). This first couple is epitomized and, indeed, reenacted by the two leading trumpets that blow throughout Yangis:

they are "husband" and "wife," in a phallic form of course. In an opening rite of masquerade, two men holding hands reenact the primordial
copulation of the primary couple. Of opposite moieties (thus father and
mother's brother), they are said to be, among the Umeda, *eli sabbra,*
two men, and the Cassowaries. But among the Yafar, the original beings
from which the Cassowaries *descended* are the *êri,* the first persons. The
Yafar Cassowaries came from *afwêeg* and *fenaw* sago palms, and these
are, for the Yafar, the most ancient generation, the sources or "mothers"
of the male and female moieties, respectively.

The mythic dismemberment of the cosmic source (coconut) was a
foreshortening that still left the source with a penis. The source of clones
was a penis (the coconut trunk) full of milk (the coconut flowers),
amniotic fluid (coconut water), breasts (the inverted penes as nuts hanging down), and a uterus (the nut fallen to that other womb, the earth).
In relation to the succeeding generations, the source with the maternal
maleness was "mother's brother", as was the secondary clone. The first
clone, being semen in origin, was a penis (sago tree trunk) full of semen
(raw sago). He was "father," appropriately enough given his vital fluid.
The moon (is the moon called "father's head"?), came from the primal
father's foreshortening of his penis. That is the origin, among other
things, of nocturnal semen, now pouring down also as mist and dew.
Similarly, the sun came from, and thus is the dismembered breast of, the
primal mother's brother. "The mother's brother is the breast", the Yafar
say, which, of course means, among other things, that the breast is *not*
the mother: "the mother's *brother* is the breast". The original, archetypal couple thus consisted of the same two *males,* from whom, *looking
backward,* any other individual originates to this day: mother's brother
and father.

It is my inference (the people do not put this into words) that the primal
couple were sexual opposites *in a male form* (on Gimi thought, see Gillison 1980:170). One was the paternal being (the origin of Yafa, the
Cassowary as father), produced asexually from a part (the penis) of the
maternal individual (the origin of the Cassowary as mother's brother). In
the beginning, in other words, was bisexual cloning. And bisexual cloning
is the primordial transformation to which Yangis returns.

The original cloning was followed by the cloning of clones, and so
forth, until not only genera and species emerged but the whole of the
universe, including the earth and the heavenly bodies. Thus the clone of
a coconut was one sago palm (*afwêeg*). This gave rise (the myth is about

a fathering penis emerging from the earth) to one moiety, the male, and also to Yafar itself. From its clone (the *fenaw* sago palm) in the alternate generation equivalent of the cloning source came the female moiety. According to the equivalence of alternate generations, the female moiety originates, like Umeda and other Waina villages, in both the coconut and the *fenaw* sago palm; it thus is prior to and yet comes after its alternative.

The ambiguity allows for two views about origins—and, moreover, alternative versions of the masquerade—which are mutually contradictory yet coordinated. It all depends on the point of view (be it from the center, the Umeda's perspective, or from the periphery, the Yafar's) and on whose origins are regarded by whom. I develop this point more fully later in my account of regionalism and the coordination of West Sepik festivals.

A moment's reflection upon these relations leads one to a sense of the conceptualizing of recursive transformation. The last is first, the first is second, and so forth in a closed dialectical spiral. In this the outcome anticipates the antecedent and the part encompasses the whole, as well as the converse. The totalizing is total such that the divisibility is organically indivisible. It all comes back to the same thing: the dialectical unity of duality. In the face of this evidence from West Sepik, the notion that New Guinea lacks cosmology in the sense of an organized, unitary conception of the universe must be rejected (see also Harrison 1990).[4]

At Umeda, according to Yafar origin myth, heroes, tired of alternatively being fed and hungry, first managed to kill that Cassowary who was the trickster to blame for their hunger cycle (the maternal Cassowary?). From this source of plenty at Umeda, a whole body was shared out among the region's peoples. The Umeda got the head or tongue (an image of "eat" as a primary category) and the Yafar, the genitals (both penis and vagina, of course, in the image of "copulation"). This is said to be the origin of sacred relics and thus of the masquerade festival itself. The myth also images organic unity: the villages of the region get, or have taken, the gift of one body, and they share in it according to their appropriate parts.

Here I must go back over what I have already said, before going forward to say more about the regional variation in the cult. I freely admit that I have not been able to tell the Yafar myth in the way Juillerat reports it to be told by the Yafar. For the sake of carrying forward my own discussion, I have had to tell the myth as if it were a narrative. My version imposed a beginning and an end, as if there were differences between them and as if the story was a progression from beginning to end. Not so for the reported myth: the beginning *is* the end.

Alternatively, with our own temporal or historical bias, we might say the beginning prefigures the end. In the beginning of a Yafar myth, Cassowary goes from village to village at night giving, like a maternal figure of nurture, coconuts or eggs.[5] The Cassowary's gift is first abundance and happiness, then the opposite for each village in turn within a hunger cycle. (Perhaps the idea is that food, coconuts, get overcome by fertility, egg.) The end of the myth returns to the beginning, since the outcome is the festival and the eternal return of the Cassowary. I make this digression to stress the continuity between the myth and the rites. In both, time turns back upon itself in the absence of the future. There is the past and there is the present, which turns out to be the same as the past. It is the future that is obliterated in the recurrence of the past. Or, rather, the outcome of the past is prefigured by the anticipation of the present. The importance of such anticipation and recursion will become even more evident in the second half of this chapter, when I say more about self-reference in my discussion of breast-feeding and weaning as an anticipated outcome of the performance of Yangis.

THE REGIONAL CONVERSIONS: INDIGENOUS AND EXOTIC

I now turn to a detailed review of the indigenous and exotic versions of Umeda and Yafar as "mother" and "daughter" villages within a regional cult. Tables 7.1 and 7.2 illustrate my view of the sequence of rites in Ida and in Yangis.

First, in myth and masquerade, one ur-ancestor emerges centrally and with the greatest priority. The figure as a source of being, though unmistakably masculine, is an "old woman," "a mother". The ur-ancestor for each separate village is its seminal source of vital potency, namely its Cassowary. Umeda and Yafar being separate villages, each has its own Cassowary. The former is recognized to be prior to the latter. Ida is the origin of Yangis, as "mother" is of "daughter".

The Cassowary accordingly emerges as penis earlier and more centrally in Umeda masquerade than in Yafar. Ida's ur-ancestor emerges as Cassowary at the very *beginning* and in the very *center* of the dance grounds. This Cassowary is the copulator with the unmistakably erect

Table 7.1.
Metaphoric Sequence of Ida

			Preliminary:	Birth
Variation	Act	Scene		
Copulation				
Thesis	I	i	Defloration	
Antithesis	I	ii	Ejaculation	
Gestation				
Synthesis	II	i	Multiplication	
Counterthesis	II	ii	Confinement	
Parturition				
Counterantithesis	III	i	Contraction	
Countersynthesis	III	ii	Release	

Table 7.2.
Metaphoric Sequence of Yangis

			Pre-Preliminary:	Origin of Self (Sago)
			Preliminary:	Nursing
Variation	Act	Scene		
Copulation				
Thesis	I	i	Defloration	
Antithesis	I	ii	Ejaculation	
Gestation				
Synthesis	II	i	Multiplication	
Counterthesis	II	ii	Confinement	
Parturition				
Counterantithesis	III	i	Release	
Countersynthesis	III	ii	Antimaternity (antisorcery)	

and more enlarged penis in the masquerade's opening act. The flesh of this Cassowary is overwhelmingly black in body paint, the color of preserved maturity, smoked meat.

By contrast, the gestation of Yafar's ur-ancestor as "Cassowary chick" is subsequent to the initial act of copulation. It is in the second act of Yangis. Yafar's ancestor is the red of the relatively immature, the newborn. Only with parturition, the third act of Yangis, is the Yafar ur-ancestor fully released. He emerges with the apparent *finale* at the *periphery* of the dance grounds. Of course, no enlarged penis for him: in the figure of the New Man, the Arrowhead, he comes with a mere penis-head. His is a part that is a dismemberment of the opening act's primal member. (The first creative act in myth, as in masquerade, was that gift of a penis-part, the semen for the head.) As befits the "Cassowary chick," his penis is foreshortened and not yet erect.

For the Yafar, this paltry Priapus is *the* Cassowary. He is *their* seminal source, the one who prefigures their own potency. The Yafar emphatically denied that either of the opening copulators was the Cassowary when Juillerat made that suggestion "in reference to Gell's book." As the Yafar saw it, the opening pair, whom they urged on with shouts of "long penis," were "big (old) women," "children's mothers".

In each festival Cassowary is imaged appropriately according to a perpetual relationship between "mother" and "daughter". The images differ according to the perspective. Nevertheless, the idea is the same, and in this respect the people are right when they insist that one festival is the same as another, *relatively* speaking.

Second, with respect to the alternation in the rites, after the masquerade of Yangis comes the second part of the Yafar festival. This part is culturally indigenous to the Yafar. It is for *roofuk* restoring the peripheral outside by closing down the passage from the underground. Not a directly borrowed part of Ida, it seems to Juillerat to be a separate ritual, the Gungwan festival of the Yafar. Hence he says little about it in his version of Yangis. Nevertheless, the second part belongs in our discussion of the Yafar festival as a coordinated revision of the Umeda festival. It is in the Yafar version no less a part of the whole festival than is the doubling of performance in the original Ida.

In the village, Ida alternates between antitheses, and so, too, does the Yafar version. Ida's first performance is in the "bush" hamlet, the second in the "village" hamlet, the most central hamlet "of the fathers". The movement is centripetal. In Yangis, the direction is centrifugal; it is reversed along with a change to the emphasis on above/below. In each case, however, the direction fits the placement of the center, the centripetal for the center of centers and the centrifugal for the peripheral center. The village movements are coordinated by being mutually polarized. Each gravitates toward the appropriate extreme of its own origins. Thus there is centralizing at the center of origins in Ida and peripheralizing at the most peripheral in Yangis, which also becomes a festival of Gungwan, more originally Yafar, rather than exotic or imported.

Similarly, the Yafar elaborate in their sanctuary the significance of the more peripheral palm, sago, from which they claim village descent, rather than the central palm, coconut, for Umeda. In the nonpublic rites of Yangis, the processing of sago is minutely and thoroughly enacted far beyond its importance in Ida. The prime concern in Ida is coconut. The reversal extends to the moieties, also, of course. In Yafar, the male moiety of the village "fathers" is sago, with coconut as the female moiety of the "mothers". The opposite holds in Umeda. ("Women" can thus be seen in each case as coming from the outside, from the other village.) Such centralizing at the center of the mother village and peripheralizing at the peripheral daughter village is consistent with each being a center of its own highest value.

Here I want to hazard a second guess, this time on the coordination of alternative perspectives and alternative forms of redoubled dual organization (see Werbner 1989). Umeda and Yafar are alike in having redoubled dual organization, both concentric and diametric forms. Their coordination with each other, through a third party, is tied to perceived resemblances, both having bush-village and sky-earth oppositions. The difference between Umeda and Yafar is in the valorization of oppositions, not in the oppositions themselves.

The inversion of organization from one village to the other is, I infer, a matter of *dominance*. Either the concentric or the diametric is the dominant form: more pervasive over a greater variety of cultural realms, organizing relations of production, consumption, and exchange. Elsewhere I demonstrate that the concentric form is dominant in Umeda (Werbner 1989). I infer that in Yafar the dominant form is diametric.

Among other things, the Yafar hamlet is not, as a whole, a central place for the exchange of women, but is divided by moieties, unlike the exogamous Umeda hamlet. Only the Umeda hamlet, not the Yafar, is highly stable, has its own name (rather than a topographic reference), is personified in terms of kinship or speciation, and is a focus for perpetual relationships. One Umeda hamlet is always *the* father, the center of centers, "of the village." There is no such paramount and fixed focus of concentricity among the Yafar. The three hamlets, each with its own sky and earth priests, are undifferentiated; the festival may be held at each. It follows from all this that the Yafar hamlet as center, the focus of the concentric form, cannot be the point around which the exchange of women and their alternative, masks, is organized in a center-periphery opposition.

In accord with an inversion in organizational dominance, Umeda and Yafar have dominant perspectives that are reversed. The bias in Umeda's is on village-bush, on the center-periphery opposition, on concentricity. Sky-earth, the above-below opposition, the diametrical prevails in the dominant perspective of Yafar. The Yafar have the above-below opposition under the control of their own priests and thus are able to acknowledge the centrality of Umeda, the center-periphery opposition being devalued from the Yafar perspective. And the converse is the case for the Umeda. As a consequence, the coordination of Yafar and Umeda (via Punda, of course) within the same regional cult is based upon differentiation and disparate values.

A point of some importance follows from all this. And here I would quarrel with what I understand Juillerat's position to be. It is a great mistake to base the comparative discussion on the idea of sameness, as if the Umeda and Yafar were fundamentally the same in cosmology, myth, or masquerade. These, like their organizational forms and dominant perspectives, are alternatives; they need to be appreciated in their coordinated differentiation.

Underlying much of my discussion so far is the importance of the gift and images of the gift in the West Sepik. Here I must make an assumption about the gift explicit in order to account for clowns and the third of my essential conversions from one festival to the other. The assumption is about discardability. It is not only that one gives a part of oneself in the gift, the *hoofuk,* so to speak, but also that in the gift a part of oneself is discardable, the *roofuk,* as it were. This is the assumption that underlies the relation between hero and clown, both of whom are transformers, as agents of the gift. Whereas the hero is the agent of the gift as *hoofuk,* the clown is the agent of the gift as *roofuk.*

In Ida it is the clown who gets pelted with the leftovers in a wild barrage of dirt and rubbish from women and children. This is the agent's expulsion from the center along with the discardable part of the center's gifts. In turn, a clown discards inedible fruit by the path outside the masquerade arena. From the fruit comes more fruit for discarding. The appropriate gift of a rotten ghost and totally unwanted by insiders, it is an external gift without exchange value, not worth any return. As such it is a perverse form of the mother's brother's exchangeable gift across hamlets to the center, namely the gift of a mother and, with her, nuts for the coconuts planted innermost within the festival hamlet. The clown who makes the unexchangeable gift is aptly called a "father's sister," in contrast to a "mother's brother." "Mother's brother" is the term used for the subject of reciprocal exchange, here the woman in sister exchange.

As I show in detail elsewhere (1984; 1989), Ida's clowns are the destructive antitheses of Ida's heroes. Four of the clowns are an embodiment of the primary category of experience "kill"; each is one of its destructive varieties of experience. They perform as isolates, and are asocial, individualist, wholly independent of others. In contrast, the heroes whom they interfere with perform as agonistic, and thus social, pairs, one from the male moiety, the other from the female. The Mudmen among the clowns are barbaric fathers of the periphery, perhaps up from the dead. They are covered with mud, sterile without the paint of primal life. This befits beings from the underground who invade from beyond the community, from outside the sacred center and its source of heroic life in the sanctuary's spring.

During the phase of gestation in the masquerade, once the clowns invade, they are driven off. Their interference, which is overcome, is with the reproductive dance of the heroes who are fishes bearing the spirits of individual and clan growth. The expulsion of these isolated clowns discards the barbaric and sterile fatherhood of the periphery. That is the prime danger to the center in Ida. Among the Umeda, the ones who call in sorcery from the outside are the aged. In Ida, the aged are clowns, and in clowning Ida overcomes both aging and the discardable part of the gift. With aging out of the way, parturition comes and Ida moves to the spectacular release of youth. A pair of newborn heroes shoots forth in the apparent finale. The successful gestation of Ida's masquerade in the mother village returns to the restoration of fecund motherhood.

No interference with gestation is tolerated in Yangis. Only in the mother village, where gestation is said to be "of the daughters," does clowning interference occur. But it is not clowning time when Umeda's ancestral Cassowary emerges during the opening copulation in Ida. So, too, when gestation is the time for the emergence of an ancestral Cassowary, the Yafar ancestor in Yangis, it is no time for clowning.

The reversal extends to aging and fatherhood. Rather than being clowns in Yangis, the aged take over the last moments of the apparent finale. Yangis does not end with the spectacular release of youth. Instead, the shooting of the newborn heroes is brought back to ground beyond the arena in the peripheral bush by aged men. They plant sago shoots in the peripheral bush, as fathers do. They are unmasked and unpainted, in contrast to the masked or mud-covered aged who are up from the underground in Ida. In Yangis, their fatherhood is still regenerative, if not in copulation then at least in caring for shoots. In contrast to Ida, therefore, the restoration to which Yangis returns is that of fecund fatherhood, not motherhood. Accordingly, Ida's focus, the maternal coconut, comes into the village center from the planting of the mother's brother, whereas Yangis's focus, the paternal sago, comes up in the bush from the father's planting.

But what of clowning in Yangis? It is literally a mere whiff of what it is in Ida. Yangis's one clown is said to be *suweegik*. That is the polluting vapor from the first and divine mother with the ineffable and thus, for us also, the unquotable name of B. . . . It is also the dangerous emanation from women during pregnancy and menstruation, obliterating an enveloping boundary. This vaginal evaporation and phallic release are incompatible. Hence, during the clown's escape back to the bush, racing across the village to the sound of the women's laughter, there is a silencing of the phallic trumpets from their otherwise constant blowing. In contrast to the barbaric fatherhood expelled in Ida, the gift part of the other that the daughter village expels is dangerous motherhood. Each village expels in its festival the part, in its gift relation as "mother" or "daughter," it has to discard from its alternative in mediated exchange.

Elimination of 4 clowns from Ida leaves Yangis with 12 out of Ida's 16 masqueraders. Elsewhere I have shown that each Ida clown is linked to the representation of the four primary modes of experience (Werbner 1984, 1989). In terms of these modes, the Yangis clowns represent three modes out of four, namely copulate, eat (as in gestation), and shoot (as in parturition). Missing from Yangis's masquerade is "kill," along with the Ida repeat performance. But for both of these to be lacking in the Yafar festival the Yafar version would have to be fundamentally unlike Ida. The Yafar festival would be incomplete and not a total whole with recursiveness or the endless quest for the eternal return. Worse still, from the Yafar point of view as the daughter village, the danger from the mother, indeed the danger from the very gift of Ida, would not be fully protected against. Instead, the Yafar complete their version of Ida and protect themselves from its dangers. They do so by the counteraction of "kill", which is associated with the bowels.

The Yafar perform this counteraction immediately after Yangis in the rest of the festival known as Gungwan. In Gungwan, the Yafar "shut the invisible roads leading down to the cosmic bowels, to stop the people's uncontrolled self (*sungwaag*) during sleep from escaping down to the Mother-Earth." Juillerat also tells us, although without reference to the mother-daughter relationship of the villages, that the aim of Gungwan "is to protect the society—and especially the Yangis performers' *sungwaag* [their uncontrolled self]—from any further contact with the maternal forces now dismissed" (chapter 1, "Gungwan: The Closing of the Mother-Earth"). In other words, their intent is to control the dangerous outside, the threat from maternal forces beyond the inner self and beyond the very society.

The Umeda and Yafar share the same intent, but accomplish it through alternatives, the paternal clowning of ghosts and the maternal countersorcery of divine priests. The Yafar festival is under the dominance of divine priests, who are absent from Ida. From Ida to Yangis, the priests are in, the clowns are out. But for both Yafar and Umeda the outside is the dangerous zone beyond their range of permanent alliance. They are, for each other, *potential* not actual affines (*awk*, in Umeda terms, Gell 1975:32). Their relationship is, of course, actually mediated by a third partner, Punda village, with whom both exchange wives directly.

Lest I obscure the actual mutuality along with the indirection in this relation, I must add that the borrowing is significantly not in one direction alone. The Umeda cannot remove sorcery by means of their own rites. For this they depend on rites performed by a pair of men from the village of Punda, the fellow Waina speakers who mediate between the Umeda and the Amanab-speaking Yafar. The countersorcery rites come from the Amanab, I infer from the Yafar. Even more to the point here, for the Umeda the exotic countersorcery rites are the deadly form of the vital arrowhead rite in the apparent finale of Yangis. In both forms, the deadly (sorcery) and the vital (fertility), a "mother's brother" (that is, from Punda as the village of mother's brothers) extracts an arrowhead from the one suffering the experience.

The indirectness and the mediation is all the more important because in the regional cult the one gives the indigenous and the other receives the exotic. Thus for one, the outside threat comes from acting as an originator or parent in the regional cult's gift relations. The originator, the "mother," has to combat the danger in the giving of the indigenous, of what is originally one's own, and thus turns to clowning about the paternal and the aged. Being affiliated into the regional cult brings the threat of the outside to the other, the "daughter." Here the threat, quintessentially represented by in-marrying wives, is from the receipt of the exotic. Hence the counteraction through countersorcery against maternal forces. In brief, the difference in the Umeda and the Yafar performance of their shared intent is relative to the outside, and thus to their relation to each other. It is this mutual relationship, from opposite sides, that in each festival the men are trying to master. In due course, more must be said about the method of self-reference that they use to convert and thus to master the relationship.

A similar point has to be made about my fourth and final essential for regional conversion, the anticipation of the outcome in both festivals. According to Umeda and Yafar common sense, neither birth nor weaning comes before parturition, yet one or the other does so in each festival. Ida does not actually begin with the copulating of the Cassowary. The preliminary rite of birth for the "new man" comes before that. The preliminary rite is for the neophyte about to wear his penis sheath for the first time and about to dance for the first time in the most junior of parts. Once masked and painted, he is a Fish in gestation, representing an eat experience. His birth is accomplished by making him crawl through his mother's brother's parted legs and slapping him on the behind (to make him cry like a newborn?) as he goes through. The male mother from whom the "new man" issues in this preliminary rite is unmasked and unpainted. So, too, is the "mother's brother" who, during parturition and its postliminary rite, labors for the release of the ultimate New Man.

But why this anticipation of the outcome? Why is there such a reversal in masquerade sequence of common sense series? Why does the sequence double back upon itself, with, as it were, the tail before the head? The questions must be asked. But I would myself be getting out of sequence, putting tail before head, were I to try to answer them immediately. First, I must show that the same questions have to be asked and in turn answered in relation to both Ida and Yangis.

The sequence in the masquerade dance of Ida is a rebirth. It has a preliminary act and three subsequent acts, each of which has two scenes. The preliminary one of birth, an act of delivery from labor, precedes (I) the act of copulation, with (i) defloration and (ii) ejaculation scenes, next (II) the act of gestation, with (i) multiplication and (ii) confinement in the womb, then (III) parturition with (i) womb contraction and (ii) womb release. The scenes of clowning (II,ii and III,i) interrupt and interfere with the act of gestation.

By now, it hardly needs to be said that Yangis cannot replicate Ida. The "daughter" village must have a version, appropriately its own, of what the "mother" village may be doing. Not surprisingly, the Yafar answered a question of Juillerat's by denying that they could perform the rite of issuing forth the New Man. Such birth of a male pushed ahead by male mothers was a privilege in the regional cult for the village of the "mothers" alone, not for the "daughters." Their preliminary rite must be the contrasting one for it to be suitable for them, the "daughters," as the offspring of "mothers." In the rite of "daughters" and offspring, the New Man has to take control of the giving, as befits the donor village. Hence the rite of nursing and weaning, in which the leading subject is the New Man himself, is the preliminary rite for the Yafar, though not, of course, for the Umeda.

The Yafar rite of nursing and weaning, with its milk gift of coconut flowers (the gift of game), is the one I have already described for the inauguration of hunting. The very same man acts again, later, having hidden throughout the masquerade in the sanctuary; he becomes the apparent finale's hero as New Man and new-born Arrowhead. Earlier, before the masquerade, he is the scantly decorated, unmasked man who releases then ties up the flowers, giving then withholding the milk and the game.

It can be seen, therefore, that as in Ida so, too, in Yangis: the preliminary rite preempts the outcome of the postliminary rite. All that comes after the preliminary rite, including the game for Yafar, as well as the subsequent copulation for Umeda, takes on the fantastic appearance of a flashback. For each the enactment of fantasy is such that the gift each most wants is secured in advance of the giving and from themselves. And that is the closest I can myself come to an answer to the questions I raised earlier.

My suggestion is that in doubling their festival sequences back upon themselves the Yafar and Umeda have their gift and give it. They complete a fantasy of self-containment. Within their own gift they find what they actually get from another. It is all in the past, and it all comes from their own ancestors. In oblivion and obliterated is the future, which is all that is not already of and within oneself. But is the autologic, the method of self-encompassment, the self-reference from alternative perspectives complete?

A doubt remains. The coconut is still in the Yafar image of the New Man returning to the mother's breast for the gift of milk and game. And the coconut, like the Cassowary, comes to Yafar from Umeda, from the "mothers," not from the daughter's themselves. For Yafar to begin at the coconut would be to privilege a source of life outside themselves, not the source of their own ancestor, and thus not the source of themselves.

The doubt is real, but it is not beyond the power of fantasy to overcome. A prior preliminary rite, again not one practiced by Umeda, restores the Yafar autologic from the very start, before the preliminary rite itself. In the Yafar's prior preliminary rite, their own ancestral source, sago, is first felled, according to clones in two subspecies, by each moiety simultaneously in the bush. This is appropriately at the periphery whence the Yafar ancestor came. Next comes the processing and consuming of the sago along with game by men in the village. Each moiety shares in exchange with the other. This village product is also the source of the vital sago jelly to be released in the masquerade's copulation at the village.

It might seem that this rite in meeting one doubt raises another. Do we now have a real beginning and a real end, in the sense of an initial moment that is not a doubling back of the last subsequent moment? What has happened to the obliteration of the future, and the ever-cyclical method of the flashback that I have suggested dominates both Ida and Yangis? The answer is in evidence of the finale. In the last moment of Yangis, two "sago shoots" as arrowheads are replanted, heads upward, by elders, one at the foot of a palm of each subspecies. One plant is said to be "the original coconut," or "the original coconut twig," the other "the original sago," or "sago twig." Thus, for the Yafar in Yangis, sago is last as it was first; there is neither beginning nor end, only the circulation of sago back upon itself. Since sago is the Yafar and the Yafar are sago, we may say that the movement represented in Yangis, like the fantasy it embodies, is self-circulation.

In returning to and from birth, the dance sequence resembles a classic minuet of the ABA form. I suggest, however, that we may best understand it as an instance of a closed dialectic. My view of it covers the fine detail of the highly specific transformations in imagery, including the patterned black, polychrome, red transformations. For ease of presentation, I take up the preliminary act after discussing the rest of the sequence.

First comes the binary passage from thesis (Act i, scene i) to antithesis (Act i, scene ii) to synthesis (Act ii, scene i) (see tables 7.1 and 7.2). The sequence here follows the ingression into the womb, with multiplication in synthesis. Next comes the alternative binary passage from counterthesis (Act ii, scene ii), then the counterantithesis (Act iii, scene i) to the countersynthesis (Act iii, scene ii). Here egression from the womb is performed leading to a countersynthesis. The dangers of such egression are overcome through clowning in Ida and through maternal antisorcery rites in Gungwaan. Leaving aside the preliminary act for the moment, the sequence can be seen to be a contrastive oscillation (see Werbner 1989) between opposite extremes of inner-directed and outer-directed movement.

The main acts are one inversion of time within another. The entire sequence oscillates back upon itself. In Ida the outcome of birth is preliminary to the labor of birth, and similarly in Yangis, with nursing as the preliminary to parturition, and with the origin of sago (in felling and thus death) prior to the antisorcery rite (counteracting death?). The relation between ingression and egression is within an infinite regression back to birth and origins. Recursion is endless.

LOOKING BACKWARD

Let me review my argument. First I want to briefly go over the logic underlying the festivals of Ida and Yangis. Is it the logic that we find in a wide class of New Guinea rites, namely the logic of gender relations, of the sexual production of a genderized individual? I think not. Instead, in my view, it is the logic of the asexual production of individuals for the sake of autogenesis, the logic of cloning; or the logic of "unilateral creation" (O'Flaherty 1980:28). These West Sepik festivals are not about the creation of gender, or "genderizing." Each festival recreates a whole cosmos, making each, in my terms, a "world renewal festival." To interpret the rites purely in terms of gender is to focus too narrowly on person and agency, and thus too little on community and cosmos, on the construction of regionalism. Yet each of the communities involved actually becomes a community, to a great extent by its celebration of the festival, by its performance of its own version of masquerade, by its differentiation of its own version of the cosmos around itself. Each performance recenters regionalism.

The method is simple: to create the cosmos in one's own image. In each version others are edited out as others and encompassed in terms of the self. This self-encompassment is not merely a method for editing out a gender opposite. Nor is it a conversion people make simply for the sake of dominance in gender relations. Their concern as insiders is too inclusively with outsiders for that to be the case.

The discourse of the West Sepik festivals of Ida and Yangis is dialectical yet it is not dialogue. It is a series of conflicting monologues. Each of the conflicting monologues takes its own course toward the representation of cosmic rebirth. The fulfillment in performance is tied to the social relations of a certain kind of gift exchange. In it the gift has a discardable and a salvageable part.

For the sake of cosmic regeneration and enhanced potency, the male villagers in each festival display their inner selves outwardly and grotesquely in a masquerade of masculine androgyny. The men mix together the inner and otherwise separate life fluids (semen and menstrual blood). This is for the sake of being complete in themselves and thus capable of autogenesis, of "unilateral creation." In so doing, they become Cassowaries, self-reproductive and autonomous. It is a paradox of their representation of autonomy, however, that they cannot be complete without others, men without women, insiders without outsiders, elicitors of a regional cult without the elicited. Hence in their method of representation they resort to self-encompassment. They resort to a way of creating a version of social reality in which the other is included solely on ego's terms. The other is in effect edited out as other.

If this appears to be a way of giving an individual gender or "genderising," that is because gender is but one instance, here perhaps a primary instance, of a social relationship between self and other. And what self-encompassment engenders is the very social relationship between self and other, including own community and other community.

I am myself doubtful that Juillerat's Freudian approach or any similar psychoanalytic approach emphasizing the classic oedipal situation is appropriate when it is applied to androgynous fantasies constructed with the method of self-encompassment in myth and masquerade. Relations of self and other of a quite different kind are needed for such an approach to apply (see also Gillison 1987).

Any other can be edited out through the method of self-encompassment. It is the method by which each and every other is encompassed on ego's own terms, and in terms *of* ego, not alter. I have neither the needed knowledge of myth among the Yafar and Umeda nor the appropriate opportunity to pursue this fully. Nevertheless, I am tempted to suggest that their myth, like their masquerade, proceeds through the contradictory and dialectical transformation of the logic of cloning and the method of self-encompassment. My argument is that together the myth and masquerade constitute the seemingly endless self-reference of self-reference. What emerges is the region *in* and *of* the self, encompassing the other.

It follows that every version created by self-encompassment is actually a counterversion. Each of the festivals is thus one alternative constituted in opposition to others, providing the greatest moments for men to trumpet their own horns, making the most of themselves. This is why a regional perspective advances our understanding of the self-serving nature of each representation of cosmic rebirth. We appreciate each in argument with the others against which it is proved. To say this is to open, without concluding, the interpretation of counterversions.

NEGATION AND AFFIRMATION

In the Epilogue, Juillerat quotes me as saying men " 'labor' not only to masculinize the cosmos [this cosmos so dominantly *feminine*] but also to divinize their masculinity" [my italics]. Nothing could be more appropriate for our discourse. Juillerat's brackets display the very negation [*roofuk*] of my own affirmation, *hoofuk*. . . .

NOTES

1. I am greatly indebted to Marilyn Strathern and Roy Wagner for what they have said, in conversation as well as in published and unpublished writing. Both let me read their contributions to the project before I wrote mine. They explained to me, at some length, their views on recursion in the light of their considerable experience in and of New Guinea.

2. The importance of immaterial barter subverts Gell's recent attempt to argue for a bride service economy among the Umeda instead of a gift economy (n.d.). It may well be that in his monograph Gell gave too little weight to services; that the stress on services among these *virtual* hunter-gatherers is more comparable to a basic stress among aboriginal hunter-gatherers and less like that among the pig-keeping agriculturalists of the Highlands. Nevertheless, Gell's recent argument, which depends upon the absence of all barter, seems to me misguided, for at least two reasons. First, it leads him into disregarding the institutionalization of immaterial barter. Second, and even more fundamentally wrong, is his disregard for the importance in social reproduction of ceremonial exchange during festivals *for* reproduction. After all, his subjects are, in their own eyes, "the people of the coconut." In storing, then giving away coconut in their festivals, they give away part of themselves for the sake of cosmic regeneration and, in our terms, social reproduction.

3. At any one time, and over a period of years villages are differentiated in their emphasis on pig rearing and breeding. In 1970 eight were slaughtered in a single Yafar hamlet (Juillerat 1986:212). That year no more than four were kept in the whole of Umeda (Gell 1975:17).

4. There is a link between this kind of cosmology and the organizational contradictions that arise where concentric and diametric dualism operate in tension with each other. But that is beyond the scope of the present discussion (see also, Werbner 1989).

5. The beginning of all experience in the primordial egg is reserved for an interlude otherwise free of dancing and dedicated to a cosmic inventory. It is a recital of world division, species and genera. At this time, the *abi* wildfowl dashes past, the songs are interrupted, and replaced by the trumpets.

Donald Tuzin

8 Revelation and Concealment in the Cultural Organization of Meaning: A Methodological Note

Bernard Juillerat is to be congratulated for an ethnographic analysis that is both astute and provocative. The care and thoroughness with which he describes the Yangis ritual among the Yafar are enough to defeat any critic who, like myself, begins small-mindedly by looking for factual omissions or inconsistencies. In the course of his analysis of the meaning of Yangis, however, Juillerat also pursues a methodological program that is admirably explicit in its assumptions. Because some of these assumptions are liable to arouse controversy, and because the theoretical stakes involved in such controversy are quite high, this would seem to be the aspect of Juillerat's study that most profitably invites comment and, perhaps, critical engagement.

To begin with, one must examine the appropriateness of a psychological metalanguage for an analysis utilizing only cultural variables. In his conclusions in chapter I, Juillerat proposes a distinction that calls to attention the *pons asinorum* of nearly all attempts to integrate cultural formations and psychodynamic processes, namely, that between "the original individual fantasies kept in the unconscious but permanently— out of historical time—inoculated into culture, and the actual psychological feelings of particular individuals performing the ritual." Like most anthropologists interested in these matters, Juillerat takes only the former level into account. It may be, however, that the "inoculation" metaphor, although arresting, actually confounds the distinction by implying a lasting vitality on the part of those fantasies initially injected into the bloodstream of—what? Where but from the continuing psychological inclinations and experiences of living individuals can such vitality come? Unless we are prepared to embrace the mystical notion of cultural vitalism, with its odd apprentice idea that cultures are capable of undergoing such things as oedipal traumas, we should be willing to take the stronger explanatory position and say that fantasies of the sort discussed in Juillerat's paper, insofar as they are meaningful at all, originate *and are maintained* through the mental acts of individuals.

The position just stated has practical and theoretical entailments. First, a complete account of Yangis symbolism would have to include, in addition to all that is contained in the present analysis, a treatment of the developmental circumstances giving rise to oedipal fantasies in at least some individuals (see Spiro 1982). This last phrase is important, for it is not my argument that the projective meanings embedded in ritual require affirmation by all, or even very many, of the performers. The frequency of psychological inputs required in order for these meanings to persist may be difficult to determine, especially under the usual constraints of ethnographic fieldwork; but this practical obstacle should not deter us from attempting a conceptual scheme that logically integrates culture and the psyche. Such a scheme would emphatically *not* simply assert that Culture is the Psyche writ large; for it is plain (and plainly a good thing) that many elements of personal fantasy never achieve cultural signification.

Which fantasies, then, get selected? Freud clearly believed that some personal symbols occur universally, most notably, those associated with the Oedipus complex. In a letter to his friend Wilhelm Fliess dated 15 October 1897, he wrote, "We can understand the riveting power of *Oedipus Rex.* . . . The Greek legend seizes on a compulsion which everyone recognizes because he feels its existence within himself" (quoted in Laplanche and Pontalis 1973:283). Anthropology, however, has learned that the existence of such compulsions must be verified and given substance in the cultural setting. As I had occasion to say in a similar context (Tuzin 1977:220), "When we shift from the expressive needs of individuals to the expressive needs of *populations,* we find that the 'regard for representation' becomes a . . . trenchant and delimiting criterion. Practically speaking, it would seem that a symbol's potential to become generalized correlates with the degree to which its form reflects unconscious conflicts and impulses that are comparably occurrent in the population—the latter being, itself, a psychocultural statistic supported by primary institutional arrangements." In addition, while private fantasy is arguably the prototype of all fantasy, before we can establish the conceptual relationship between it and various forms of culturally constituted fantasy, certain anthropological ideas are required.

Primary among these is the recognition that culture *organizes,* or, if you will, encodes, ideas authentic to itself, including those that interact with psychodynamic functioning. A hallmark of classical psychoanalysis is that manifest thoughts and actions express latent ideas only in a disguised form, this because normal ego functioning depends upon a balance being maintained between the simultaneous expression and concealment of primary-process materials. The whole of psychoanalytic theory and method is built on the notion that our mental products are influenced—sometimes decisively so—by thoughts we possess unawares. What, then, becomes of this arrangement when its manifest elements are transposed to the level of *cultural* products?

By implication at least, Juillerat addresses this question in the context of advocating the methodological importance of exegetical materials. Exegesis, he argues, inhabits a level intermediate between the public understanding of a performance and the deeper meanings sought for by the anthropologist or psychoanalyst. Thus, "the revelation of important exegetical material may lead us to discover the genuine signification of a ritual (myth, cosmology, etc.) and help in the elaboration of a more scientific interpretation."

Without denying the value of exegetical materials—after all, the analyst should use any materials at hand for the purpose—there are questions to be asked of Juillerat's formulation. First, it is the sad lot of some ethnographers to fall among people who are apparently devoid of exegetical insight, who exhibit an exasperating lack of curiosity or stubborn ignorance about the "meanings" of their words and deeds. Are we to say of such people that their performances are without meaning, or merely that whatever meaning they have is inaccessible by any known interpretive procedure? In rejecting both alternatives—as, I believe, we must—we are led to conclude that exegesis is essential neither to the generation of meaning nor to its scientific determination.

What, then, is the explanatory status of exegetical materials in societies, such as the Yafar, where they do exist and can be elicited? Juillerat unsympathetically cites Barth's refusal (1975:225) to admit such materials into the interpretive enterprise. In my view, and somewhat contrary to Juillerat's reading of it, Barth's objection is at once too harsh and too mild. It is too harsh because it would discredit the valid and judicious use of exegesis on the purely technical grounds that informants are liable to be adulterated by the anthropologist's ways of looking at things. It is too mild because there are more serious, nontechnical reasons for doubting that exegesis is the royal road to the Unconscious in Culture.

Consider, for a start, the kinds of persons who typically provide the ethnographer with exegetical insights. By his own account, Juillerat relied mainly on "two men [his] best friends among the Yafar," with additional information episodically provided by the two "priests" of Yangis. It is surely a natural tendency among ethnographers in the field to associate most closely with persons who are relatively well informed about the subject at hand. But there is a hazard in this that goes beyond Barth's worry that the ethnographer might be inadvertently "training" his key informants. Whether the exegetical tradition is received from the ethnographer himself or from the informant's own forebears, the analytic danger is that the insights obtained from someone with specialized knowledge may have little bearing on the way in which, say, ritual symbols are apprehended by the population at large. Indeed, it is clear that the danger increases in step with the crystallization of exegesis *as a cultural form.* Thus, a Jesuit priest may be learned on the "meaning" of the Holy Sacrament, but this is neither here nor there as regards the thoughts and associations of parishioners during the ritual Enactment. To the extent that the knowledge gap between adepts and others widens, the former might well be seen as increasingly in the service of the ego, providing historically refined, defensive functions that lead the analyst away from, rather than toward, the level of meaning sought.

The illustration of the Holy Sacrament may seem remote from the Yafar situation until it is remembered that the element of ritual *secrecy* delineates a knowledge gap that is, if anything, wider than that separating the Jesuit and his flock. If the Yafar are anything like the Ilahita Arapesh (Tuzin 1980), there is a broad spectrum of exegetical sophistication among the male cult insiders; but this variation pales to insignificance when compared with differences between the men and the (excluded) women as regards the meanings of ritual objects and performances. In Ilahita at least, under the terms of ritual secrecy, all men were potential sources of exegetical insight—and no woman was. Does this mean that the women's understandings were irrelevant to the meanings that the men invested in the cult? No and yes. On the one hand, the ritually prescribed, sometimes violent, separation of the women from cult affairs gave the men a feeling of privilege that was quite central to the delicious naughtiness, combined with a sense of lofty mission, they enjoyed during their conclaves. Without the meaningful exclusion of women, the whole point of what the men did would be lost. Thus, an adequate interpretation of ritual meaning must take account of the women's understandings, if only as characterized by fearfulness, willful deception and enforced ignorance brought about by the men.

On the other hand, the separation between cult insiders and outsiders was real, and to a great extent the meanings invested in the ritual symbols were peculiar to the men. I have used the past tense in referring to Ilahita because, in 1985–86, I returned there after an absence of 13 years, arriving 10 months after the cult secrets had been revealed to the women. Ilahita's ethnographic present had, indeed, become its past. For the first time it was possible to discuss the cult openly with the women. Somewhat to my surprise, I found them to be largely indifferent to the particulars of this institution from which they and their foremothers had for so long been excluded. They were impatient over the ritual excuses that had mandated this exclusion and wrathful at having been duped. Although some women voiced pity over the ritual ordeals and disciplines that, they now learned, the cult had imposed on the men, even they were not impressed by the claim that all this was borne of cosmological necessity. In general, the women's view was that the men's ritual understandings were at best irrelevant to their interests; at worst, inimical to them; and, in all likelihood, were fallacious.

The manifest meanings of Yangis are likewise held secret by the men, for which reason the women are all the more excluded from its *latent* significances. This accords with Juillerat's interpretation that the latter are oedipal in character, in that such fantasies appear to have a distinctly masculine bent. Indeed, it may be that the secrecy itself was and is prompted by the men's intuition that the ritual's nuclear meanings could be neither understood nor accepted by the women. This construction certainly applies to the Ilahita Arapesh case, in which the men frequently worried among themselves that the revelation of cult secrets would expose them to the women's ridicule, *because no amount of explaining would ever make them understand*. The secrets of the men's cult are not just secrets, they are *men's* secrets. If this interpretation is valid for these two societies, it would perhaps be interesting to see whether the ideology of secrecy in other Melanesian male cults is likewise traceable to oedipal or other psychodynamic complexes peculiar to men.

Before undertaking such a project, one should heed the warning, implicit in Juillerat's analysis, that flexibility is necessary in the application of Freudian concepts to a Melanesian setting—or, indeed, to any society in which close affective ties regularly extend beyond the conjugal family. Thus, among the Yafar, the "mother's brother" figures importantly into the ritual projection and resolution of oedipal anxieties. A complication exists here, however, in the need to recognize the relativity of perspective that can arise when we shift from personal to collective fantasy. With rare exception, the "I" of a dream is recognizably the dreamer himself. In cases such as the Yangis ritual performance, however, the implied vantage point is not obvious, nor is it necessarily unitary or stable. A common (and questionable) assumption by ethnographers is that the symbolic import of an initiation ceremony is to be evaluated from the point of view of those being inducted. Similarly, Juillerat casts the youthful *ifegê* as the hero in his hypothesized oedipal drama. In Ilahita, on the contrary, the perspective is explicitly taken to be that of the men conducting the ceremony. There, it is said that one's initiation is only truly complete when one has performed the role of initiator (Tuzin 1980), because the understanding acquired upon induction is confused and partial. "Years later," they say, "when you have prepared and conducted the initiation—only then do you know what it is all about." It is arguable, indeed, that the elements of reminiscence and renewed, heightened awareness are powerfully present in all initiation rites (see Crapanzano 1981). Seen as a drama mainly enacted by and for the adult actors, the issue of whether Yangis is or is not an "initiation" ritual loses most of its significance. And, if Ego is assumed to be not the *ifegê* but one or another class of adult male participants, then the entire oedipal argument would have to be scrapped or, as I will suggest below, reformulated.

Another possibility is that the perspective is decentered, that it shifts from one position to another during the ritual sequence, or occupies more than one position simultaneously. Paradoxes and figurative puns are among the tricks that ritual devises, so to speak, in order both to appeal to the greatest number in the collectivity and to disguise its meanings. One result is that a psychologically complex image such as "mother" can be split into two or more affectively specialized female representations—rather in the way the museum guide might show you the skull of Charles I displayed next to the skull of Charles I in his old age. In Ilahita ritual and mythology, such splitting can be seen in the composite representations of both Nambweapa'w, the Cassowary-Mother of all mankind, and her consort, the culture-hero Baingap (Tuzin 1980). In both cases, the split centers on the difference between these mythic figures depicted in youth and in old age. Depending on which life-stage is being momentarily highlighted, the terms of the analysis may have to be radically adjusted, in that, say, the oedipal implications of an aged mother are very different from those of a youthful mother. Compounding this with the possibility of a shifting or composite Ego perspective, one can appreciate how far Melanesia takes us from the "family romance" scenario of classical psychoanalysis.

The need to remain flexible in applying such standard psychoanalytic concepts to Melanesian settings is, of course, engendered by the fact that Freud could never have anticipated the kinds of relationships and images that exist there (Tuzin 1975). Take, for example, the "Great Mother" of Yangis ritual. This is the figure toward whom the *ifegê* is dissuaded from feeling incestuous impulses, in favor of regarding "her" as a source of nurturance. Consider, though, how this supposedly sexually desirable female is depicted: she had a single, central breast, suspended in the heavens by her mythic husband: "this phallic characteristic and the fact that her body was covered with hairs gives the Great Mother a rather terrifying aspect. The way [Juillerat's] informants talked about her showed that her image provoked reluctance and fright" (chapter 1, note 46). Following Juillerat's interpretation, we would say that the horrific features of this projection are counterphobic in origin, arising from the unacceptable nature of the impulses being felt. But if we take this description for what it is—an image of towering *phallic* threat—and consider it in terms of the fear of femininity that is widespread in Melanesian male cults, we are led to suspect that this fantasy is not oedipal in any straightforward sense but involves, rather, an imagined threat originating in the mother figure itself. This threat is, of course, a projection; but is it a projection by the *ifegê* or by the adult males who actually design and orchestrate Yangis? If, as I suspect, it is the latter, then the sexual component would be bound up with what Devereux (1980:117) has called the "Laius complex," manifest here in the men's psychically self-serving wish to convince adolescent boys that sexual contact with the Mother (and, indeed, with women in general) is a lethal, castrative prospect.

Support for this line of interpretation comes from considering, first, that Juillerat's evidence gives us no basis for supposing that oedipal (or even counter-oedipal) fantasies are alive in the minds of the *ifegê* cele-brants; second, that the symbolism of Yangis is, as earlier suggested, a production by and very likely *for* the adult men; and, third, the impliction of Juillerat's rendering of the summary significance of Yangis: "In order to understand how these cultures see society as freed from the natural realm, it is imperative to consider the two conditions for the imposition of a new society: male control over fertility, and the sublima-tion of the Oedipus complex." What, then, would be the "natural" condi-tion of these relationships? Nothing less than the domination of men by women *and* the sexual congress of mother and son. The two images together comprise a projection in which incest is instigated by the terrify-ing, predatory mother figure. Contrary to Juillerat's interpretation, then, the arrow shot heavenward at the Great Mother's breast-cum-penis, the triumphant climax of Yangis, would be an act of masculine power and assertion against a feminine threat that is, by psychodynamic reckoning, castrative. The metamessage would be that for protection and guidance in such matters the youth must commit himself to membership in the solidary male society.

This interpretation is only skeletal and suggestive, and on closer test-ing may prove to be quite wrong. My intention is merely to illustrate the need for flexibility in the application of concepts such as the "Oedipus complex" and the analytic possibilities that such flexibility can open up.

Returning, finally, to the issue of exegesis and the cultural organiza-tion of meaning, I suggest that Juillerat has omitted an important ele-ment from his tripartite methodological scheme of public, exegetical, and latent meanings. This is the level that my colleague Theodore Schwartz (personal communication) has called "cultural annotation," and it accords with the tendency for meanings to be widely distributed in the cultural repertoire of ideas. Consider, for example, the symbolic significance of "stinging insects" in Ilahita Arapesh ritual and myth. This detail crops up frequently in Arapesh texts (including dream reports) and in any given context may appear to be trivial or obscure. Its signifi-cance, however, often crucial to the interpretation of the text, is discov-ered in the realization that in *other* symbolic contexts "stinging insects" is plainly an image of coitus. This sort of indexing (or cross-referencing) activity goes on constantly in the generation of meaning, as preconscious associations are utilized unconsciously by the cultural actor in respond-ing to a given stimulus. Accordingly, to interpret such a stimulus the ethnographer must retrace the steps followed in its generation—in the first instance, by annotating its constituent details with the significances attaching to them elsewhere in the body of cultural ideas and scenarios. Exegetical remarks by informants may furnish some of these annotations, as may the direct questioning of informants; but in the nature of the case many of them will be found scattered in one's notebooks, in and among the diverse bits of information that are the fieldworker's daily bread. Viewed by some as a measure of the flaccidity of interpretive ethnography it is, on the contrary, the technique that most closely mirrors the way in which meaning is deployed in culture.

There is nothing essentially new or original about this annotating procedure: it was central to the hermeneutic methodology of Wilhelm Dilthey's *Geisteswissenschaften* (Rickman 1979) and continues to be used routinely by structuralists, symbolists, Turnerians, and other anthropologists interested in the constitution of meaning in culture. Juillerat, himself, diligently pursues this procedure in developing his interpretations of Yangis but, importantly, fails to identify it as being associated with a distinct level in his methodological framework. In view of the psychoanalytic thrust of his interpretations, this omission causes a valuable *theoretical* point to be missed: namely, that the distribution of meanings occasioning this method may be seen as a culturally constituted defense mechanism (Spiro 1965)— a device that here displaces, diffuses, and thereby disguises meaning in the service of primary-process functioning.

In these remarks, I have tried to indicate those features of Juillerat's analysis that touch on general problems of theory, method, and conceptualization in the anthropology of ritual symbols. Is it appropriate to analyze culturally constituted meanings in psychodynamic terms? Yes, I think, but only in the context of a conceptual scheme that integrates the levels of personal and public fantasy and appreciates the mutuality of psychogenesis and ethnogenesis in symbolic processes. In these terms the testimonies of native exegetes might be seen as unwitting defenses against, rather than simply as revelations of, the deeper meanings of ritual; cultural systems might be understood both as repositories of such meanings and, in the way they are organized, as structures for their concealment; and, conversely, models taken from classical psychoanalysis might be tailored to suit the exteriorization of fantasy amidst the peculiar sociocultural conditions of faraway places. These are some of the thoughts aroused by Juillerat's excellent study.

Andrew Strathern

9 Exegesis, Comparison, and Interpretation

From time to time a particular anthropological study provokes a wide range of comment. This has been true of Evans-Pritchard's classic ethnography on the Nuer people of Africa. The work of Alfred Gell and Bernard Juillerat in the West Sepik Province of Papua New Guinea is now generating a similar spate of reinterpretive comment, with the interesting variation that both of the original ethnographers are themselves making their own commentaries! This circumstance gives us a unique opportunity to assess the work of two ethnographers working in closely related areas and to see how other anthropologists set about reinterpreting what the ethnographers have written. I must indicate, however, a skeptical stance on my part with regard to the enterprise of reinterpretation, because it is not always clear to me how we are to situate the type of knowledge thereby obtained. Precisely how much is due to the imagination of the author doing the reinterpretation and how much to valid inference from the data? Problems of this sort multiply in my mind when I see the rich substantive rereadings and reformulations that commentators have produced on the ethnography. Why is it, also, that studies of ritual, in particular, tend to attract such elaborate recensions? Is it perhaps that the subjective element in interpretation finds in ritual its freest region (under the sign of the Cassowary, as Alfred Gell himself disarmingly notes)? In my own comments, I do *not* propose to undertake any such rewriting of the ethnography, but only to make remarks on general questions arising from reconsiderations of this kind. I am surprised that the commentators, on the whole, show little concern for the possible impact of the work in the West Sepik itself. They appear to see the ethnography simply as a disembodied entity with no possible relevance for the local area itself. But this is to lay anthropology open once more to charges of academic insensitivity. Having said this, I return to my academic "last."

GENERAL

This is an absorbing study, both for its ethnographic details and for the interpretations to which these lead. It is also a remarkable commentary on Alfred Gell's assertion that there was no indigenous exegesis for Ida; equally, it is a no less remarkable testimony to many of the insights that Gell applied to that ritual. The combined effect of Gell's and Juillerat's ethnography now gives us a new means of evaluating Ron Brunton's claims about order and disorder in Melanesian religions. Juillerat's present study also enables us to evaluate Gell's earlier comment that his method of elucidating the meanings of ritual sequences enables us to make comparisons with other cultures, whereas Juillerat's reliance on exegesis does not.

EXEGESIS

In an honest and thoughtful testimony at the beginning of this study Juillerat makes it quite clear how he got his information and what its status was. It was secret and dangerous, and his male informants' classic fear was that it might get back to the village where women could learn about it and thus men would lose their ritual and magical control. No wonder, then, that Gell would not gain access to this type of information, especially since he had only one field trip as against several over the years by Juillerat. Moreover, when Gell worked in Umeda in 1969–70 he was an unmarried bachelor of an age that would not have allowed him access to these secrets anyway.

Juillerat's discovery that there were two hereditary priesthoods, Master of the Sky (male moiety) and Master of the Earth (female moiety) is itself something of a revelation, but it was not, apparently, from these two priests that the major secrets were obtained. Rather, it was from two other men of the community whom he names simply A and B. (Similarly, he gives only the first letters of the names of the two original male and female deities in mythology.) It would be interesting and perhaps significant, however, to know if these two men in turn had any special role or status or were special guardians of this sacred knowledge, or if their knowledge was shared by all other men of their age. How did they themselves learn it? How will they transmit it, aside from Juillerat committing it to paper (not to the tape-recorder, which could be played back to those who should not hear it)? Why was it important to maintain the fiction that the two did not know of each other's contribution? Finally, what overall systematic differences, if any, emerged in their viewpoints on the system? Juillerat gives hints of these matters as he goes along, but it would be helpful if he could pull these references together. Finally, should there be some sort of coding for degrees of secrecy of the information? Surely, there is a danger of the book getting back to Amanab, so at least the degree to which the information in it is "classified" needs to be made plain.

The composite exegetic picture that emerges from a myriad of details that Juillerat has quarried is one of a rich and ramifying set of connections between myth and ritual practice, like a flowering jungle beneath which the ground plan of the garden can still be seen in terms of opposing dualities such as male (line)/female (line), sago tree/coconut, vital force/skin, central/peripheral, black/red, and so on. These dualities also emerged clearly in Gell's earlier account. It is their explicit underpinning and symbolic elaboration that is now revealed to us. To that extent, the artificial distance between ethnographer and informants is properly collapsed, and in writing down the meanings for his informants Juillerat becomes simply a literate "assistant" rather than a superior "observer." (This is not to downplay his role as an intelligent questioner and interpreter but simply to note how his work demystifies aspects of the relationship between the ethnographer and the people studied.)

The kind of issues that can be extracted from this account can be exemplified by reference to the famous theme of the cassowaries. Gell thought that the *eli* masks were mature "cassowaries;" incipiently "peripheral," and representing one end point of the cycle of reproduction. In this, and their general understanding of the ritual, he and Juillerat are at one. However, Juillerat says explicitly that "Yafar informants did not identify them with cassowaries." The explicit associations made are that they are the 'mothers;' or, in another mode, that they represent the original couple W . . . and B . . .; or, that they are the male and female sago palm clones. One of these dancers apparently bears a white design under the neck representing the severed breast of the mother. Although the dancers are not cassowaries, they "keep in their mouths a piece of cassowary meat given to them by the two moiety priests." These pieces of meat are later passed onto the "sago jelly" dancers who replace the *eli*. What is the significance of this?

It is another mark of Juillerat's honesty that when he comes back to the question of cassowary symbolism he admits that his information on this topic "is still confused." The *êri* or *eli* dancers were not explicitly described as cassowaries by his informants. Yet the involute series of mythological and ritual facts that he gives in this section do demonstrate an association between the cassowary and maternal feeding, and in one piece of myth an eye of the cassowary is said to have become the sun, otherwise identified in the ritual cycle with the mother's breast. Gell's guesswork that the cassowary is central to the symbolism of Ida (Yangis) is then seen to have some foundation. However, there appear to be overlapping or meshing symbols that *"overdetermine"* the symbolic system as a whole and perhaps have a reinforcing and mnemonic function. Thus the bowmen dancers[' masks] may be called "original cassowaries," but are *also* known as "sago shoot" and "coconut shoot" (= new male and female growth). Juillerat hints that the final key to this problem may be found in the creation myth. Cassowary could be "the most secret identity" in this myth.

It would in addition be interesting to survey the surrounding cultural areas for their shared or distinctive ideas regarding the cassowary (similarly for the Highlands). Sepik mythology commonly links the death of an original cassowary mother with the origin of yams: a theme Bernard Narokobi has dramatized in his play *Death of a Muruk*. The cassowary definitely takes on a maternal aspect. Gell's idea that it is male fits better with the range of associations it has in the Highlands cultures, in fact.

Of the other commentators, Werbner seems to lay his finger on a possible *reason* why there should be an exegetic discrepancy between Umeda and Yafar with regard to the *eli;* that is, that these villages explicitly differentiate themselves in terms of such varying details of mythology. Werbner adopts what he calls a regional rather than a culture area approach. He is interested to see that the two places studied by Gell and Juillerat may contain ritual discourses that *negate* each other. So if *eli* is a cassowary in Umeda, it is *not* one in Yafar. Was this negativity in fact *created* at the point when Juillerat quoted Gell's version to the Yafar people? There are too many imponderables here. Can we be sure that this difference between the two versions is a systematic, 'meant' difference? What if it should prove to be a random matter? Again, I evince skepticism, not a refutation. In general, Werbner's stress on regionalism is a productive one for New Guinea. Stephen Frankel's study of the Huli shows that there is a much wider regional network of ritual and mythology in that area than has before been supposed (Frankel 1986). We are familiar by now with the ritual centrality of Telefolip in the Telefomin area. The regional significance of the constantly diffusing Female Spirit or Goddess cult in the Western Highlands also fits into the picture here. Ritual experts for this cult specialize in minor parts of the ritual that mark them out as practitioners from others. I have wondered if there might be deliberate innovations of this kind in rituals such as Ida or Yangis.

ORDER AND DISORDER

The exegeses that Juillerat carefully obtained indicate quite clearly the richness of the ideas on which Yangis is based; their ground-plan in terms of symbolic dualities is also clear. What does this tell us about the problem of order and disorder in Melanesian religions as broached by Brunton? Two points can be made:

1. To revert to the original metaphor I have used in this context, the details of associations proliferate strongly and become entangled like jungle plants. Yet the divisions of the "garden" in which they "grow" remain clearly marked out. There is therefore an appearance of disorder and an underlying reality of order.

2. Proliferation occurs through the transmission and mixing of traditions and peoples and through the secrecy of the information so there are no opportunities for people to check up and compare their knowledge. This side of the matter (the sociology of knowledge about Yangis) is something Juillerat should take up further. For *whom* is the system "ordered"? And what does this order do?

COMPARISON AND INTERPRETATION

Juillerat moves from exegesis to interpretation through one crucial detail of the ethnography, the severing of the breast of the mother and its placement in the sky. At the end of the ritual the bowmen shoot at the sun, and thus covertly at the mother's breast, as a mark of their claim on it. To further his discussion of these facts, Juillerat adopts a specifically Freudian viewpoint. "That is what Yangis discloses: to leave the womb for the breast is envisaged as the first phallic enterprise undertaken by the child and the oblique shooting of the *ifegê*'s arrows (a symbolic erection) is its ritual realization." Following his general contrast between myth and ritual, Juillerat shows how this ritual differs from a myth in which oedipal themes are plainly displayed.

The problem that arises here is the same as with Freudian analysis in general. What kind of privilege can we give Freud's notions in the face of New Guinea mythology? How much of Freud's scheme is peculiar to his own milieu and how much can be used cross-culturally? Short of a prior demonstration of the appropriate boundaries here, only a piecemeal approach can be taken: look at each case and argue about it. It is good to see François Manenti going over the point in this empirical state of mind. He finds that oedipal themes are definitely present (indeed, we can tell this also from the famous and in Melanesia widespread myth of the ogre-killing child); but I am not sure I understand the reason he gives for why this should be so. Surely, we need in each case to look at family dynamics? That Ida/Yangis is in some way concerned with reproduction, succession, replacement, and recursion is abundantly clear, and in this context the question of whether and how the son replaces the father inevitably does arise. Whether it is necessary to look at this narrowly in terms of the Oedipus theme or not is another question.

Tuzin's extremely thoughtful reconsideration is relevant here. Picking his way with care through the minefields of Freudian scholastic theory, he comes out with the suggestion that perhaps we should be looking for a "Laius complex." I would like to endorse that from a Highlands perspective. Senior men in Hagen put out two contradictory messages to their juniors. One is that in general they should not be afraid of sexual relations: "you came out of there, so why should you be afraid to go back in," they say, making a playful confusion between mother and wife. But the other message is that they *should* be afraid because of women's menstrual powers. This idea is used to exert moral control. Young men should not "sleep around," because with a strange woman you do not know what her menstrual state is. By inculcating a fear of menstrual blood, they may be exerting an inhibiting effect on their juniors' sexuality.

The other level of interpretation that Juillerat uses is also one that may lead to more discussion. This has to do with the role of secrecy in ritual. One type of secrecy supports the creation of hierarchy; here it does not matter much what the content of the secrets is, he suggests. Another type, that found in Yangis, strives for the "elaboration of a total representation of the society within the cosmos." He goes on to say that "the most striking fact about Yangis . . . is its very low level in practical sociological implications." I wonder about this. What is meant by "sociological" here? Surely the ritual has all kinds of social and even natural implications, some of which are listed by Juillerat himself. However, his suggestion of the two types of secrecy could be extended into comparisons with Highlands cults where ritual knowledge is relatively unelaborated but hierarchies and boundaries are created, thus supporting Juillerat's generalization.

I am still puzzled here about the correlation between the two supposed types of secrecy and their sociological implications. Is it *necessary* that where ritual creates political identities meaning is absent or sparse? I should not have thought so. Juillerat goes on to argue that in Yangis also exegetic knowledge is kept secret, or "socially repressed." He adds that this is done "partly for properly sociological reasons (such as male dominance over women)", but also because "its deepest meaning is close to universal unconscious symbolization in man." Two different interpretive steps are being taken here. One is functionalist, the other is psychological: both come from the author, not directly from the data. But the first reason, I think, controverts the proposition that Juillerat has just made, because here it shows that there *is* a politics of meaning in the Yangis case. In his commentary, Gell also notes that for Umeda it is simply not true that the Ida has a low level of practical social implications. He suggests that there is a difference between Umeda and Yafar in this regard, because in Yafar Yangis is irregular whereas in Umeda Ida is normal and regular. This seems to me to be a vital difference and it may well be related to the differing degrees of exegesis in the two cases as well. All in all, I think that Juillerat's dichotomy, while interesting, requires some rethinking. It is at least a testable proposition, and there should be someone now with the creative energy to take it up and test it across a number of detailed cases within Melanesia; perhaps a project for a latter-day aficionado of the cross-cultural area files? Anyone who does so, however, will have to begin by pondering Roy Wagner's witty review of the earlier Brunton-Gell-Juillerat exchanges (Wagner 1984). It is certainly time now for a systematic reexamination of all we know about exegesis, secrecy, and nonverbal as against verbal communication in Melanesian rituals. Juillerat, from start to finish of his massive enterprise (a labor of love, if ever there was one), has stuck firmly to the idea that exegesis *is* present, and it acts as a bridge between public and possibly unconscious meanings. Other commentators, for example Tuzin, note that because the meanings given by exegesis may be highly specialized it is unlikely to give us access to the unconscious thoughts of ordinary participants. What it comes down to is that "exegesis" is a broad term and can refer to varying patterns of shared or specialized explication of knowledge. As Wagner intimates in his commentary on Barth, broken or partial exegesis may be a tool by which informants control the curiosity of anthropologists and also keep their own juniors confused. Partial exegesis leaves room on the one hand for mystery and on the other for maneuverability and innovation. I would characterize it in fact as *the* Melanesian form of communication in ritual, while recognizing that it may be possible, in ideal terms, to make the kind of dichotomy Juillerat has proposed between "thin" and "thick" ritual traditions.

Bernard Juillerat

I0 Epilogue

I do not want to abuse the privilege I have of concluding this book by imposing my personal interpretation of Ida-Yangis. Although this is, to a certain extent, inevitable, I shall try to restrict myself to a reassessment of various theoretical concepts that have been proposed by the contributors to this volume. I shall then reconsider some crucial stages in Yangis or in the mythology that, as a "subtext" (Green), sustains it. This will also give me an opportunity to report some new pieces of ethnographic material only recently uncovered.

INFORMANTS AND EXEGESIS

But first I would like to respond to a few questions formulated by some of my colleagues. Andrew Strathern and Donald Tuzin have commented on the conditions in which the Yafar esoteric material was collected, the identities of my informants, and the way knowledge is shared and transmitted. The reply to the last remark is developed in *Les Enfants du sang,* and here I can provide only slightly more precision. On a few occasions I was able to work with the two specialized "Masters" because their responsibilities prevented them from revealing the esoteric knowledge of which they were the custodians in and for the society. But, as knowledge is shared in an informal and unequal way among adult males, I was able to work with informants A and B; A was, moreover, the best possible informant among the Yafar (he was a ritual specialist but was not in charge of any inherited office). Concerning "the fiction that the two did not know of each other's contribution" (A. Strathern), this was due to their respective fear of being discovered: B by A, and A by the Master of the Sky, whom the whole community saw as a powerful man. To reply to Tuzin's (and indirectly Barth's) objection that the ethnographer "might be inadvertently 'training' his key informants," I agree that this is a risk; but I do not see how information of the kind provided during my enquiry on Yangis might, in my interlocutor's mind, be a product of my own influence. There is, nevertheless, a risk that an informant, to please the ethnographer—and this occurred a few times with B—might provide a reply in spite of his ignorance. But cross-checking of the material rapidly isolates the faulty information and shows it to resist integration into the general meaning being elaborated. Tuzin suggests that "the testimonies of native exegetes might be seen as unwitting defenses against, rather than simply revelations of, the deeper meanings of ritual." This point raises a complex problem that deserves close attention; it seems, first of all, necessary to distinguish the informant's idiosyncratic defenses that surface in the course of conversations with the anthropologist, on the one hand, and the defensive aspects of the local male ideology that are an integral part of the exegetical comments, on the other hand. A defensive process can also be found in the nonesoteric explanations provided by any young man. It should, however, be possible to unveil all defensive reactions using a psychoanalytically oriented approach. And, to the extent that they are part of what is usually called ideology, as opposed to the imaginary, it is possible that defensive images may be less imperatively subjected to secrecy.

The problem of the validity of calling on local exegesis, for a better understanding of ritual or myth, has already been extensively discussed (see *Man* 1980 and chapters 2, 7, 8, and 9 herein), but I would like to express a doubt here, not concerning the importance of interpretation through exegetical (secret) material, which, I think, has been sufficiently demonstrated in my analysis of Yangis, but concerning the word "exegesis" itself. I see now that I have used the notion in a somewhat abusive way, and that this may have been misleading. My use of the term "exegesis" does not, in fact, correspond to a cognitive category that would confine that part of the more general ethnographic material within the limits of a special methodological status. Exegesis is simply the more or less secret part of *local knowledge,* potential information that is not widely shared in the community. It is the local interpretation of ritual and myth that are, in a Ricoeurian spirit, already in themselves an interpretation of reality (Ricoeur 1969). The question of whether that kind of native commentary should or should not be taken into account is then meaningless: local exegesis belongs to the whole corpus of ethnographic material and thus must be considered with a no less critical eye than any other information. Andrew Strathern notes that "reliance on exegesis" precludes comparisons between societies. Why should that be so? Comparison has only to operate, as far as possible, on the same level, that is, on "exegetical" or "public" material.

LOSS, GIFT, AND SPLITTING

I would now like to examine a central notion in Yangis, that of "loss" (Manenti) or "gift" (M. Strathern). The *êri* discard a part of themselves (blood) into the *rawu-inaag;* the *yis* discard the *ware-inaag* (remains of sago jelly); the *ogomô*'s dance produces the *sawôg,* the *koor,* the "Termites" and finally the *ifegê.* The latter dispatch their arrow toward the sun and lose its head (the *anuwanam* shaft is headless); and the sun is the severed main part (breast) of the Great Mother (the socially salvaged part seems to be the breast; the rest of the dismembered body, that is, the discarded part/s, return to nature), and so forth.

In the Lacanian approach proposed by François Manenti, the notion of loss (Fr. *perte*) refers to what the subject experiences in the sexual relation, insofar as it designates unfulfillment, and allows him to feel intimately related to death, or that something is lacking (Fr. *manque*). The loss or lack, then, is the expression of two levels of repression (Fr. *refoulement*), one bearing on the body image, ("things representation") and the other on the signifier ("words representation"). Manenti thus distinguishes the loss related to the act of nomination by the father (entry into the symbolic), and the relation to the subject's body in its separation from the mother. The "work of the *hoofuk*" corresponds to "losses necessary to the *ifegê*'s birth." This is what I tried to show in Figure 1.1, where black personages produce colored ones as discarded substances or beings, and where the chronological list of the latter starts with virginal blood and ends with the newborn bloody totemic sons on their way toward socialization. This dual opposition is the equivalent of Marilyn Strathern's distinction between "reproductive" and "produced," in which she demonstrates that to be reproductive is to be able "to detach a part" of oneself. M. Strathern considers the sexual relationship possible because each bisexual or androgynous figure can give to and receive from the other that detachable part. Here—and this is in opposition to the Lacanian view, which considers the loss irremediable—the "loss" is transformed into a double gift, that is, an exchange. The relationship between pure loss and exchange may be established through the notion of debt: paradoxically, the subject may integrate the loss as a debt (Manenti, personal communication). Whereas the psychoanalyst sticks close to the ontogenetic unconscious experience, the anthropologist here proposes to define the loss endured by the mythico-ritual figures as a gift and to integrate this process into a more general theory of exchange and gender.

Richard Werbner, who acknowledges his debt to both Marilyn Strathern and Roy Wagner, stresses that gift supposes a salvageable and a discardable part, the first associated with the *hoofuk,* the second with the *roofuk.* I would prefer to say that the detachable part is discarded in a salvageable way by becoming transformed into a creature (*bana* fish from the virginal blood; *ifegê* from the discarded maternal blood; *bêêbi* liana from the cassowary's severed penis; metamorphoses of the dismembered Mother; and so on), or by being given to or incorporated into the other (exchange of *hoofuk* by the *êri* at the opening of the festival, shooting of the *ifegê*'s arrows at the celestial breast, and so on). Both *hoofuk* and *roofuk* can be discarded, but they will then transmit their respective particular properties (see chapter 1, note 47). The point is that the opposition seems to be between a discarded part, which is the object of a transformation into some natural species, and the owner, who proceeds toward sexuation and individuation and thus is propelled toward a more socialized, and also a more sterile, destiny. The separated part is the object of a metamorphosis, on the side of nature, while the subject thus deprived of that fertile and regressive part of himself will have to fight for his saving integration into the social world.

What is described here is a splitting of the self between two tendencies: the one regresses toward the imaginary, the maternal, unrestricted gratification or narcissismus; the other progresses toward the "reality principle" (Freud 1966 [1920]), the restraining social law (Ricoeur 1965), and the object relationship. The Yafar mythical hero succeeds in discarding his regressive self and proceeds toward society. In this sense, Yangis or some Yafar myths are actually, as André Green rightly suggests, a "recapitulation" of the ontogenetic experience.

However, some myths may place the emphasis on the personage incarnating the released part and ignore the destiny of the one who is supposed to become the social subject. The myth of the *abi* wildfowl is a case in point: both the younger brother and the younger sister, in disobeying the elder brother's "paternal" law, become the discarded parts of the respective pairs of siblings. They are thus subjected to a powerful transformation leading to the birth of the *ogomô* (male principle at work in pregnancy and growth), while their elder siblings proceed slowly (without any apparent transformation) within the narrow limits and under the infertile constraint of the social rule. Death, insofar as it is a corollary of maternal incest, is thus, as Green writes, reintegrated into the life forces, but exclusively on the natural, nonsocialized side. As I try to demonstrate in more detail elsewhere (1991a), Yafar myths are the expression of an ideology of the subject, who is described as building up his sociality by separating himself successively from his "discarded parts" or regressive instincts. The pair of siblings represents (and this is another emphasis Melanesian cultures put on the same-sex relation; see chapter 5) duplicity of the self; and only the subject relieved of his (sometimes her) negative double (younger or elder sibling of the same sex) can become the (unique) hero. As a male Ego, he is then the representative of society. This "image in transformation" (as Wagner would say) of a splitting Ego may be superimposed on the oedipal scheme (the two brothers in the myth of the *abi* wildfowl being related as father and son), or it can be juxtaposed to it, as in the myth of the three oedipal sons, where the group of brothers opposed to their fathers is divided into the three incestuous sons and their youngest brother, who alone will achieve his social destiny.

I see, in the personal trajectory of the Yafar mythical heroes—and of the *ifegê* in Yangis—the mirrored image of all human individuals in their own experience. This is perhaps what Alfred Gell felt so obscurely to be convincing when he himself was working "under the sign of the cassowary": the impression of being in the presence of "the uncanny" (Freud's *Unheimliche*), of slowly identifying, through the decoding of symbols, with something already known and experienced, but forgotten. This presumption of universality concerns only the very basic, "primordial" (Green's term) mental image inscribed at the core of the Yafar culture; it does not preclude the properly Melanesian, or Yafar, formulations concerning gender, gestation, or filiation. Gell identified with the cassowary as the male symbol of autonomy; below we shall see how new ethnographic evidence brings us to understand that to be "under the sign of the cassowary" means primarily to be under the sign of the (both phallic and feeding) Mother.[1]

CASTRATION AND PHALLIC REGENERATION

In the present collection of essays, the idea of loss also calls up the idea of castration. Manenti gives the Great Mother's unique breast the status of an "imaginary phallus" (Lacan). For Green, castration is only discreetly mentioned during Yangis and always concerns both sexes (in the *rawsu-inaag* mythology, for instance); it never takes the form of a sanction operated by a jealous father: castration is "annulled in its dimension as amputation." Green relates castration to the loss of the *roofuk,* and thus to the notion of a discarded part, as discussed above. The presence of a phallus in the Mother's body and the loss of a part of the male organ in different personages could be regarded as an effort to cancel out sexual differentiation, but it appears closer to a (male) desire to masculinize female gestation and nurturance; as Werbner nicely puts it in chapter 7, "men 'labor' not only to masculinize the cosmos [I would add: this so dominantly feminine cosmos] but also to divinize their masculinity." In 1986, during my most recent stay in Yafar, informant A talked to me about a tiny intrauterine breast that feeds the fetus (perhaps a metaphor empirically inspired by the possum's nipples concealed within the marsupial pouch). This is not *the* second breast, of course, but an internal version of the unique (male?) breast, and is perhaps an alternative to the Umeda theory (unknown in Yafar) of the fetus being fed by the father's semen (Gell 1975). To the external phallic breast corresponds the internal feeding phallus. The two breasts are thus endowed with a double and successive function, and the "search for the breast" by the *ifegê* may be seen also as the result of a first weaning coinciding with birth. After her dismemberment, the Mother is metonymically divinized into a phallic celestial breast—an "all-encompassing synecdoche" (Werbner, chapter 7)—whereas the rest of her body (apart from a couple of stars; see chapter 1, note 47) is definitively attached to a terrestrial destiny. I shall add to my comments in chapter 1 that the recurrent Yafar theme of the separation from the mother is expressed twice, first in the dismemberment of the Mother's body performed by the "father," second in the search for the breast and the shooting conducted by the "mother's brother" (MB).

On the male side, the phallus does not have to be fantasized, but it can be adorned and enhanced, as during the *ifegê*'s sequence. This is actually the main theme of the totemic sons' ritual behavior: the emergence of the phallus from the maternal blood. Marilyn Strathern sees, in the father's intervention on his sons' weak and bloody penes, the reiterated conditions of conception: the bandaged penis is a fetus. This interpretation does not contradict the explanation that calls upon the necessity of the father's action to strengthen the virility of a male infant born of female blood. The symbol of the "bloody sago shoot" is thus certainly not a sign of castration, in the usual sense, but appears as an original and natural stigmate of the phallus born out of the womb, that is, phallic regeneration. Castration—in a Yafar reformulation—could be identified in the image of the *anuwanam*'s (MB) headless arrow, but it appears to be more specifically the castration of the regenerating phallus, the loss of its growing head. On this point, I would concur with M. Strathern and Werbner and say that the *anuwanam* lost his arrowhead (as a detachable part of his penis) when, as an *ifegê* or neophyte, he shot his then complete arrow at the sun, in a previous festival (remember that the same man must perform the two parts successively). The arrowhead may then be seen as the sign of the growing phallus (sago shoot, *ifegê*'s penis, or child), the headless shaft being the grown-up phallus endowed with that unspecified new "experience" (actually sexual and reproductive) attached to the *anuwanam*. In this context, arrowheads are the sign of growth in the making. Here again Marilyn Strathern's interpretation sheds a subtle light on the commonly accepted opposition "not yet reproductive/reproductive" by transforming it into "reproductive/no longer reproductive." In this case, however, I would persist in seeing the loss of the arrowhead as the result of the inaugural introduction to reproductivity. Achieved reproductivity is ensured by that which has grown up, not by that which is still growing. Let us recall that, in the *rawsu-inaag* sequence, reproduction is accompanied by the loss of the hymen *and* by the loss of a small skin of the male figure's penis (see Green, chapter 3). I understand these images of apparent castration as meaning achieved sexuality. The cultural hero Wefroog shortens his penis when he finds the nice melon-woman who will become his wife;

however, the male Cassowary father is also said to shorten his penis *after* the Great Mother's death. The action of making the right size or shortening implies self-control over sexuality, in the first instance, renunciation of sexuality in the second. The remote time of long penes and long clitorises was the age of unsocialized reproductivity. Wefroog submits himself to self-control and performs on his own body a "socialization of sexuality"; the father Cassowary displaces his lost phallus into nature to become the celestial liana linking the East to the West. As the representatives of the potent father (chapters 3 and 5), but of the "potent society" as well, the *ifegê* have also to undergo restraint by losing their arrowheads at the very moment they realize, "for the first time," their reproductive potency.

BREAST, PHALLUS, AND MOTHER'S BROTHER

The meaning to be given to the heavenly breast as a target, within the context of the dismemberment of the Great Mother's body or in relation to the implicit opposition between father and mother's brother, and to the identification between mother's brother and mother has also been discussed by most of the contributors. Green (chapter 3) suggests that, at this stage of the mythico-ritual chronology, the breast is no longer the feeding organ, but the mother's very body, which is to be penetrated and filled; he adds that the distance and the father's mediation (he has placed the severed breast in the sky) allows the bowmen to dare shoot at the mother; the breast thus becomes an authorized part of the mother to be penetrated, accompanied, however (I would add), by the ambivalent feelings of incest and guilt, which explains the terrified attitude of the *ifegê* once their arrow has been dispatched. The breast would then be the transitional object, no longer the mother's womb, but not yet the "other woman." In accepting the importance of a polysemy of meaning in Yangis (chapter 3) and of a polysemy of roles in the family romance (chapter 8), one is led to integrate Wagner's proposition to see the shooting at the sun "as the penetration of the birth orifice from within by the neonates" (chapter 6); we remember that the exegetical comment states that the arrows are tearing open the totemic coconut fiber. The *ifegê*'s arrows could then be seen as being shot toward the breast from within the womb.

The association of the mother's brother with the breast, specified in the Yafar maxim and in the title of my essay, has been the object of various interpretations. Relative uncertainty persists as to whether it should be understood that the mother's brother (and consequently *not* the mother; Werbner, chapter 7) *is* the breast; or that the mother's brother is only the keeper or representative of the mother's breast (my own view); or again, that he is that, but appears also as a "male mother" as well as a "nonmother" (Green, chapter 3); or even whether the Yafar saying means that the mother's brother *has* the (mother's) breast as his own detachable female part (M. Strathern, chapter 5). The latter interpretation is the exact symmetrical opposite of Manenti's view, which states that the unique breast is an imaginary male part of the mother with which the mother's brother can thus be identified (chapter 4). Let me add that the literal translation of the Yafar maxim, *nonoog ba tot ogwa* is "Mother's brother / then / breast / stands." The word *ogwa* or *ogo* belongs to the triad *ogo* (to stand), *aga* (to sit), *igi* (to lie). Here *ogo* should be translated simply by "is," but it could also advantageously be understood as "stands for." Now the sentence is not specifically formulated in the Yangis context, but is usually given as moral advice to the sister's son (ZS), who must pay back his uncle for his mother's milk. Second, it must be made clear that, in Yangis mythology, the sun-breast is never presented as *being* the mother's brother, or the *anuwanam* as *being* the breast. The MB/ZS pair remains on earth and looks-shoots at the sun-(Mother's) breast in the sky. They are linked in the differentiated attitude already described (neophyte/initiated) with respect to a distant object.

I would add here that the mother's brother knows where the breast is, not only because, as an *ifegê*, he was introduced to it in a previous ritual, but too because he *is* also the father who has placed the breast in heaven. Before the dismemberment of the maternal body, father and mother's brother (husband and brother) may have been a single person. The *ifegê*'s birth and the separation of the breast from the rest of the Mother's body would then call for the parallel separation of the mother's brother from the father. As Green puts it, "no less than two men are needed in order to 'frame' the mother/child relationship" (chapter 3). And Manenti adds that it is the dismemberment and the nomination that actually promote the passage to language and to the symbolic level; the socialized father, that is, the mother's brother, is substituted for the imaginary father of the primal scene. In a more complex and perhaps somewhat enigmatic way, Marilyn Strathern says that the father produces a sister's son for his wife's brother, and that the mother's brother thus disappears ("becomes a corpse") while transforming his sister's son into a father.

THE FATHER

The concomitant point of the absence of the father during the ritual finale has also been discussed by some of the contributors. The father's absence corresponds symmetrically, one may notice, to the mother's brother's absence before the bowmen's birth, which seems to confirm that both men cannot be present simultaneously because they are one and the same person whose two complementary facets exclude each other. During my 1986 stay in Yafar, informant A often referred to the Mother-Earth and to the necessity of closing its underground roads by the Gungwan ritual. It appeared in his comments that this not only prevented the sleeper's *sungwaag* from going down and becoming "ripe," but also stopped the possible reemergence of the *awarehak,* the "rotten father," castrator and cannibal, now definitively incorporated, but mobile, in the Great Mother's body (Juillerat 1986:379). This "barbaric father" could actually be allowed to appear in Ida in the shape of the Mudmen clowns, as Werbner has probably rightly guessed. This is one of the negative products of the Mother. But, as paternal duality is here in conformity with the image of the splitting of the self into a regressive and a progressive Ego, the question is where is the "fecund father"?—"He has disappeared, we don't know, he didn't say where he was, he is hiding," were among the first replies from informant A to my question (about "the father," without mention of the opposition bad/fecund). But later, when we were both alone with no indiscreet ears around, I learned that the primordial father was just a bundle of bones irrevocably concealed within the Mother's terrestrial body, which envelops it completely and forever. That is where he is hiding, as a dry indestructible and sterile debris at the center of a huge, fertile, and fleshy female body. Yafar cosmology also supposes an idealized and potent father-in-heaven, rooted in perpetual copulation with the Earth. In both cases, dead or castrator in the underworld, or virile in the sky, the father as genitor is kept outside society; within society he is replaced by the mother's brother, the first socialized personage in Yangis. We understand here that "bad father" and "fecund father" are not opposites, but that they are the same presocial entity. The fecund or

individuals are actually initiated (remember, however, the *nemetod,* "new man," who is the only "real" novice in the Ida performance), but that the idea of "initiation" is enacted in the transformation of the *ifegê* into an *anuwanam* through the use of the same actor for both parts. Both parts are, in fact, two successive states of the same personage before and after the transformation represented by the shooting of the arrow: the *ifegê* shoots his arrow and rushes out of the arena to reappear, in the next festival finale, personified in the *anuwanam*-mother's brother, while a new pair of bloody totemic sons has just been produced. The shooting has transformed the son still covered in his mother's blood into a socialized adult. I acknowledge that, during my field inquiries, the problem of the individual (the performer's) experience was not sufficiently tested, and I ignore whether the Yafar or Umeda who have performed the preceptor's (mother's brother's) part would speak like the Ilahita who have "performed the role of initiator" (Tuzin, chapter 8).

A REGIONAL CULTURAL SYSTEM?

Now, let us turn to the crucial question of "regionalism." First, I agree wholeheartedly with Werbner that we must look to the regional level for elements of a cultural system. But I would note that the idea of "regional cultural system" must be distinguished from that of the borrowing process (for the Southern Border Mountains, see Huber 1990). And I would also heed Andrew Strathern's warning about the significance of differences. The absence in one village of a feature present in another does not necessarily mean that this lack is meaningful and that the difference is the reflection of a system. And, of course, the absence of a feature in an anthropologist's work is no proof that it is really lacking in the culture. For instance, ritual responsibilities ("priests") do exist in Umeda and Punda, as well as in Yafar (from Yafar and Punda informants); they seem to be an integral part of the Ida-Yangis cult, and I have never heard that the other Amanab groups or the Anggor and Abau to the south had similar religious offices. On this point, Werbner states that Gell could not have "missed" the existence of such priests in Umeda and suspects me of knowingly pointing out my colleague's inability to discover that institution. Gell knows perfectly well that I had no such intention. I can only reply to Werbner that I myself "missed" the existence of ritual inheritance statuses in Yafar during my first four periods of fieldwork (1970–78), and that I learned about it only in 1981—even if I had vaguely *guessed,* in 1976, that a pair of men were responsible for each moiety during the performance—*because* informant A spontaneously *decided* to present me with this "gift" (see Juillerat 1986:102). Such a secret institution is not "too hard to miss," as Werbner thinks, but it is impossible to discover without the people's help. Thus, before construing a regional model on the existence/nonexistence of priests in Yafar and Umeda, respectively, let us have the patience to wait until an observer checks the situation in Umeda; this is also valid for Werbner's supposition that Umeda men do not perform the "coconut ritual" to open the hunting season. Such questions can be answered only by facts.

The problem of the cassowary looks much more pertinent for a regional approach. First, the systematic identification of the *eli* with cassowaries, mentioned by Gell, and the fact that the *eli* sequence is the most important moment of the Umeda festival appear quite significant when compared with the fact that the Yafar do not associate their *êri* with cassowaries (or prefer to keep such an association a secret), and seem to consider the *ifegê* the most sacred personages and their appearance the most crucial moment (even if the *êri*'s dance is also treated with great respect). In 1986, two men from Sowanda (Umeda's western neighbors) told me, with relative facility, that the mythological primordial Mother was a cassowary (appearing in Ida), that her male companion was the *afur* (Yafar *afwêêg*) sago palm, and their daughter the coconut. Such cosmogonic differences between groups could explain why the Yafar identify the Great Mother primarily with the coconut and do not associate *êri* and cassowaries. But one may guess here that the coconut is to the cassowary as the Yafar are to the Umeda; that is, they share a daughter-mother relationship (see also Werbner, chapter 7). This could be a part of the system; as "daughter" group, the Yafar (but this should also hold true for the Punda and Sowanda) should not be related directly to the Cassowary, but only to its "daughter." However, we have seen that the Yafar exegesis presents the traveling cassowary in a nurturing role. As Gell implies, this story, like its cassowary, has probably also traveled from north to south, starting with the Waris (Walsa) groups.

For a better regional understanding, Gell points to the need for information concerning the Waris communities of the Wasengla Valley, to the north of the Waina speakers. Recently I was able to obtain some scanty but quite significant material about this group (same linguistic family as the Waina and Amanab) from Florence Vidal, a graduate student of

Nanterre University (Paris X), who did fieldwork there in 1984–85. The Waris have different rituals using Cassowary figures, the most prominent being the *xwemda wevti* (a rough translation would be: "big-cassowary/ritual"), in which, following several Cassowaries, an ultimate personage shoots an arrow (probably at the sun).[2] Another tiny language group, the Simog (East of the Walsa) are said to have had their own ritual that they, too, called *Yangis;* however it has not been performed for the last generation.

One of Vidal's Waris informants made a surprising comment about the natural cassowary: it is said to suckle its chicks with its wattle (what I would call a "pseudo-belief"). This would be a good reason for the cassowary "not to be a bird" (Bulmer 1967), but also for that bird (Yafar and Umeda classify it as a bird) to be dominantly female, because males also have wattles. The Mianmin of the Upper Sepik actually assert that male cassowaries simply do not exist (Gardner 1984). The association cassowary-mother does not end here, however; and a further identification can be established with the *êri* [*eli*], the "mothers" of the first night of Ida-Yangis: ornithologists state that double-wattled cassowaries (*Casuarius casuarius* L.) have been observed only in southern New Guinea, whereas northern New Guinea, "West of Astrolabe Bay," is inhabited by *Casuarius unappendiculatus* Blyth (plate 17), a single-wattled cassowary (Rand and Gilliard 1967). The Yafar *uneg tot,* the unique "breast of the neck" of the Great Mother, reproduced on the *Angwaneri êri* performer's body by a white triangle, would thus be inspired by the real bird's "single club-shaped wattle on the fore neck" (Rand and Gilliard 1967: 24), the lower tip of which hangs loose like a nipple or a penis (Rand and Gilliard 1967: ill. 1, p. 246). The *eli* are in fact cassowaries, as Gell has reconfirmed in this book, and Yafar *êri* "should be" as well. The opposition shown in Table 10.1 can be interpreted as a small piece of one possible regional system, unless it constitutes merely different fragments of a more homogeneous regional view.

This modest discovery could give a new impetus to the argument concerning the origin of the unique central-breast image, and some readers will perhaps see in this empirical evidence a good reason for discarding the psychoanalytic explanation. I tend to think that a mental representation, in order to become materialized in ritual, must be imaged empirically in a concrete fact. Nature then provides a botanical or animal species with a convenient attribute. There is no more reason to consider that the central-breast image is due only to the existence in the

Plate 17. *Casuarius unappendiculatus* (Blyth). "Single-wattled cassowary:
Height about 5ft. Adults: plumage black; casque high and triangular, flattened on the back; a single club-shaped wattle on the fore neck; small wattles
near the corners of the gape; colour of bare skin of head and neck mostly
blue, with some red and yellow" (Rand and Gilliard 1967). (Copyright ©
Bibliothèque Centrale du Muséum National d'Histoire Naturelle, Paris)

Table 10.1.
Some Elements for a Regional Comparison

Umeda "mother"	*Eli* = cassowaries (more sacred than *ipele*) Mythical mother = ? cassowary	*Ipele* ≠ (?) sago shoots
(Sowanda	Mythical mother = cassowary Mythical daughter = coconut)	
(Waris	Real cassowaries suckle chicks)	
Yafar "daughter"	*Eri* ≠ cassowaries = mothers Mythical mother = coconut	*Ifegê* = red sago shoots (more sacred than *êri*)

area of single-wattled cassowaries, than to see in the red color of the sago shoot the explanation for the invention in Yangis of bloody male infants (*ifegê*), or in the morphology of the coconut (palms growing out of the coconut fiber) the origin of the emphasis that these cultures put on the idea of phallic regeneration, of maleness freeing itself from femaleness. I would even suggest that, on the contrary, the Waris "belief" that female cassowaries feed their chicks at the breast is a consequence of a more archaic mental image that found its apparent confirmation in nature and consequently could be expressed in ritual. The existence of the single-wattled cassowary can explain the ritual formulation of the idea of a single breast only, not the fantasy itself. Or better: the existence, in reality, of that cassowary's attribute has made possible the passage of the unconscious idea of single breast into the conscious; in the same way, the fact that sago shoots are all red made possible the association of sago palms with totemic sons born of their mother's blood. This could explain why the very reality of such peculiarities in natural species are kept secret and revealed only through exegesis.

CULTURE AND SOCIETY

These concluding pages have not elucidated all the ethnographic uncertainties, nor have they answered all the theoretical questions raised by the discussion. But the whole of the present book, to use Andrew Strathern's metaphor, has cleared much of the disorder produced by the multitude of "jungle plants" and has covered it by different superposed orders. They are more complementary to than exclusive of each other. The order imposed by the oedipal representations (Juillerat, Green) or that based on the opposition between imaginary and symbolic (Manenti) remains close to more universal mental images, whereas the proposition of a "mother's brother's child" syndrome (M.Strathern) as well as the brilliant formal elaboration of image transformations, or obviation (Wagner), introduce the reader deeper into the Melanesian world. Werbner worked more on the ethnographic material provided by Gell and myself, with the aim of revealing new differential meanings, while Tuzin and Andrew Strathern raised important methodological questions, to which I could give only very brief replies.

Alfred Gell again stressed his faith in what he calls his "sociological" approach, as opposed to my "intellectualist-cum-psychoanalyst considerations." Our divergence is, in my view, partly due to a lack of methodological distinction between three levels of interpretation: social integration, cultural meaning, and individual experience. These domains are, of course, not independent from each other and do overlap on many points. The difference between our sociological views of Ida-Yangis stems, as Gell has emphasized, from the fact that Ida is (or at least was when my colleague was in the field) completely integrated into the seasonal cycle (see also Werbner), whereas the Yafar Yangis is quite an exceptional and isolated event. This difference can also explain the degree of sacredness and secrecy attributed to the cult by the two respective societies.

Now, before proceeding to further considerations on the "sociology" of the festival, and defining ritual, as Gell does, as an inversion of mundane social life or as "a series of denials of normative expectations" (chapter 2), it would first be useful to establish clearly whether we are speaking of ritual as simply a break in the continuity of daily life, or whether we are considering the ritual contents as a language endowed with a special message (clear or confused, known by many or only a few) to deliver (or to keep secret). In the first case, we are still dealing with sociology, and I agree with Gell on this point; but in the second case, we are dealing with cultural meaning. Now, as I have tried to explain in my essay, that meaning concerns procreation and fertility, but it also enacts a sociogenesis, in the sense that Ida-Yangis, as a totemic festival, tells something about the emergence of the "original man" (*ifegê* ‹*ifêêg êri*) out of nature. Curiously, no contributor has commented on the literal sense of *ifegê* [*ipele*] as "first man" or "original person": Ida-Yangis is ritual theater that deals with the appearance of humanity; and what does Man come out of if not nature? But this is not true sociology; it is rather a cultural fantasy on the idealized ontogenetic conditions for the promotion of Society, an ethnosociology. This "individual" process is a cultural image and has nothing to do with the individual experience in ritual. The Ida performer is not a puppet (Gell), but if he does not know the deep meaning of his role, he is a little— to use Werbner's metaphor—like an opera singer who does not understand a word of the libretto, but fully enjoys the music and the staging. That is what young men are doing when they perform a "Fish" role, for instance, while older men and priests try to dissimulate the anguish that is inherent in their ritual responsibilities. Nonetheless, Gell's interest (see also Tuzin, chapter 8) in the intrapsychic feelings of ritual participants is not only legitimate, it became a field of psychosociological anthropology only recently (Herdt and Stoller 1989; Poole 1982) and, as I have already confessed, completely neglected in my own research. I have, however, the impression that Gell has confused cultural meaning (here religious symbols) and individual experience; the first may influence the second (a learned man or priest playing the *êri* or *ifegê* part does not have the same feelings as a youngster beneath a *rawsu-inaag* mask), but I do not think the reverse holds true. For instance, the oedipal model in Yangis belongs to culture and does not correspond to any particular incestuous desire (in the full sense of the word) on the part of the performers or in the community at large (see also Paul 1987), but only to the cultural expression of a nostalgia for the lost mother. The cultural meaning, in this respect, is the result of a transformation, in nonindividualized cultural terms, of a general ontogenetic inner experience not actually present in any individual consciousness. Even if I do not follow Robert Paul (1987) in his rather extreme interpretation of Freud on the primacy of cultural fantasies over the individual psyche, I think one cannot simply state, as Tuzin seems to do, that only individuals can perpetuate such fantasies through their idiosyncratic patterns. I have, however, no new theory to propose for the complex problem of the relation between culture and personality, and I

can only suggest that the three approaches exposed above are all necessary to give ritual its full significance and should be envisaged as an
"enacted regulation" (Wagner 1984) of meanings.

NOTES

1. In *Metamorphosis of the Cassowaries,* Gell notes that the designation "of the mothers" is applied to the Cassowary *dancers,* but that the
cassowary itself remains "emphatically male—but . . . belongs to the
mothers more or less as an emblem" (1975:226). I have the intuition that
Gell is describing, in this ambiguous comment, the Umeda image of the
phallic mother. Numerous Papua New Guinea cultures mention a mythical cassowary ancestress, sometimes with androgynous characteristics:
see, for instance, Tuzin (1980), Herdt (1981), Poole (1982), Gardner
(1984), and Tuzin and A. Strathern in this book. Herdt makes some interesting comments on the image of the cassowary among the Sambia, defining the bird as "a masculinized female," "fundamentally 'female,' " and
"identical to women"; the descriptive names for the two subspecies he
distinguished contain a segment meaning "female breast" (Herdt 1981:
chap. 5).

2. The first personage of the *xwemda wevti* ritual would seem to be a
Cassowary figure called *okumbe xwemda,* Sun Cassowary. However, the
Waris do not spontaneously compare their festival with the Ida of the
Umeda, which they know. I thank Florence Vidal for having allowed me
to publish these points from her field notes before she had the opportu-
nity to do so herself.

Glossary

Amanab	Waina	
aba	*aba*	Sago (raw or cooked ≠ jelly)
	aba	Ritual personage in Ida (Yangis: *yis*)
abi	*ab*	Wildfowl (*Talegalla* sp.)
afaag	*ava*	Mother
afwêêg	*afur, avul*	Sago palm clone; symbolically "male" and totemic sp. of "male" moiety (Yafar)
akba	*akaba*	Sun
amof	*amov*	Termite; ritual personage in Ida/ Yangis
angô, angwa	*ag, agwa*	Lexical segment for "female," "peripheral"
Angwaneri or Angwatuar	*angwatod(na)*	"Female" moiety.
anuwanam		Who has acquired a particular experience, initiated to
anuwanam	*kwanugwi*	Ritual role of the preceptor or "mother's brother" leading the *ifegê/ipele*
Araneri or Aratuar	*edtod(na)*	"Male" moiety
awaag		Father, owner, master of ritual

aya	*aiya*	Father (term of address)
bêêbi		*Calamus* liana
besa	*wata*	Coconut petiole fiber
boof	*subove*	Orange colored fruit used for mask and dancer's decoration (*Rejoua aurantiaca*)
êr, êri	*ed*	People, person, man
êri	*eli*	Ritual personage in Ida-Yangis: Cassowary figure (Ida), Mother figure (Yangis)
fenaw		Sago palm clone, symbolically "female" and totemic sp. of "female" moiety (Yafar)
fuf	*fuf, huf*	Wooden trumpet
hoofuk	*hofoy*	Sago pith, tuber flesh, etc.; fecund white substance in the womb (Yafar), principle of fecundity; connotes the idea of "origin" and "inside"
hoofuk fatik		"To drop the *hoofuk*": ritual throwing to the ground of two moiety's *hoofuk* in the opening of Ida-Yangis
hwig		Penis
ifêêg, mwig, fut		Original, primordial
ifegê (<*ifêêg êri*)	*ipele*	Ritual personage in Ida-Yangis, "red bowmen" (Gell), "totemic sons" (Juillerat)
-inaag		In, within
	ida	Ritual
ira		Women's dance style
koor	*kwod*	Ritual personage in Ida-Yangis
	koor	Ghost (in Sowanda ?)
kwoy	*kwi, yapa*	Cassowary
mô	*mo*	Word, language, talk; gullet (Waina)
na	*na*	Sago palm
-na	*-na*	Of, with
naya	*naia*	Mother (term of address)
nonoog	*na*	Mother's brother
ogomô	*ahoragwana*	Ritual personage in Ida-Yangis; sago palm growth spirit (Yafar)
raw		Hymen (?)

rawsu-inaag	*molna tamwa*	Ritual personage in Ida-Yangis
	mol	Daughter
roofuk	*tofoy*	Skin, bark, envelope of the *hoofuk/hofoy;* connotes the idea of "caducity" and "sterility"
ruwar		Child, children
sa (say)	*sa*	Coconut; mother symbol and totemic sp. of the "female" moiety (Yafar)
sabaga	*sabbra*	Two
sangêk	*awsego*	Sacred songs in the 2d night of Ida-Yangis
sawôg	*tawmego, tamwa*	Fish
	tamwa	Fish mask in Ida (Am.: *ogomô mesoog*)
sawôg	*tetagwa*	Ritual personages (body polychrome painting) in Ida-Yangis
sööb	*sub*	Black palm ssp.
suwê	*sue*	Fire
suhig, suh-	*-suh*	Connotes the idea of full maturity, strength, blackness
suh-wagmô	*pedasuh*	Ritual, elongated and black phallocrypt
taf	*tof, tov*	Blood
tot		Female breast
wagmô	*peda*	Daily, ovoid and yellow phallocrypt
ware		Wild pitpit canes
ware-inaag	*teh, ulateh*	Ritual personage in Ida-Yangis
wura	*ula*	Net bag
wurag		Womb
yis	*yis*	Sago jelly
yis	*aba*	Ritual personage in Yangis
yug		New shoot of a plant

References

Anzieu, D. 1966. "Oedipe avant le complexe ou de l'interprétation psychanalytique des mythes." *Les Temps Modernes* 245:675–715. And in *Psychoanalyse et culture grecque*. Paris: Société d'Edition "Les Belles Lettres," 1980.

Baal, J. van. 1966. *Dema. Description and analysis of Marind Anim culture.* The Hague: Martinus Nijhoff.

Barth, F. 1975. *Ritual and knowledge among the Baktaman of New Guinea.* New Haven, Conn.: Yale University Press.

———. 1987. *Cosmologies in the making. A generative approach to cultural variation in inner New Guinea.* Cambridge: Cambridge University Press.

Bateson, G. 1936. *Naven. The Culture of the Iatmul People of New Guinea as Revealed through a Study of the "Naven" Ceremonial.* Stanford: Stanford University Press.

Bausch, C. 1978. "*Po* and *Ao*. Analysis of ideological conflict in Polynesia." *Journal de la Société des Océanistes* 61:169–85.

Biersack, A. 1982. "Ginger gardens for the Ginger woman: Rites and passages in a Melanesian society." *Man* (n.s.) 17:239–58.

Brunton, R. 1980a. "Misconstrued order in Melanesian religion." *Man* 15(1): 112–28.

———. 1980b. "Order or disorder in Melanesian religion?" Correspondence. *Man* 15(4): 734–35.

Bulmer, R. 1967. "Why is the cassowary not a bird? A problem of zoological taxonomy among the Karam of the New Guinea Highlands." *Man* 2(1): 5–23.

Craig, B. 1969. *Houseboards and warshields of the Mountain Ok,* 3 vols. M.A. thesis, University of Sydney, Sydney.

———. 1990. "Is the Mountain Ok culture a Sepik culture?" In *Sepik heritage. Tradition and change in Papua New Guinea,* edited by L. Lutkehaus et al. Durham, N.C.: Carolina Academic Press, 129–49.

Crapanzano, V. 1981. "Rites of return: Circumcision in Morocco." In *The psychoanalytic study of society,* vol. 9, edited by W. Münsterberger and B. Boyer. New York: Psychohistory Press, 15–36.

Damon, F. H. 1983. "Muyuw kinship and the metamorphosis of gender labour." *Man* (n.s.) 18: 305–26.

Devereux, G. 1980. "The voices of children: Psychocultural obstacles to therapeutic communication." In *Basic problems of ethnopsychiatry,* translated by Basia Miller Gulati and George Devereux, edited by G. Devereux. Chicago: University of Chicago Press, 105–21.

Douglas M. 1973 (1970). *Natural symbols. Explorations in cosmology.* Ringwood: Penguin Books Australia.

Forge, A. 1962. "Paint: A magical substance." *Palette* 9: 9–16.

———. 1970. "Learning to see in New Guinea." In *Socialization, the approach from social anthropology,* edited by P. Mayer. London: Tavistock, 269–91.

Frankel, S. 1986. *The Huli response to illness.* Cambridge: Cambridge University Press.

Freud, S. 1900. *The interpretation of dreams.* In vols. 4/5 of the standard edition of the complete psychological works of Sigmund Freud. London: Hogarth Press.

———. 1905. "Jokes and their relation to the unconscious." In vol. 8 of the standard edition. . . .

———. 1912–13. *Totem and taboo.* In vol. 13 of the standard edition. . . .

———. 1966 [1920]. "Beyond the pleasure principle." In vol. 18 of the standard edition. . . .

———. 1923a. "The Ego and the Id." In vol. 19 of the standard edition. . . .

———. 1923b. "The dissolution of the Oedipus complex." In vol. 19 of the standard edition. . . .

Galis, K. W. 1956. "Ethnografische notities over het Senggigebied (district Hollandia)." Hollandia, Gouvernement van Nederlands Nieuw Guinea, Kantoor voor Bevolkingszaken, 86, 32p.

———. 1956–57. "Ethnologische survey van het Jafi district." Hollandia, Gouvernement van Nederlands Nieuw Guinea, Kantoor voor Bevolkingszaken, 102, 84 p.

Gardner, D. 1981. *Cult ritual and social organization among the Mianmin.* Ph.D. diss., Dept. of Prehistory and Anthropology, Australian National University, Canberra.

———. 1984. "A note on the androgynous qualities of the cassowary: Or why the Mianmin say it is not a bird." *Oceania* 55(2): 137–45.

Geertz, C. 1973. *The interpretation of cultures.* New York: Basic Books.

Gell, A. 1971. "Penis sheathing and ritual status in a West Sepik village." *Man* (n.s.) 6(2): 165–81.

———. 1975. *Metamorphosis of the cassowaries. Umeda society, language and ritual.* L.S.E. Monographs on Social Anthropology 51. London: Athlone Press.

———. 1978. "The Umeda language poem." *Canberra Anthropology* 2: 44–62.

———. 1979. "Reflections on a cut finger: Taboo in the Umeda conception of the self". In *Fantasy and symbol: Studies in anthropological interpretation,* edited by R. H. Hook. London: Academic Press, 133–48.

———. 1980. "Order or disorder in Melanesian religion?" Correspondence. *Man* 15(4): 735–37.

———. In press. "Inter-tribal commodity barter and reproductive gift exchange in Old Melanesia." In *The anthropology of barter,* edited by C. Humphrey and S. Hugh-Jones. Cambridge: Cambridge University Press.

Gillison, G. 1980. "Images of nature in Gimi thought." In *Nature, culture and gender,* edited by C. P. McCormack and M. Strathern. Cambridge: Cambridge University Press, 143–73.

———. 1987. "Incest and the atom of kinship: The role of the mother's brother in a New Guinea Highlands society." *Ethos* 15: 166–202.

Godelier, M. 1986. *The making of great men. Male domination and power among the New Guinea Baruya.* Cambridge: Cambridge University Press.

Green, A. 1968. "Sur la mère phallique." *Revue française de psychanalyse* 32: 1–38.

———. 1977. "Atome de parenté et relations oedipiennes." In *L'identité,* edited by C. Lévi-Strauss. Paris: Grasset, 81–108.

———. 1980. "Le mythe: un objet transitionnel collectif. Abord critique et perspectives psychanalytiques." *Le Temps de la Réflexion* 1: 99–131.

———. 1986. *On private madness.* London: Hogarth Press.

———. 1990a. *Le complexe de castration.* Paris: Presses Universitaires de France (Coll. "Que sais-je?").

———. 1990b. *Le folie privée. Psychanalyse des cas-limites.* Paris: Gallimard.

Gregory, C. A. 1982. *Gifts and commodities.* London: Academic Press.

Harrison, S. 1984. "New Guinea Highland social structure in a Lowland totemic mythology." *Man* (n.s.) 19: 389–403.

———. 1985. "Ritual hierarchy and secular equality in a Sepik river village." *American Ethnologist* 12: 413–26.

———. 1990. *Stealing people's names: History and politics in a Sepik river community.* Cambridge: Cambridge University Press.

Herdt, G. H. 1981. *Guardians of the flutes: Idioms of masculinity.* New York: McGraw-Hill.

Herdt, G. H., and R. Stoller, 1990. *Intimate Communications. Erotics and the Study of Culture.* New York, Columbia University Press.

Holy, L. 1987. *Comparative anthropology.* Oxford: Basil Blackwell.

Huber, P. B. 1975. "Defending the cosmos: Violence and social order among the Anggor of New Guinea." In *War and its social correlates,* edited by M. A. Nettleship, R. Dalegivens, and A. Nettleship. Paris: Mouton, 619–61.

———. 1980. "The Anggor bowman: Ritual and society in Melanesia." *American Ethnologist* 7: 43–57.

———. 1990. "Masquerade as Artifact in Wamu." *Sepik Heritage. Tradition and Change in Papua New Guinea,* edited by L. Lutkehaus et al. Durham, N.C.: Carolina Academic Press, 150–59.

Huyghe, B. 1982. "La violence: une réciprocité manquée?" *Culture* 2(2): 15–29.

Jedrej, M. C. 1980. "A comparison of some masks from North America, Africa, and Melanesia." *Journal of Anthropological Research* 36: 220–30.

Johnson, R. 1981. "Order or disorder in Melanesian religion?" Correspondence. *Man* 16(3): 472–74.

Jones, E. 1916. "The theory of symbolism." *Britain Journal of Psychology* 9(2). And in *Papers on psycho-analysis,* edited by E. Jones. Boston: Beacon Press, 1961; London: H. Karnac, 1977.

Jorgensen, D. 1981a. *Taro and arrows: Order, entropy, and religion among the Telefolmin.* Ph.D. diss., University of British Columbia, Vancouver.

———. 1981b. "Order of disorder in Melanesian religion?" Correspondence. *Man* 16(3): 470–72.

Juillerat, B. 1978a. "Techniques et sociologie de la couleur chez les Iafar (Nouvelle-Guinée)." In *Voir et nommer les couleurs,* edited by S. Tornay. Nanterre: Université de Paris X, Labethno, 477–95.

———. 1978b. "Vie et mort dans le symbolisme iafar des couleurs." In *Voir et nommer les couleurs,* edited by S. Tornay. Nanterre: Université de Paris X, Labethno, 497–523.

———. 1980. "Order or disorder in Melanesian religion?" Correspondence. *Man* 15(4): 732–34.

———. 1981. "Organisation dualiste et complémentarité sexuelle dans le Sépik occidental." *L'Homme* 21(2): 5–38.

———. 1986. *Les enfants du sang. Société, reproduction et imaginaire en Nouvelle-Guinée.* Paris: Maison des sciences de l'homme.

———. 1988. " 'Une odeur d'homme': évolutionnisme mélanésien et mythologie anthropologique à propos du matriarcat" ("An Odour of Man." Melanesian evolutionism, anthropological mythology and matriarchy). *Diogenes* 144: 65–91.

————. 1990. "Male ideology and cultural fantasy in Yafar society." In *Sepik heritage. Tradition and change in Papua New Guinea,* edited by N. Lutkehaus et al. Durham, N.C.: Carolina Academic Press, 380–84.

————. 1991a. *Œdipe chasseur. Une mythologie du sujet en Nouvelle-Guinée.* Paris: Presses Universitaires de France (Coll. "Le Fil Rouge").

————. 1991b. "Complementarity and Rivalry: Two contradictory principles in Yafar society." In *Big men and great men: Personifications of power in Melanesia,* edited by M. Godelier and M. Strathern. Cambridge: Cambridge University Press, 130–41.

Keesing, R. M. 1982. "Introduction." In *Rituals of manhood. Male initiation in Papua New Guinea,* edited by G. H. Herdt. Berkeley: University of California Press, 1–43.

Kelm, A., and H. Kelm. 1975. *Ein Pfeilschuss für die Braut. Mythen und Erzählungen aus Kwieftim und Abrau, Nordostneuguinea.* Wiesbaden: Franz Steiner Verlag.

————. 1980. *Sago und Schwein. Ethnologie von Kwieftim und Abrau in Nordost-Neuguinea.* Wiesbaden: Franz Steiner Verlag.

Kuper, A. 1982. *Wives for cattle.* London: Routledge & Kegan Paul.

Lacan, J. 1966. *Ecrits.* Paris: Editions du Seuil.

————. 1984 [1938]. *Les complexes familiaux dans la formation de l'individu. Essai d'analyse d'une fonction en psychologie.* Paris: Navarin.

Laplanche, J., and J.-B. Pontalis. 1973. *The language of psycho-analysis.* Translated by Donald Nicholson-Smith. New York: Norton.

Laycock, D. C. 1975. *Languages of the Sepik region.* Canberra: Australian National University, Pacific Linguistics, Series D, 26.

Lee, R. 1976. "!Kung spatial organization." In *Kalahari hunter-gatherers, studies of the !Kung San and their neighbors,* edited by R. Lee and I. DeVore. Cambridge, Mass.: Harvard University Press.

Lévi-Strauss, C. 1963a [1958]. "The structural analysis in linguistics and in anthropology." In *Structural anthropology.* New York: Basic Books.

————. 1963b. *Totemism.* Boston: Beacon Press.

————. 1966. *The savage mind.* Chicago: University of Chicago Press.

Lewis, G. 1980. *Day of shining red. An essay on understanding ritual.* Cambridge: Cambridge University Press.

Lewis, I. M. 1977. "Introduction." In *Symbols and sentiments. Cross-cultural studies in symbolism,* edited by I. M. Lewis. London: Academic Press, 1–24.

Lienhardt, G. 1961. *Divinity and experience: The religion of the Dinka.* Oxford: Oxford University Press.

Lyotard, J.-F. 1984. *The post-modern condition: A report on knowledge.* Manchester: Manchester University Press.

McCormack, C. P., and M. Strathern, eds. 1980. *Nature, culture and gender.* Cambridge: Cambridge University Press.

Maddock, K. 1983. *Your land is our land: Aboriginal land rights.* Ringwood: Penguin Books Australia.

Mitchell, W. E. 1978. "On keeping equal: Polity and reciprocity among the New Guinea Wape." *Anthropological Quarterly* 51(1): 5–15.

Morren, G. E. B. 1979. "Seasonality among the Miyanmin: Wild pigs, movement and dual kinship organization." *Mankind* 12: 1–12.

Obeyesekere, G. 1990. *The work of culture. Symbolic transformation in psychoanalysis and anthropology.* Chicago: University of Chicago Press.

O'Flaherty, W. 1980. *Women, androgynes, and other mythical beasts.* Chicago: University of Chicago Press.

Paul, R. A. 1987. "The question of applied psychoanalysis and the interpretation of cultural symbolism." *Ethos* 15(1): 82–103.

Paz, O. 1978. *Claude Lévi-Strauss: An introduction.* New-York: Dell; repr. from 1970 edition.

Pepper, S. 1942. *World hypotheses.* Berkeley: University of California Press.

Peter, H. 1973–74. "Vorstellungen über Krankheiten und Krankenbehandlungen bei den Gargar im West-Sepik-Distrikt." *Wiener Völkerkundliche Mitteilungen* XX.–XXI. Jahrg., Band XV–XVI: 27–62.

Poole, F. J. P. 1876. *The Ais Am.* Ph.D. diss., 5 vol. Ann Arbor, University Microfilms.

———. 1982. "The ritual forging of identity: Aspects of person and self in Bimin-Kuskusmin male initiation." In *Rituals of manhood. Male initiation in Papua New Guinea,* edited by G. H. Herdt. Berkeley: University of California Press, 99–154.

Radin, P. 1948. *Winnebago hero cycles.* Indiana University Publications in Anthropology and Linguistics Memoir I. Bloomington: University of Indiana.

———. 1953. *The world of primitive man.* New York: Henry Schuman.

———. 1956. *The trickster. A study in American Indian mythology.* New York: Philosophical Library.

Rand A. L., and E. T. Gilliard. 1967. *Handbook of New Guinea birds.* London: Weidenfeld and Nicolson.

Rappaport, R. A. 1974. "The obvious aspects of ritual", *Cambridge Anthropology* 2(1): 3–69. And in R. A. Rappaport. *Ecology, meaning and religion.* Richmond, Calif.: North Atlantic Books, 173–222.

———. 1984. "Epilogue." In *Pigs for the ancestors. Ritual in the ecology of a New Guinea people.* New, enlarged edition. New Haven, Conn.: Yale University Press.

Rickman, H. P. 1979. *Wilhelm Dilthey: Pioneer of the human studies.* Berkeley: University of California Press.

Ricoeur, P. 1965. *De l'interprétation. Essai sur Freud.* Paris: Le Seuil. Translated edition, *Freud and philosophy: An essay on interpretation.* New Haven, Conn.: Yale University Press, 1977.

————. 1969. *Le conflit des interprétations: Essais d'herméneutique.* Paris: Le Seuil. Translated edition, *Hermeneutics and the human sciences,* edited by J. B. Thompson. Cambridge: Cambridge University Press.

Sahlins M. 1976. *Culture and practical reason.* Chicago: University of Chicago Press.

Sanger, P., and N. Sorrell. 1975. "Music in Umeda village." *Ethno-musicology* 19(1): 67–89.

Schieffelin, E. L. 1976. *The sorrow of the lonely and the burning of the dancers.* New York: St-Martin's Press.

————. 1982. "The *Bau* a ceremonial hunting lodge. An alternative to initiation." In *Rituals of manhood. Male initiation in Papua New Guinea,* edited by G. H. Herdt. Berkeley: University of California Press, 155–200.

Schwimmer, E. 1984. "Male couples in New Guinea." In *Ritualized homosexuality in Melanesia,* edited by G. H. Herdt. Berkeley: University of California Press.

Sørum, A. 1984. "Growth and decay: Bedamini notions of sexuality." In *Ritualized homosexuality in Melanesia,* edited by G. H. Herdt. Berkeley: University of California Press.

Spiro, M. E. 1965. "Religious systems as culturally constituted defense mechanisms." In *Context and meaning in cultural anthropology,* edited by M. E. Spiro. Glencoe, N.Y.: The Free Press, 100–13.

————. 1982. *Œdipus in the Trobriands.* Chicago: University of Chicago Press.

Strathern, A. J. 1970. "The female and the male spirit cults in Mount-Hagen." *Man* 5(4): 571–85.

————. 1979. "Men's house, women's house: The efficacy of opposition, reversal, and pairing in the Melpa *Amb Kor* cult." *Journal of Polynesian Society* 88: 37–51.

Strathern, M. 1980. "No nature, no culture: The Hagen case." In *Nature, culture and gender,* edited by C. P. McCormack and M. Strathern. Cambridge: Cambridge University Press, 174–222.

————. 1985. "Kinship and economy: Constitutive orders of a provisional kind." *American Ethnologist* 12: 191–209.

————. 1986. "Dual models and multiple persons: Gender in Melanesia." Paper presented to the American Anthropological Association, Session on Melanesian ethnography in the production of anthropological theory.

————. 1987. "Increment and androgyny. Reflections on recent developments in the anthropology of Papua New Guinea." Paper presented on the New Guinea Workshop. Nijmegen, Centre for Australian and Oceanic Studies, Catholic University.

————. 1988. *The gender of the gift. Problems with women and problems with society in Melanesia.* Berkeley: University of California Press.

———. 1991. "Partial connections." ASAO Special Publication 3. Savage, Md.: Rowman and Littlefield.

Swadling, P., ed. 1979. *People of the West Sepik coast.* Port-Moresby: Records of the National Museum and Art Gallery 7.

Thomas, K. H. 1941. "Notes on the natives of the Vanimo coast, New Guinea." *Oceania* 12: 163–86.

Todorov, T. 1982 [1977]. *Theories of the symbol.* Oxford: Basil Blackwell.

Turner, V. W. 1967 (1964). "Symbols in Ndembu ritual." In *The forest of symbols. Aspects of Ndembu ritual.* Ithaca, N.Y.: Cornell University Press.

———. 1974. *Dramas, fields, and metaphors: Symbolic action in human society.* Ithaca, N.Y.: Cornell University Press.

Tuzin, D. F. 1975. "The breath of a ghost: Dreams and the fear of the dead. *Ethos* 3(4): 555–78.

———. 1977. "Reflections of being in Arapesh water symbolism." *Ethos* 5(2): 195–223.

———. 1980. *The voice of the Tambaran. Truth and illusion in Ilahita religion.* Berkeley: University of California Press.

Wagner, R. 1972. *Habu. The innovation of meaning in Daribi religion.* Chicago: University of Chicago Press.

———. 1977. "Analogic kinship: A Daribi example." *American Ethnologist* 4:623–42.

———. 1984. "Ritual and communication: Order, meaning, and secrecy in Melanesian initiation rites." *Annual Review of Anthropology* 13: 143–55.

———. 1986a. *Symbols that stand for themselves.* Chicago: University of Chicago Press.

———. 1986b. *Asiwinarong. Ethos, image, and social power among the Usen Barok of New Ireland.* Princeton, N.J.: Princeton University Press.

Weiner, A. B. 1980. "Reproduction: A replacement for reciprocity." *American Ethnologist* 7: 71–85.

———. 1982. "Sexuality among the anthropologists, reproduction among the informants." *Social Analysis,* Spec. Issue 12. In *Sexual Antagonism, gender, and social change in Papua New Guinea,* edited by F. J. P. Poole and G. H. Herdt, 52–65.

Weiner, J. 1987. "Diseases of the soul: Sickness, agency and the men's cult among the Foi of New Guinea." In *Dealing with inequality. Analysing gender relations in Melanesia and beyond,* edited by M. Strathern. Cambridge: Cambridge University Press, 255–77.

Werbner, R., ed. 1977. *Regional cults.* A.S.A. Monographs 16. London: Academic Press.

———. 1979. " 'Totemism' in history: The ritual passage of West African strangers." *Man* 14: 663–83.

————. 1984. "World renewal: Masking in a New Guinea festival." *Man* (n.s.) 19(2): 267–90.

————. 1985. "The argument of images: From Zion to the wilderness in African churches." In *Theoretical explorations in African religion,* edited by W. van Binsbergen and M. Schoffeleers. London: Routledge & Kegan Paul.

————. 1989. *Ritual passage, sacred journey: The form, process and organization of religious movement.* Washington, D.C.: Smithsonian Institution Press.

————. n.d. "The reworking of root-metaphor: More reflections on Sepik festivals". Author's manuscript.

Wurm, S. A., and S. Haltori, eds. 1981. *Languages atlas of the Pacific area.* Part 1, *New Guinea area, Oceania, Australia.* Canberra: Academy of the Humanities.

Young, M. 1987. "The tusk, the flute and the serpent: Disguise and revelation in Goodenough mythology." In *Dealing with inequality: Analysing gender relations in Melanesia and beyond,* edited by M. Strathern. Cambridge: Cambridge University Press.

Contributors

ALFRED GELL was educated at Cambridge and London universities. He has worked in West Sepik Province, Papua New Guinea, and in central India. His monograph on the Umeda, *Metamorphosis of the Cassowaries,* was published in 1975, and he has published other papers on Umeda symbolism and ritual. More recently he has written on markets and consumption in central India, including a contribution to the volume *The Social Life of Things,* edited by Arjun Appadurai (1986). His monograph entitled *Wrapping in Images: A Study of Tattooing in Polynesia* is in press, as is another monograph, *The Anthropology of Time;* both are scheduled to appear in 1992. Since 1980, he has been reader in anthropology at the London School of Economics, where correspondence may be addressed.

ANDRÉ GREEN received his M.D. from the Paris University. He has worked in psychiatry and psychoanalysis. He is a former director of the Paris Institute of Psychoanalysis and former president of the Paris Psychoanalytic Society. He has held the Freud Memorial Chair at University College, London. He has worked intensively in clinical and applied psychoanalysis (primarily literature and mythology). His major publications are *Le discours vivant. La conception psychanalytique de l'affect* (1973); *The Tragic Effect. The Oedipus Complex in Tragedy; Narcissisme de vie Narcissisme de mort* (1983); *The Private Madness* (1986); *Le complexe de castration* (1990); *La folie privée. Psychanalyse des cas-limites* (1990); and *La déliaison. Psychanalyse, anthropologie et littérature* (1992). Correspondence should be addressed to 9, Avenue de l'Observatoire, 75006 Paris (France).

BERNARD JUILLERAT first conducted fieldwork among a non-Islamic society of northern Cameroon and in 1969 received his Doctorat de 3e cycle in anthropology from the University of Paris. He then dedicated himself to the study of the Yafar in West Sepik Province, Papua New Guinea. His major publications are *Les bases de l'organisation sociale chez les Muktele, Nord-Cameroun* (1971); *Les enfants du sang. Société, reproduction et imaginaire en Nouvelle-Guinée* (1986, his monograph on the Yafar); *Oedipe chasseur. Une mythologie du sujet en Nouvelle-Guinée* (1991, a psychoanalytical study of Yafar mythology); and *La révocation des tambaran; les Banaro et Richard Thurnwald revisités* (in press). He has been affiliated with the National Center of Scientific Research in Paris since 1972, where he is now directeur de recherche; between 1980 and 1987, he was responsible for the research unit "Anthropologie du monde océanien contemporain." Correspondence should be addressed to 19 rue de l'Odéon, 75006 Paris.

FRANÇOIS MANENTI is psychoanalyst, lecturer in clinical psychopathology at the University of Paris VII. Sometime researcher for the laboratory of Prehistoric American Anthropology at the Ecole de Hautes Etudes en Sciences Sociales in Paris. Former member of the Franco-Brazilian archeological mission to Piaui, Brazil. Member of the Scientific Committee of the European Foundation for Psychoanalysis. His early research focused on prehistoric rock-art painting in Europe and northern Brazil. Over and above his clinical work, his recent research has led him to question the link between the structure of the subject and the notion of culture. Correspondence should be addressed to 10 rue Charles Divry, 75014 Paris.

ANDREW STRATHERN is Andrew W. Mellon Professor of Anthropology at the University of Pittsburgh. He has previously held positions at Cambridge University, the Australian National University, the University of Papua New Guinea, University College London, and the Institute of Papua New Guinea Studies, where he was director from 1981 to 1986. Since 1964 he has conducted extended fieldwork in the Highlands of New Guinea. His major publications include *The Rope of Moka* (1971); *One Father, One Blood* (1972); *Ongka* (1979); *Inequality in Highlands New*

Guinea (1982); and *A Line of Power* (1984). Correspondence should be addressed to the Department of Anthropology, University of Pittsburgh, Pa. 15260.

MARILYN STRATHERN is professor of social anthropology at Manchester University. Her publications on Melanesia include New Guinea Research Bulletins on legal change (1972) and migration (1975) and *Women in Between* (1972), and she coauthored *Self-Decoration in Mount Hagen* (1971). The two edited collections, *Nature, Culture and Gender* (1980) and *Dealing with Inequality* (1987), indicate some of her interests. A general critique of Melanesian anthropology appeared in 1988 under the title *The Gender of the Gift*. Correspondence may be addressed to the Department of Social Anthropology, University of Manchester, Brunswick Street, Manchester, England M13 9PL.

DONALD TUZIN is professor of anthropology and director of the Melanesian Archive at the University of California, San Diego. In addition to numerous papers on Melanesian topics, he is the author of *The Ilahita Arapesh* (1976) and *The Voice of the Tambaran* (1980), and co-editor, with Paul Brown, of *The Ethnography of Cannibalism* (1983). Correspondence should be addressed to the Department of Anthropology, University of California at San Diego, La Jolla, Calif. 92093.

ROY WAGNER is professor of anthropology at the University of Virginia. He has carried on field research among the Daribi of Mount Karimui and the Usen Barok of central New Ireland. Pertinent works to this discussion include *Lethal Speech* (1978) and *Symbols That Stand for Themselves* (1986). Correspondence may be addressed to the Department of Anthropology, University of Virginia, Charlottesville, Va. 22903.

RICHARD P. WERBNER, reader in African anthropology, University of Manchester, has done extensive fieldwork in Botswana and Zimbabwe. He was a Fellow at the Smithsonian Institution in Washington in 1989–90. He is the founder of the Satterthwaite Colloquium on African Religion and Ritual, which meets annually in England. His books include *Tears of the Dead: The Social Biography of an African Family* (1992); *Ritual Passage; Sacred Journey: The Process and Organization of Religious Movement* (1989); *Land Reform in the Making* (1982); and *Regional Cults* (1977). Correspondence should be addressed to the Department of Social Anthropology, University of Manchester, Brunswick Street, Manchester, England M13 9PL.

Index